PR 3730 THO

The Castle of Indolence
and Other Poems

JAMES THOMSON

The Castle of Indolence
and Other Poems

edited by

Alan Dugald McKillop

UNIVERSITY OF KANSAS PRESS
LAWRENCE, 1961

FOR ALISON

PREFACE

The present edition undertakes a full study of those poems of James Thomson's, other than *The Seasons*, which may be considered to have some special claim to attention. The high literary value of *The Castle of Indolence* need hardly be reasserted, yet this important poem has never heretofore been critically edited or fully discussed and annotated. Even J. Logie Robertson's excellent Oxford edition (1908) does not provide a critical text for the poems here included. Thomson will always be for us primarily the author of *The Seasons*, yet the pieces which I have reëdited further attest his significance and his varied powers.

The work for this edition was largely carried on in the Fondren Library of Rice University and in the British Museum, and more than perfunctory thanks are due to the officials and staff of those libraries for their continued friendly aid. The cordial encouragement and invaluable advice of Professor Clyde K. Hyder of the University of Kansas Press, who has extended editorial hospitalities unique in my experience, are again gratefully acknowledged.

ALAN DUGALD McKILLOP

Rice University
March 17, 1961

Contents

Illustrations

The Castle of Indolence

INTRODUCTION

i

The Castle of Indolence has usually been enjoyed and admired rather than analyzed. Readers take particular delight in Canto I, setting it apart from the rest of Thomson's work and perhaps wondering how the poet happened to fall into such a felicitous vein. Criticism has been concerned largely with the nature and the effects of the Spenserian imitation, and Professor Wasserman's study has well brought out the different aspects of Spenserian imitation to be found here: the poem "burlesques, moralizes, and sheds a dreamworld atmosphere."[1] The situation is fairly complex, and the literary motives behind the work deserve careful consideration.

When we take the two cantos together we find that Thomson's formal and professed purpose is to present his views on morals and religion, material and cultural progress, simplicity and luxury, solitude and society, the active and the contemplative life—all this in the form of a simplified Spenserian allegory. The Knight of Arts and Industry must eventually vanquish the enchanter Indolence. Professor Havens has connected this opposition with the opposition between primitivism and progress in *The Seasons*.[2] Thomson, really a Whig panegyrist of progress, allows himself to be pleasingly beguiled by the idyl of a virtuous Golden Age in *The Seasons,* and again by a vision of sybaritic retirement in Canto I of *The Castle.* There is a blending of different themes here, and a cultural contradiction. Entrance into the Castle is not merely a return to simple nature, but a cultivation of the delights of rural retirement, traditionally preferred to the promptings of ambition or the tumult of the city, and endlessly extolled by the Augustan poets. Yet on the didactic level the delights of Canto I are disapproved. "The Castle hight of Indolence,/And its false Luxury" are identified with self-indulgence, and pseudo-simplicity proves to be over-refinement. This moral scaffolding is closely related to the basic

---

[1] Earl R. Wasserman, *Elizabethan Poetry in the Eighteenth Century* (Urbana, 1947), p. 111. University of Illinois Studies in Language and Literature, XXXII, Nos. 2-3.

[2] Raymond D. Havens, "Primitivism and the Idea of Progress in Thomson," *SP,* XXIX (1932), 41-52, especially 50-51.

ideas of Thomson's other poems, particularly *Liberty*. *The Castle*, like *Liberty*, presupposes the traditional cycle of cultural history: active virtue progresses and succeeds to the point of luxury, then sinks into vice and corruption. The early career of the Knight of Arts and Industry is in large part identical with the progress of Liberty, and culminates in British imperial power; the campaign of the Knight against the enchanter is the reform called for by dissident Whig panegyric. And like *The Seasons*, *The Castle* operates with a pattern of man in retirement and man in action, man immersed in nature and man in society.

But here the pattern is associated with a simplified form of Spenserian allegory, and with what the age took to be the special Spenserian manner. We view some of the special effects with particular pleasure, and are perhaps too ready to reject the general scheme as dead lumber, not making enough allowance for the possibility that the scheme may be the ladder by which the poet ascends. Norman Callan has recently urged the importance of the total program for this poem: "Whatever 'didactic' may imply, the second canto, telling of the destruction of the enchanter by the Knight of Industry, forms the essential complement of the first, which, by itself, would be a freak, however delightful. The reader who is looking for surprises will prefer the first canto; the reader who values Augustan poetry for its own sake will sense that a piece of writing such as [the description of the enchanted land of Indolence] needs something to complete it."[3]

At least a preference for Canto I over Canto II should not keep us from recognizing the poet's need for a validating moral purpose, and the logical and structural relevance of that purpose, even when we are concerned with special aesthetic effects. The fusion is not complete here, and in our experience of the poem we do not find that the progress of society, the state of the nation, or even the cause of virtue, are fully presented in the private history of the poet in the Castle, the part that interests us most. Our preference might be for a poem more completely taken up with dreams and visions, for a controlling plan more unequivocally related to the movement toward subjectivity which can be traced from Locke through Sterne to

---

[3] Norman Callan, "Augustan Reflective Poetry," in *Pelican Guide to English Literature: IV, From Dryden to Johnson* (1957), p. 366.

Wordsworth.[4] But what we actually have here is of great and subtle, though uneven, interest.

The subjective and the objective sides, the aesthetic and the moral aspects, are both covered by the term Indolence. There are really two histories or sequences, the inner history of the poet in the Castle, and the external course of events. The Indolence enjoyed in Canto I is not exactly the Indolence vanquished in Canto II, just as the Melancholy enjoyed in *Il Penseroso* is not identical with the Melancholy banished in *L'Allegro*. We may make out three meanings, though of course they cannot be kept completely separate:

(a) Indolence as mere inertia, sluggishness, or apathy. Thomson's early associate Joseph Mitchell wrote a poem called *The Charms of Indolence,* ironically praising Dullness in the manner of *Mac Flecknoe*.[5] Here belongs the "dismal vacuity" of which Samuel Johnson incessantly complained, and which he would no doubt have treated in his unwritten "Palace of Sloth—a vision."[6]

(b) Indolence as refined self-indulgence, the cultivation of the choicest pleasures that nature and art can give. Thomson often associates this with a dreaming mood which we may call imaginative, though it is never so active as the "visionary bustle" or the indulgence of "the power of fiction" which Johnson censures.[7]

(c) Indolence as virtuous and philosophic retirement. This ideal is described in various terms, and may combine with or shade into sense (b) above. Thomson's Indolence or "Idless" is closely connected with what the age called "ease." "We seek happiness, in which ease is the principal ingredient, and the end proposed in our most restless pursuits is tranquillity." "To be at ease is the greatest of happiness (at ease, I mean, both of mind and body), but to be *idle* is the greatest of unhappiness."[8] Of Dorothea Mallet Celesia's *Indolence* (1772), no doubt directly inspired by Thomson's poem, the *Monthly Review* re-

---

[4] See Ernest Tuveson, "Locke and the 'Dissolution of the Ego,'" *MP*, LII (1955), 159-74.

[5] Joseph Mitchell, *Poems on Several Occasions* (1729), I, 55. The poem was originally published in January 1722, and thus precedes *The Dunciad*.

[6] Boswell, ed. Hill-Powell, IV, 382 n.

[7] *Rambler*, No. 89; *Rasselas*, chaps. iv, xliii.

[8] *Guardian*, No. 22; Owen Ruffhead, *Life of Pope* (1769), p. 248. I owe these references to Maynard Mack's note on Pope's phrase, "the sage's indolence," *Essay on Man*, II, 172—Twickenham edition, p. 75.

marked: "The Indolence which is the subject of the present panegyric, is not 'sordid sloth,' nor the 'lazy apathy of the stoics,' but, in the words of the poem itself,

> Philosophic rest,
> The inward sunshine of th' unruffled breast;
> Passions, just fann'd, not roughen'd by desire,
> These are my theme, for these I touch the lyre."[8a]

More broadly, the poet of the Castle is a Virgilian swain, a meditative poet in retirement, an artist who has his own way of attaining this ideal. In Thomson's generation the ideal of philosophic retirement could be easily combined with the ideal of refined hedonism not only by such ancient precedents as the Horatian view of life but also in particular by Addison's account of the pleasures of the imagination, which offer a middle way between hard toil and inglorious sloth, and make it possible to be at the same time "idle and innocent." "The Pleasures of the Imagination have this Advantage, above those of the Understanding, that they are more obvious, and more easie to be acquired. It is but opening the Eye, and the Scene enters. The Colours paint themselves on the Fancy, with very little Attention of Thought or Application of Mind in the Beholder." Again, they "do not require such a Bent of Thought as is necessary to our more serious Employments, nor, at the same Time, suffer the Mind to sink into that Negligence and Remissness, which are apt to accompany our more sensual Delights, but, like a gentle Exercise to the Faculties, awaken them from Sloth and Idleness, without putting them upon any Labour or Difficulty" (*Spectator,* No. 411). There is a somewhat similar gradation in the pleasures of the Castle, from the passive enjoyment of the pleasures of the senses to the "gentle Exercise" of the faculties, and so on to the construction of larger syntheses in memory and reverie, inspired both by art and nature,—a construction which is itself a reassertion and serious pursuit of a way of life. Yet it all comes under the head of Indolence.

It would be superfluous, indeed impossible, to point out in detail the various modes of philosophic retirement inspired by Lucretius, Virgil, Horace, Ovid, and Milton, to name no others, but special note may be made of some clues in Thom-

---

[8a] *Monthly Review,* XLVI (1772), 454.

son's earlier work. A favorite passage had always been the praise of the simple rural life at the end of the second *Georgic*. In the Preface to the second edition of *Winter* (1726) Thomson translates the lines (II. 475-86) in which Virgil says that he longs to know the secrets of nature, but that he may have to give up this quest and resign himself to rural retirement. The last four lines, in Thomson's rather awkward version, read thus:

> But, least I should these mystic-Truths attain,
> If the cold Current freezes round my Heart,
> The *Country* Me, the brooky *Vales* may please
> Mid Woods, and Streams, *unknown*.

In adapting this passage at the conclusion of *Autumn* (1730) Thomson reads into it a general farewell to ambition and a longing for the delights of reverie:

> But if to that unequal; if the blood,
> In sluggish streams about my heart, forbids
> That best ambition; under closing shades,
> Inglorious, lay me by the lowly brook,
> And whisper to my dreams.
>
> *(Autumn,* 1367-71)

This is consonant with the more elaborate development of the theme of Miltonic retirement in the "Hymn on Solitude" (1725), but the words "sluggish" and "inglorious" also hint at the ambivalence of Indolence, the ignoble side of the poet's repose. In another context innocent retirement could be censured as "a fugitive and cloistered Virtue," in the phrase of *Areopagitica*. Thomson edited *Areopagitica* in 1738, and a few weeks later published his lines *To the Memory of the Right Honourable the Lord Talbot,* in which he wrote:

> Nor could he brook in studious Shade to lie,
> In soft Retirement, indolently pleas'd
> With selfish Peace. The SYREN of the Wise,
> (Who steals th' *Aonian* Song, and, in the shape
> Of Virtue, wooes them from a worthless World)
> Tho' deep he felt her Charms, could never melt
> His strenuous Spirit, recollected, calm,
> As silent Night, yet active as the Day.
>
> (39-46)

This brings us close to the "Syren Melody" of the Enchanter Indolence, the song in praise of the Epicurean *ataraxia* ("What,

what, is Virtue, but Repose of Mind?") with which he lures his victims (I. ix-xix). On one level *The Castle of Indolence* repudiates the ambition and indulges in the reverie; on another level it disowns the reverie and reasserts the ambition. But even the word "ambition" is ambiguous here. The moral obligation to attempt to realize the ambition that makes for public progress is not the same thing as poetical ambition or realization. In yielding to the delights of Indolence in a pregnant sense the poet may attain a success not known to Whig panegyric.

ii

Thomson did not proceed directly to the central theme and its implications, but began very casually. What little we know of the history of the poem suggests improvisation and piece-meal composition. Thomson's biographer Patrick Murdoch writes: "It was, at first, little more than a few detached stanzas, in the way of raillery on himself, and on some of his friends, who would reproach him with indolence; while he thought them, at least, as indolent as himself."[9] Murdoch goes on to describe the development of the poem very briefly: "But he saw very soon, that the subject deserved to be treated more seriously, and in a form fitted to convey one of the most important moral lessons." We are left in doubt as to just how soon Thomson began to take the project seriously and resolved to push on with his moralizing. His letter to William Paterson, April 1748, indicates that the origin of the poem goes back to 1733 or 1734 and gives us the only statement we have from the poet himself about the social experiences and the private jests among friends that gave the original incentive: "Now that I am Prating of myself, know that, after fourteen or fifteen Years, the Castle of Indolence comes abroad in a Fortnight. It will certainly travel as far as Barbadoes. You have an Apartment in it, as a Night-Pensioner; which, you may remember, I fitted up for you during our delightful Party at North-Haw. Will ever these Days return again? Dont you remember your eating the raw Fish that were never catched?"[10] The Reverend Thomas Morell's stanzas addressed to Thomson "On his unfinish'd Plan of a Poem call'd *the Castle of Indolence.*

---

[9] Thomson, *Works* (1762), I, xiv.
[10] *LD*, 197.

In Spenser's Stile" seem to be the only other surviving record
of the raillery on the subject that passed between the poet and
his friends.

> As when the Silkworm, erst the tender Care
>> Of *Syrian* Maidens, 'gins for to unfold
> From his Sleek Sides, that now much Sleeker are,
>> The glossy Treasure, & soft Threads of Gold;
>> In Various Turns, & many a winding Fold,
> He spins his Web; &, as he spins, decays;
>> Till within Circles infinite enroll'd,
> He rests supine, imprison'd in the Maze;
> The Which himself did make, the Gathering of his Days.

> So Thou, they say, from thy prolific Brain,
>> A Castle, hight, of Indolence, didst raise:
> Where listless Sprites, withouten Care, & Pain,
>> In idle Plesaunce spend their jocund Days,
>> Nor heed rewardfull Toil, nor seeken Praise.
> Thither thou didst repair in luckless Hour,
>> And lulled with thine own enchanting Lays
> Didst lie adown; entranced in the Bow'r,
> The which thyself didst make, the Gathering of thy Pow'r.

> But Venus suffring not her fav'rite Worm,
>> For aye to slepen in his silky Tomb;
> Instructs him to throw off his pristine Form,
>> And the gay Features of a Fly assume.
>> When lo! eftsons from the surrounding Gloom,
> He vigorous breaks, forth issuing from the Wound,
>> His horny Beak had made; & finding Room
> On new-plum'd Wings he flutters all around,
> And buzzing speaks his Joy in most expressive Sound.

> So may the God of Science, and of Wit,
>> With pitying Eye ken Thee his darling Son;
> Shake from thy fatty Sides the slumbrous Fit,
>> In which alas! Thou art so Woe-begone!
>> Or with his pointed Arrows goad Thee on,
> Till Thou refeelest Life in all thy Veins;
>> And on the Wings of Resolution,
> Like thine own Hero dight, fliest o'er the Plains,
> Chaunting his peerless Praise in never-dying Strains.[11]

---

[11] *LD*, 135-36. There are two transcripts of these lines in the Richardson papers
at the Victoria and Albert Museum (XVI, 2, ff. 59-60, and XII, 1, f. 60), and one
in the Cole papers at the British Museum (Addit. MS. 5832, f. 129ᵛ). They first

These stanzas are no doubt connected with the passage in *The Castle of Indolence,* I. ix, beginning:

> See her bright Robes the Butterfly unfold,
> Broke from her wintry Tomb in Prime of May.

In one of the Richardson transcripts these lines are dated "1742." The conclusion probably indicates that at the time Morell was writing Thomson had planned the campaign of his Knight but had not yet got very far into Canto II. In William Cole's transcript a note is added to the next to the last line, "The Knight of Resolution, the Hero of the Poem," and this may indicate that Thomson originally intended to give this name to his hero.

Though the portraits of Thomson's circle at the end of Canto I must include early burlesque stanzas (notably lxi and lxix), they also show the effects of the fully developed theme and include references of later date, so that they cannot as a group be taken as the early nucleus.

The use of the Spenserian form would lend itself to an early period of piecemeal composition; stanzas might be carefully wrought and yet remain "detached," as Murdoch says in his report. Playful Spenserian imitation invited triviality and small-scale work—the *jeu d'esprit,* the short descriptive bit, the little exercise in style, with considerable emphasis on the supposedly ludicrous or quaint diction. The result might be broad or heavy burlesque, as in Pope's "The Alley" and Shenstone's early piece called "The Virtuoso"; but at the other extreme the possibility of a light and delicate burlesque verging on the idyllic had been brilliantly exemplified in Shenstone's *School-Mistress.* Shenstone's Advertisement describes the effect aimed at: "What particulars in Spenser were imagined most proper for the author's imitation on *this occasion,* are his *language,* his *simplicity,* his manner of *description,* and a peculiar *tenderness*

---

appeared in print, as far as I know, in the *Works of the English Poets* with Johnson's Lives, XLVIII (1779), 252-53. They appear in Chalmers' *English Poets,* XII, 467, and in *The Cabinet of Poetry* (1808), IV, 179-80. Robert Burns, in his letter to Stephen Clarke, 16 July 1792, may had had these lines in mind, as well as *The Castle of Indolence* itself and the opening of *The Dunciad,* Book III, when he writes with humorous sarcasm of "Mr. C— . . . in the drowsy hours of slumbrous repose, in the arms of his dearly beloved elbow-chair, where the frowsy but potent Power of Indolence, circumfuses her vapours round, & sheds her dews on, the head of her DARLING SON" (*Letters,* ed. Ferguson [Oxford, 1931], II, 115).

of *sentiment* remarkable throughout his works."[12] As Thomson's Advertisement shows us, the idea of "a Simplicity of Diction . . . which borders on the Ludicrous" was prominent in his mind also, particularly at the earliest stage of the project. The humorous sketches of individuals with which Thomson began are paralleled in Richard Owen Cambridge's *Archimage,* written in Thomson's lifetime but not published until later.

The verses on Spenser which Thomson added to *Summer* in 1744 do not cover the whole effect of Spenser's genius, but dwell on fancy, magic, and a pleasing flow of verse:

> Nor shall my Verse that elder Bard forget,
> The gentle SPENCER, Fancy's pleasing Son;
> Who, like a copious River, pour'd his Song
> O'er all the Mazes of enchanted Ground.
>
> (1572-75)

Robert Shiels, remembered if at all only as Dr. Johnson's amanuensis and as a collaborator in the *Lives of the Poets* called "Cibber's," was an ardent admirer of Thomson and was evidently much impressed by the poet's references to Spenser in private conversation. A note in Shiels' elegy for Thomson, *Musidorus* (October 1748) says: "Mr. *Thomson* being the best descriptive Poet in our Age has frequently own'd, that in this Respect he form'd his Taste upon *Spencer"* (p. 23). He repeats this statement in his Life of Spenser, and elaborates it in his Life of Thomson: "He is indeed the eldest born of Spenser, and he has often confessed that if he had any thing excellent in poetry, he owed it to the inspiration he first received from reading the Fairy Queen, in the very early part of his life."[13] We must not take this literally, but it probably indicates a personal response to Spenser which goes beyond the repetition of the current clichés, such as we find in the passage from *Summer* just quoted, or in William Thompson's lines:

> Father of fancy, of descriptive verse,
> And shadowy beings, gentle Edmund hight

---

[12] Shenstone's supposed change from mere burlesque of Spenser to sympathetic and delicate imitation is studied by Virginia F. Prettyman, "Shenstone's Reading of Spenser," in *The Age of Johnson: Essays Presented to C. B. Tinker* (New Haven, 1949), pp. 227-37. But Richmond Bond rightly warns against exaggerating this change (*English Burlesque Poetry 1700-1750* [Cambridge, Mass., 1932], pp. 133-35).

[13] Cibber-Shiels, *Lives of the Poets* (1753), V, 217.

Spenser! the sweetest of the tuneful throng,
Or recent, or of eld. Creative bard,
Thy springs unlock, expand thy fairy scenes,
Thy unexhausted stores of fancy spread,
And with thy images inrich my song.[14]

The idea of a didactic poem in strict Spenserian form, on a
somewhat larger scale than Shenstone's and with a more serious
professed moral, would still be relatively novel in the 1730's,
but had presented itself more than once. As has been said, the
delights of retirement and ease would inevitably be viewed by
the Augustans from a social and moral point of view. Spenser's
example would encourage a firm moral judgment, and temptation and enticement would be natural themes for almost any
imitation of Spenser that tried to sound a serious note. Such a
pattern had already developed, and an "Archimage" or malign
enchanter becomes a central figure. *The Castle of Indolence*
belongs to this small group of early imitations, immeasurably
superior to the others though it is. A precedent for this didactic
approach, though not for the two-canto plan, is Gilbert West's
Canto of the Fairy Queen (1739), later reprinted under the
unpromising title *On the Abuses of Travelling* (Chalmers'
English Poets, XIII, 175-80). The particular theme of West's
poem, the grand tour as a mode of luxurious idleness, calls
forth a speech from an enchanter Archimage:

Behold, says *Archimage,* the envied Height
Of Human Grandeur to the Gods allied!
Behold yon Sun of Power, whose glorious Light,
O'er this rejoicing Land out-beaming wide,
Calls up those Princely Flowers on every side:
Which, like the painted Daughters of the Plain,
Ne toil, ne spin, ne stain their silken Pride
With Care or Sorrow, sith withouten Pain,
Them in eternal Joy those Heav'nly Beams maintain.

Them morn and evening Joy eternal greets,
And for them thousands and ten thousands moil,
Gathering from Land and Ocean honied Sweets
For them, who in soft Indolence the while
And slumbring Peace, enjoy the luscious Spoil;
And as they view around the careful Bees

---

[14] William Thompson, *Sickness* (1745), I. 275-81.

10

Forespent with Labour and incessant Toil,
With the sweet Contrast learn themselves to please,
And heighten by compare the Luxury of Ease.

These stanzas are close enough to the theme of *The Castle of
Indolence* to cast some light on the origins of the poem.

Dr. Johnson's comments on Spenserian imitation, though
of course somewhat later in date, show in a striking way how
the problem of dealing with style and allegory, the "artifice of
the copy" and the "sentiments," might present itself to contemporary poets and critics. In *Rambler* No. 121 he approved
of the allegory but, as we might expect, sharply rejected the
stylistic imitation.

To imitate the fictions and sentiments of Spenser can incur no
reproach; for allegory is perhaps one of the most pleasing vehicles
of instruction. But I am very far from extending the same respect
to his diction or his stanza. His style was in his own time allowed
to be vicious, so darkened with old words and peculiarities of phrase,
and so remote from common use, that Jonson boldly pronounces
him *to have written no language.* His stanza is at once difficult and
unpleasing; tiresome to the ear by its uniformity, and to the attention by its length. . . . Perhaps, however, the style of Spenser might
by long labour be justly copied; but life is surely given us for higher
purposes than to gather what our ancestors have wisely thrown
away, and to learn what is of no value, but because it has been
forgotten.

Yet in the *Lives of the Poets* Johnson is surprisingly favorable
to Spenserian imitators, and approves the performances of West,
Shenstone, and Thomson, with whatever reservations.

[West's] *Imitations of Spenser* are very successfully performed,
both with respect to the metre, the language, and the fiction; and
being engaged at once by the excellence of the sentiments, and the
artifice of the copy, the mind has two amusements together. But
such compositions are not to be reckoned among the great atchievements of intellect, because their effect is local and temporary; they
appeal not to reason or passion, but to memory, and pre-suppose
an accidental or artificial state of mind. An Imitation of Spenser is
nothing to a reader, however acute, by whom Spenser has never
been perused. Works of this kind may deserve praise, as proofs of
great industry, and great nicety of observation; but the highest
praise, the praise of genius, they cannot claim. The noblest beauties
of art are those of which the effect is co-extended with rational
nature, or at least with the whole circle of polished life; what is less

11

than this can be only pretty, the plaything of fashion, and the amusement of a day.[14a]

He repeats the idea of the "two amusements" in his comment on Shenstone: "The *School-mistress,* of which I know not what claim it has to stand among the Moral Works, is surely the most pleasing of Shenstone's performances. The adoption of a particular style, in light and short compositions, contributes much to the increase of pleasure: we are entertained at once with two imitations, of nature in the sentiments, of the original author in the style, and between them the mind is kept in perpetual employment."[15]

Of *The Castle of Indolence* Johnson says only that it was "at last finished with great accuracy," and that "the first canto opens a scene of lazy luxury, that fills the imagination."[16]

iii

Current comment seems to indicate that the diction was the first thing to attract attention. Thomson's Advertisement broaches the subject by referring to "the obsolete Words, and a Simplicity of Diction in some of the Lines, which borders on the Ludicrous." When he goes on to say, quite inaccurately, that the style and measure of Spenser are "appropriated by Custom" to allegory, he leaves us to adjust the ludicrous and the allegorical as best we may. His list of obsolete words is drawn directly and almost exclusively from John Hughes' "Glossary Explaining the Old and Obscure Words in Spenser's Works."[17] The following item, for example, is identical in both glossaries: "The Letter Y is frequently placed in the Beginning of a Word, by Spenser, to lengthen it a Syllable." In some cases where Thomson uses a word or form which occurs only once, twice, or three times in Spenser, and which is to be found in Hughes' Glossary, it also seems likely that he depended on this source. The eighteenth century Spenserians took over without

---

[14a] *Lives of the Poets* (1783), IV, 307.

[15] *Ibid.,* IV, 335-36.

[16] *Ibid.,* IV, 258-59.

[17] For a fairly full record of Spenserian archaisms in the eighteenth century imitators, see Karl Reuning, *Das Altertümliche im Wortschatz der Spenser-Nachahmungen des 18. Jahrhunderts,* Strassburg, 1912, Quellen und Forschungen, 116; and especially for Thomson, Gustav Cohen, *Thomson's Castle of Indolence eine Nachahmung von Spenser's Faerie Queene,* Bonn, 1899. Neither of these studies considers the special influence of Hughes' edition of Spenser.

any misgivings the general modernization of the poet's vocabulary in Hughes' text. The discriminating Thomas Edwards was perhaps the first to complain of the defects in this edition:

In these seasons your Spenser has been of great entertainment to me; I have gone through him at leisure hours with some care, and am surprised to see how negligently Mr. Hughes who was a man of learning performed the part of an Editor to that fine Author. The faults of the press are exceedingly numerous whereas the old Edition of 1611, which is not scarce, is very correct; many of his peculiar spellings are arbitrarily altered which is giving us Spensers works not as he wrote them but as the Editor thought he should have written; and the Glossary is very imperfect; a great many words obsolete or used by Spenser in an uncommon sense are not to be found there, very seldom is there any authority produced for the interpretations he gives, or any references to the places where they are used, and very often he is mistaken in them.[18]

Of course a complete Spenserianizing of the vocabulary of the imitators would have been impossible and impracticable. The glosses provided by editors and by archaizers in verse show that many words which we take as poetic commonplace were at that time felt to be daring innovations. Thus Gay in his *Shepherd's Week* explains *erst, glee, ken, ween, welkin;* Hughes glosses *aghast, ay* (ever), *baleful, craven, doff, don, fare* (go), *glade, guise, ire, miscreant, tournament, uncouth, ween, wight;* we may note in Thomson's "Explanation" *bale, carol, gear, lea, sheen.* There developed a little group of archaisms used in common by practically all the Spenserians— such words as *ay* or *aye, carle, dight, eftsoons, erst, gan, hight, lout* (verb), *mote, ne, ween, weet, wot, whilom.*

On the whole the imitators were extremely cautious in taking over excessively rare words, and avoided crowding a passage with archaisms. Gloster Ridley's *Psyche* (Dodsley's *Museum,* III [1747], 80-97) is exceptional in its occasional grouping of strange words to the point of grotesqueness, producing something like a touch of Lewis Carroll or Joyce:

He, like her Parent and her Belamour,
Sought how she mote in Sickerness remain,
From all Malengine safe, and evil Stour.
Go, tender Cosset, said he, forray ore
These Walks and Lawnds; Thine all these Buskets are.

---

[18] MS. Bodl. 1010, p. 92. Thomas Edwards to John Clerke, April 27, 1744.

Most of the Spenserians depended for their effects on the current stock of archaisms, an occasional rare word, an occasional quaint spelling, and notably on the random use of an extra syllable for the sake of the meter—"emove," "I passen," "to trippen," "withouten," and of course the prefix y-, not felt to be specially the mark of the past participle. When they are following a Spenserian allegorical pattern closely, or else seeking marked grotesque and ludicrous effects, the archaisms are likely to be more numerous. An allegorical sequence supported by one or two prominent archaic words in each of a series of stanzas is occasionally found, as in *The Castle of Indolence*, II. v-vii; but such a grouping is exceptional, and we have stanza after stanza without marked archaism.

The composite purpose of the poem, playful, descriptive, and didactic, produces an agreeable if not always entirely successful compromise in diction. Thomson continues to draw on the stock poetic diction employed in *The Seasons* and *Liberty*— the special vocabulary derived in a complex way from literary, philosophical, and scientific sources. This is particularly true of the moralizing passages of Canto II. A mild infusion of such words is not at odds with the Spenserian vein. In Canto I, for example, the following words are in Spenser: *spacious, cumbrous, continual, rigour, perfection;* the following are not in Spenser: *torpor, arduous, roseate, enamelled, congress, vernal.* From Canto II we can make up a list of Latinate words which belong more markedly or particularly to the diction: *compressed, strenuous, mechanic, fabrick, agriculture, tranquillize, quintessence, ruptured, gelid, illusive, obdurate, latent, impervious, rapacious.* The presence of one or two of these words in a line has widespread effects; they are, for better or worse, likely to be operative. It cannot be said that Thomson is entirely successful in floating this special vocabulary, but his Spenserian project imposes restraint. There are no lines strikingly dominated by Latinisms, such as we can find elsewhere in his work:

> And ruminate in the contiguous shade

or

> His eyes effulging a peculiar fire.

Specific details of diction often fall into the background as compared with Thomson's skilful use of various metrical effects and his general command of the economy of the stanza.

14

His lavish use of alliteration, assonance, and internal rime need hardly be illustrated. Space would fail for the elaboration of such points as the interplay of the sounds *l, m, n,* and *s* in these lines:

> Full in the Passage of the Vale, above,
> A sable, silent, solemn Forest stood;
> Where nought but shadowy Forms were seen to move,
> As *Idless* fancy'd in her dreaming Mood.
>
> (I. v)

Thomson makes extended use of Spenser's device of repeating a word within the line, as in

> Yet nothing did he dread, but ever was ydrad—
> Though fair as ever living Wight was fair—. . . .

In Thomson this device is often, though not exclusively, used in the final Alexandrine:

> The murmuring Main was heard, and scarcely heard to flow—
> With woody Hill o'er Hill encompass'd round—
> To toil for what you here untoiling may obtain—
> Ne ever find they Rest from their unresting Fone.

The characteristic stanza is free from harsh inversions and extended periodic constructions; the units are loosely put together, one line often following another like an afterthought or slight and casual elaboration; and yet the reader feels an unbroken continuity and a remarkable cumulative effect within the stanza. Meanwhile, from one stanza to another the movement may be subtly retarded (as in I. v and I. xxx) or markedly accelerated (as in I. xxxi and II. iii). Thomson's original effects here go far beyond mere imitation; at his best he makes the Spenserian stanza his own.

iv

Without delay Thomson proceeds to some of his richest Spenserian effects. The opening scene comes directly from his model:

> In lowly Dale, fast by a River's Side,
> With woody Hill o'er Hill encompass'd round,
> A most enchanting Wizard did abide,
> Than whom a Fiend more fell is no-where found.

15

The first line is virtually a Spenserian formula for landscape, as in

> Down in a Dale forby a River's side
> (*FQ* VI. iii. 29. 6)

and the passage is essentially an adaptation of the description of the "little lowly Hermitage"

> Down in a Dale, hard by a Forests side
> (*FQ* I. i. 34. 1-2)[19]

where Spenser's Archimago dwells. Thomson's enchanter is later called "that Villain Archimage" (II. xxxii). The elaborate delights of the castle and its surroundings are suggested largely by Acrasia's Bower of Blisse (*FQ*, II. xii), as is the story of the attack on the enchanter by the Knight of Arts and Industry and his rescue of the victims in Canto II.

One of the most interesting links between Thomson and Spenser appears in the important group of passages in which we have garden, rural, and woodland imagery blended in a harmony of sound. From Spenser it will suffice merely to refer to the sounds that produce sleep in the house of Morpheus (I. i. 41), the lulling sound of the stream in the earlier description of the Bower (II. vi. 30), the birdsong in Phaedria's garden (II. vi. 13), and the cumulative harmony of the Bower of Blisse, where

> Birds, Voices, Instruments, Winds, Waters, all agree.
> (*FQ* II. xii. 70.9)

Thomson makes the hypnotic effect pervasive, and "slumbrous Influence" unifies his opening stanzas (I. ii-v). It should be noted that this is not mere onomatopoeia; there is not only the reproduction or imitation of sound, but the delicate assertion or domination of sound, still so muted as to counteract the effect it might have as a symbol of the active and varied life of nature. This effect appears in I. iii:

> Mean time unnumber'd glittering Streamlets play'd,
> And hurled every-where their Waters sheen;
> That, as they bicker'd through the sunny Glade,
> Though restless still themselves, a lulling Murmur made.

---

[19] Since Thomson used Hughes' edition, all quotations from Spenser in the introduction and notes are from Hughes' text.

Here Thomson uses as his material stock pastoral detail—quiet lawns, glittering streams, sunny glades, purling rills. There is such a composite, for example, in the paradise which Spenser arranges for happy lovers (IV. x. 24). But the fusion of sound is far from commonplace.

There is a parallel orchestration in *Spring,* always as a manifestation of the pervasive vitality of nature. Thus, in the course of the great sun-after-rain passage:

> Full swell the Woods; their every Musick wakes,
> Mix'd in wild Concert with the warbling Brooks
> Increas'd, the distant Bleatings of the Hills,
> The hollow Lows responsive from the Vales,
> Whence blending all the sweeten'd Zephyr springs.
> ([1744], 198-202)

In another important passage in *Spring* sound becomes of central importance as an expression of natural and cosmic harmony:

> Lend me your Song, ye Nightingales! oh pour
> The mazy-running Soul of Melody
> Into my varied Verse! while I deduce,
> From the first Note the hollow Cuckoo sings,
> The Symphony of Spring.
> (575-79)

The elaborate account of birdsong that follows, with a catalogue of songsters, culminates again in "full Concert" (582-610). We pass easily from circumstantial natural description to world harmony, and we should also note at the end of each of these passages a light evocative touch—the zephyr that blends the sounds, and, at the conclusion of the passage on birdsong, a new overtone—

> while the Stock-dove breathes
> A melancholy Murmur thro' the whole.

Similarly, full natural description in the angling passage added to *Spring* in 1744 ends in a woodland reverie which approaches the dominant tone of Canto I of *The Castle:*

> Or catch thy self the Landskip, gliding swift
> Athwart Imagination's vivid Eye:
> Or by the vocal Woods and Waters lull'd,
> And lost in lonely Musing, in a Dream,
> Confus'd, of careless Solitude, where mix

Ten thousand wandering Images of Things,
Soothe every Gust of Passion into Peace,
All but the Swellings of the soften'd Heart,
That waken, not disturb the tranquil Mind.
(458-68)

At this point the landscape becomes a floating pageant which
blends with the shifting imagery of dreams, dominated by the
hypnotic sounds of nature.

In place of the fully developed landscapes of *The Seasons*,
with their attendant universal view, we have in *The Castle of
Indolence* a "nest," an "island," or a "bower," with a wider
setting lightly sketched in the Spenserian manner. The ante-
cedents of the setting of *The Castle* may further be seen in
another landscape associated with Archimago:

So now he *Guyon* guides an uncouth way,
Through Woods and Mountains, till they came at last
Into a pleasant Dale, that lowly lay
Betwixt two Hills, whose high Heads overplac'd,
The Valley did with cool shade overcast;
Through midst thereof a little River roll'd.
(*FQ* II. i. 24. 1-6)

And also in the pleasant retreat to which the wounded Timias
is taken:

Into that Forest far they thence him led,
Where was their Dwelling, in a pleasant Glade,
With Mountains round about environed,
And mighty Woods, which did the Valley shade,
And like a stately Theatre it made,
Spreading it self into a spacious Plain;
And in the midst a little River play'd
Emongst the pumy Stones, which seem'd to 'plain
With gentle Murmur, that his Course they did restrain.
(*FQ* III. v. 39)

Thomson now makes the simple framing landscape of wood
and hill the setting and the substance of a reverie:

Full in the Passage of the Vale, above,
A sable, silent, solemn Forest stood;
Where nought but shadowy Forms were seen to move,
As *Idless* fancy'd in her dreaming Mood.
And up the Hills, on either Side, a Wood
Of blackening Pines, ay waving to and fro,

18

> Sent forth a sleepy Horror through the Blood;
> And where this Valley winded out, below,
> The murmuring Main was heard, and scarcely heard, to flow.
>
> (I. v)

With the environing Spenserian setting Thomson has fused an allegorical, meditative, and Gothic strain developed from *Il Penseroso,* and has produced something different from either. As early as the autumnal opening of the original version of *Winter* (a passage later transferred to *Autumn*) he had approximated such an effect:

> Oh! bear me then to high, embowering Shades,
> To twilight Groves, and visionary Vales;
> To weeping Grottos, and to hoary Caves;
> Where Angel-Forms are seen, and Voices heard,
> Sigh'd in low Whispers, that abstract the Soul,
> From outward Sense, far into Worlds remote.
>
> (*Winter,* first ed., 74-79; *Autumn,* 1030-36)

The topographical setting for the reverie is more definitely given in the following passages:

> Still let me pierce into the midnight Depth
> Of yonder Grove, of wildest largest Growth;
> That, forming high in Air a woodland Quire,
> Nods o'er the Mount beneath. At every Step,
> Solemn, and slow, the Shadows blacker fall,
> And all is awful listening Gloom around.
>
> (*Summer,* 516-21)

> Oh talk of HIM in solitary Glooms!
> Where, o'er the Rock, the scarcely-waving Pine
> Fills the brown Shade with a religious Awe.
>
> (*A Hymn,* 42-44)

It will also be helpful for comparison and contrast to cite the familiar lines from Pope's "Eloisa to Abelard":

> But o'er the twilight groves, and dusky caves,
> Long-sounding aisles, and intermingled graves,
> Black Melancholy sits, and round her throws
> A death-like silence, and a dread repose:
> Her gloomy presence saddens all the scene,
> Shades ev'ry flow'r, and darkens ev'ry green,
> Deepens the murmur of the falling floods,
> And breathes a browner horror on the woods.
>
> (163-70)

The *persona* of Melancholy is central for Pope's lines, and dominates all with the transitive verbs, whereas personification in Thomson becomes evanescent and shadowy. The passages from *The Seasons* imply a human observer or participant ("bear me," "let me pierce," "talk of Him"), and at the same time more elusive equivalents of the *persona* ("Angel-Forms," "Voices," "listening Gloom"). In the stanza from *The Castle* the two come together: the "shadowy Forms" are "fancy'd" by *"Idless."* The simple ordering of the ideal landscape comes to be more like the disposition of images in a descriptive lyric, less like the massing of the forces and the scenes of nature in *The Seasons.* Moreover, the poet goes beyond the easy passive role assigned to the observer in Addison's theory of the pleasures of the imagination, yet he is not constructing an allegory. He is both recording and creating the experience. The images are in the landscape and in the mind, and perception and creation merge. There is a kind of circularity here, and who can say which comes first? As Lemonnier remarks of this poem: "Il a cru faire seulement l'éloge du repos et du sommeil, mais il a fait aussi implicitement l'éloge des visions qu'apporte le sommeil. Avec lui, le sens du mot 'rêve' commence à changer; il ne s'agit plus de beaux projets d'avenir, de ces rêveries de bonheur que l'on fait tout éveillé, mais d'un foisonnement d'images incomprehénsibles, venue peut-être d'une réalité autre que celle que nous révèlent la raison et l'expérience courante."[20]

Thus the most characteristic effects of this poem appear when the imagery is partly detached both from the landscapes and the philosophical framework of *The Seasons* and from the settings and actions of *The Faerie Queene,* and is used by the poet in such a way as to produce a self-sufficient structure by its own generative power. Thomson avoids elaborate and enriched Spenserian settings, and long descriptive sequences and pageants. He makes a truly independent use of his model. The transition from the world of *The Seasons* to the world of *The Castle* may be further illustrated by some rejected lines in *Spring:*

> 'Tis *Harmony,* that World-embracing Power,
> By which all Beings are adjusted, each
> To all around, impelling and impell'd

---

[20] Léon Lemonnier, *Les Poètes anglais du xviii⁰ siècle* (Paris, 1947), pp. 76-77.

In endless Circulation, that inspires
This universal Smile. Thus the glad Skies,
The wide-rejoycing Earth, the Woods, the Streams,
With every *Life* they hold, down to the Flower
That paints the lowly Vale, or Insect-Wing
Wav'd o'er the Shepherd's Slumber, touch the Mind
To Nature tun'd, with a light-flying Hand,
Invisible; quick-urging, thro' the Nerves,
The glittering Spirits, in a Flood of Day.

(Spring [1728], 865-76)

Here, within the cosmic scheme, we have the varied pattern of nature impinging on the mind, with a suggestion of the cumulative effect of these varied stimuli in spontaneous human response. Of this passage Professor Dobrée has acutely remarked that it "expresses the kind of sentiment later generations have wished [Thomson] had explored and developed," adding that "even had he felt impelled to do so, it is doubtful whether the prosody into which he had built his sensations, and the diction he had so whole-heartedly inherited, could have communicated it."[21] Of the general truth of this comment there can be no doubt, and yet in *The Castle of Indolence,* Thomson goes some distance toward elaborating and refining this suggestion, responding to the influence of Spenser in his own way. Harmony as a *persona* or a philosophic concept becomes harmony as "proved upon the pulses," in the diction, imagery, and structure of the culminating passages of Canto I. Sights, sounds, and dominant mood work together to the same effect. At times they exercise the bewitchment said to be wrought by the song of the enchanter. They are in, of, and about the poet's dream. The long literary tradition of the dreamer comes into play here, but with a subjectivity unknown to earlier poets, even to Spenser himself. The dreamer dreams for himself an appropriate land to dream in. The poet is in the vision which he sustains and elaborates, though the time is to come when he must break the spell and get outside the vision. The "indolence" of the poet is so closely connected with the creation of poetry as to be virtually identical with it; the mode of life which produces poetry is taken to be the poetry. If this sounds extravagantly romantic, we may pause to

---

[21] Bonamy Dobrée, *English Literature in the Early Eighteenth Century 1700-1740* (Oxford, 1959), pp. 488-89.

consider that Pope in his way can set forth this situation as well as Thomson. As Pope translates Homer he writes to Jervas:

I have the greatest proof in nature at present of the amusing power of Poetry, for it takes me up so intirely that I scarce see what passes under my nose, and hear nothing that is said about me. To follow Poetry as one ought, one must forget father and mother, and cleave to it alone. My *Rêverie* has been so deep, that I have scarce had an interval to think my self uneasy in the want of your company. I now and then just miss you as I step into bed; this minute indeed I want extremely to see you, the next I shall dream of nothing but the taking of *Troy,* or the recovery of *Briseis.*[22]

Though the beginning of Canto I is thus dominated by the subtle interfusion of landscape and mood, the song of the enchanter (I. ix-xix) introduces complex moral and social issues which are merely insinuated here, insidiously presented in such a way as not to break the prevailing spell. The song begins with three stanzas inspired by the song of Spenser's Phaedria, inviting the hearer to sleep amidst the delights of her garden. Phaedria, Spenser says, stands for "Immodest Mirth," but her island is situated in the "Idle Lake," and she is called "Idleness" in Hughes' Introduction to his edition (I, lxxix-lxxx). The parallel between the songs in Spenser and Thomson may be shown by quoting the opening lines of each stanza. Spenser's sequence goes:

> Behold, O Man, that toil-some Pains dost take,
> The Flowers, the Fields, and all that pleasant grows—

> The Lilly, Lady of the flowring Field—

> Why then dost thou, O Man, that of them all
> Art Lord, and eke of Nature Sovereign,
> Wilfully make thy self a wretched Thrall,
> And waste thy joyous Hours in needless Pain,
> Seeking for Danger and Adventures vain?
>
> (*FQ* II. vi. 15-17)

Corresponding to these we have in Thomson the successive openings:

> Behold! ye Pilgrims of this Earth, behold!
> See all but Man with unearn'd Pleasure gay—

---

[22] Pope, *Correspondence*, ed. Sherburn (Oxford, 1956), I, 243. Maynard Mack quotes this passage to illustrate Pope's attitude towards the poetic imagination (*PQ*, XXXVI [1957], 395).

Behold the merry Minstrels of the Morn,
The swarming Songsters of the careless Grove—

Outcast of Nature, Man! the wretched Thrall
Of bitter-dropping Sweat, of sweltry Pain— . . . .
(I. ix-xi)

In stanza x Thomson goes to the passage in Matthew used by Spenser, but substitutes "the fowls of the air" for "the lilies of the field."[23] In stanza xii, at the beginning and the end, we have an adaptation of Matthew xi:28: "Come unto me, all ye that labour and are heavy laden, and I will give you rest." Thus the enchanter quotes Scripture for his purpose, and likewise adapts a text of Ecclesiastes in I. xix. But his inducements are manifold; he argues for the delights of retirement in such various ways that his song gives an *aperçu* of the entire poem. He hints at the Golden Age (I. xi), strikes the note of grotesque Spenserian realism (I. xiv), and satirizes *negotium* as against *otium* (I. xiii), attaining for a moment the genial social position elaborated later in Canto I. His versatility and plausibility are at their height in his adaptation and perversion of moral philosophy:

What, what, is Virtue, but Repose of Mind?
A pure ethereal Calm! that knows no Storm;
Above the Reach of wild Ambition's Wind,
Above those Passions that this World deform,
And torture Man, a proud malignant Worm!
But here, instead, soft Gales of Passion play,
And gently stir the Heart, thereby to form
A quicker Sense of Joy; as Breezes stray
Across th' enliven'd Skies, and make them still more gay.
(I. xvi)

Here he uses for his own ends the moral philosophy which is presented in good earnest in Thomson's plays. He bypasses the moral program expounded by Siffredi in *Tancred and Sigismunda,* I. iv:

---

[23] Matthew vi:26-29. One of Thomson's early poems is a paraphrase of this passage. See *LD,* p. 21. Cf. also the stanza from West quoted above, p. 10. For Thomson's use of scripture in this passage and elsewhere, see John M. Aden, "Scriptural Parody in Canto I of *The Castle of Indolence,*" *MLN,* LXXI (1956), 574-77.

Nothing so easy as in Speculation,
And at a distance seen, the Course of Honour,
A fair delightful Champian [*sic*] strew'd with Flowers.
But when the Practice comes; when our fond Passions,
Pleasure and Pride and Self-Indulgence throw
Their magic Dust around, the Prospect roughens:
Then dreadful Passes, craggy Mountains rise,
Cliffs to be scal'd, and Torrents to be stem'd:
Then Toil ensues, and Perseverance stern;
And endless Combats with our grosser Sense,
Oft lost, and oft renew'd; and generous Pain
For others felt; and, harder Lesson still!
Our honest Bliss for others sacrific'd;
And all the rugged Task of Virtue quails
The stoutest Heart of common Resolution.
Few get above this turbid Scene of Strife,
Few gain the Summit, breathe that purest Air,
That heavenly Ether, which untroubled sees
The Storm of Vice and Passion rage below.

In these lines the landscape of *The Castle* is disposed of as an illusion; the devotee of virtue must make his way through a hard country. Disillusion and error come through the passions; their malign influence is described as a "magic Dust," a phrase also used of the illusion produced by Thomson's enchanter (II. xli). His spell is a short cut to the calm above the storm, the ultimate repose of mind or "ease" which is set up as the goal. The influence of the Lucretian figure of the detached philosopher viewing the storm (*De Rerum Natura* II. 1-13) appears in both passages, but the enchanter offers ease without struggle as his version of the Epicurean *ataraxia*. He also has an alluring distinction between harsh and easy passions, and commends the enjoyment of "soft Gales of Passion." The stock "passion is the Gale" formula is more regularly applied to the instability and irrationality of human life, as in Thomson's *Coriolanus*, IV. i:

> What is the Mind of Man? A restless Scene
> Of Vanity and Weakness; shifting still,
> As shift the Lights of our uncertain Knowledge;
> Or as the various Gale of Passion breathes.

The song is repeated and reinterpreted in II. xli-xlii:

24

With magic Dust their Eyne he tries to blind,
And Virtue's tender Airs o'er Weakness flings.
What Pity base his Song who so divinely sings!

. . . .

But they instead, as if transmew'd to Stone,
Marvel'd he could, with such sweet Art, unite
The Lights and Shades of Manners, Wrong and Right.

Here, at least, Thomson has skilfully connected the two cantos, without breaking the dominant tone of Canto I, by constructing a simulacrum of virtue within the dream.

V

One of the most important and characteristic modes of elaborating and prolonging the vision is to be found in the continuity and identity of life and art, or nature and art. The Castle, in offering a retirement at once pastoral, sentimental, voluptuous, and picturesque, becomes a "Palace of Art." There is a long tradition, endlessly exemplified since Homer's description of the shield of Achilles, in which the poet or onlooker views works of art, sees figures and objects in characteristic movement and action, and is affected by them as by real life.[24] Thomson's use of this situation, familiar and obvious though it is, adjusts the convention to the dream vision of Canto I. In Spenser's Castle Joyeous, where everything invites to love, the walls are hung "with costly Clothes of Arras and of Tour," representing the story of Venus and Adonis (*FQ* III. i. 34 ff.). Thomson's tapestries woven with stories of pastoral love attenuate and sentimentalize the theme:

The Rooms with costly Tapestry were hung,
Where was inwoven many a gentle Tale;
Such as of old the Rural Poets sung,
Or of *Arcadian* or *Sicilian* Vale:
Reclining Lovers, in the lonely Dale,
Pour'd forth at large the sweetly-tortur'd Heart;
Or, looking tender Passion, swell'd the Gale,
And taught charm'd Echo to resound their Smart;
While Flocks, Woods, Streams, around, Repose and
Peace impart.   (I. xxxvi)

---

[24] See Hagstrum, *The Sister Arts*, pp. 18 ff., for an excellent account of this tradition in poetry, which he calls "iconic."

25

The last line blends the vision of the tapestries with the immediate pastoral setting of the Castle itself, and repeats the theme of the muting or subduing of sound in reverie. The next stanza extends the vision backward in time to the Golden Age. And then follows a stanza of great visual and spatial extension:

> Sometimes the Pencil, in cool airy Halls,
> Bade the gay Bloom of Vernal Landskips rise,
> Or Autumn's vary'd Shades imbrown the Walls:
> Now the black Tempest strikes the astonished Eyes;
> Now down the Steep the flashing Torrent flies;
> The trembling Sun now plays o'er Ocean blue,
> And now rude Mountains frown amid the Skies;
> Whate'er *Lorrain* light-touch'd with softening Hue,
> Or savage *Rosa* dash'd, or learned *Poussin* drew.
>
> (I. xxxviii)

Attention is caught by the references in the last two lines, but this much-quoted stanza is more than a *locus classicus* for the names of favorite picturesque painters. The pictures here stand in relation to the tapestries somewhat as the wider ranges of hill and vale stand in relation to the gardens immediately surrounding the Castle. There is a release of the imagination in time and space; it ranges the cycle of the seasons, of changes of weather, of the play of light and shadow over wide prospects. Yet the phrase "in cool airy Halls" puts all this action within the confines of the Castle. The paintings remain *in situ,* and the effect is somewhat like that indicated by an essay in the *Lay-Monk:*

Another Species of Painters delineate *Landskips,* and convey to the Eye pleasant Prospects. They abbreviate Space, contract a Country, and grace the Apartments of a City-Palace with a Variety of Rural Scenes; Groves spread their Branches, Rivers flow, Fountains weep, and Shepherds tend their Flocks, in Rooms of State; and sometimes the Spectators are entertain'd with the Views of solitary Desarts, harmless Monsters and unfrightful Terrors. And this Sort may be justly compar'd to the Writers of Pastorals, whose Province it is to exhibit to the Imagination the same Objects.[25]

The special effect of the sudden irruption of active verbs in the stanza is to be noticed: there is varied movement of air, water, and light, and furthermore the "pencil" moves—the

---

[25] No. 31, January 25, 1714, repr. as *Lay-Monastery* (1714), p. 184.

painters are at work with vigorous impromptu stroke, light touch, or precise draughtsmanship. The action is variously translated in the painter, in the picture, in the poem, and in the observer or dreamer, and all are identified. As compared with the slow tempo of the earlier stanzas there is acceleration here, but the spell is not broken.

The artistic traditions underlying this stanza have been fruitfully studied by Miss Manwaring, Christopher Hussey, and most recently by Jean Hagstrum, and the full analysis need not be repeated. But in illustration of the fusion of influences —the iconic tradition as found in Spenser, the modification and extension of the pastoral, Italian landscape painting, the ideals of contemporary landscape gardening—we may refer to the work of William Kent, architect, landscape gardener, illustrator of Thomson's *Seasons* and later of an edition of *The Faerie Queene*.[26] It is of particular importance to notice that the theory of painting which Thomson inherited would encourage a subjective treatment of landscape, and could easily blend with Spenserian and Miltonic influence. Thus Roger de Piles works toward a view of the painter as creator and dreamer of and within a landscape:

Among all the pleasures which the different talents of painting afford to those who employ them, that of drawing landskips seems to me the most affecting, and most convenient; for, by the great variety, of which it is susceptible, the painter has more opportunities, than in any of the other parts, to please himself by the choice of his objects. The solitude of rocks, freshness of forests, clearness of waters, and their seeming murmurs, extensiveness of plains and offskips [*Lointains*], mixtures of trees, firmness of verdure, and a fine general scene or opening [*les Sites tels que le Paisagiste les veut représenter dans ses Tableaux*], make the painter imagine himself either a hunting, or taking the air, or walking, or sitting, and giving himself up to agreeable musings. In a word, he may here dispose of all things to his pleasure, whether upon land, or in water, or in the sky, because there is not any production either of art or nature, which may not be brought into such a picture. Thus painting, which is a kind of creation, is more particularly so with regard to landskip.[27]

---

[26] See Margaret Jourdain, *The Work of William Kent* (1948), pp. 73, 76 ff.

[27] Roger de Piles, *The Principles of Painting* (1743), pp. 123-24. For convenience I have used the English translation, though Thomson had the French original in his library (Sale Catalogue, No. 121)—*Cours de Peinture par Principes* (Paris, 1708). In this edition the passage quoted is at pp. 200-01. At two points I have tried to clarify the translation by adding the original wording in brackets.

27

Thomson heightens the subjectivity here explicitly claimed for the *paisagiste*.

There follows a similar translation of sound. The next three stanzas (I. xxxix-xli) correlates the sounds of nature and the highest effects of art in the account of the Aeolian harp.[28] Art and nature again find common ground; the harp at the same time represents spontaneous natural force and surpasses the effects of art. As in Thomson's "Ode on Aeolus's Harp," the music is said to range through the expression of love, sorrow, pensive melancholy, religious ecstasy. Nature expresses the whole range of human mood and feeling with incomparable power. "Ah me! what Hand can touch the Strings so fine?" Thomson here transposes and uses to his own end the "celestial voices" and music heard by night in Milton's Paradise.[29] In I. xlii the music undergoes another metamorphosis and blends with the luxurious dreams of the Arabian Nights, only to merge in I. xliii with the sounds of nature again—"soft-tinkling Streams," "dashing Waters," and "sobbing Breezes" (a reprise of the Aeolian harp). The reverie is enriched by the presentation of storm and danger as excluded and remote; "the Demons of the Tempest" threaten without, but gain no entrance. The wizard plays a double role here; he seems to conjure up the threatening storms in collusion with the demons (I. xliii. 4), but the exclusion of the danger is also part of his policy and his insidious spell.[30] There is at least a remote parallel here to the distancing of the storm scenes in the pictures, and once again we have the subduing and blending of natural sounds in reverie, be it sleeping or waking. In the next stanza the heightening of the dream is effected in visual terms:

> And hither *Morpheus* sent his kindest Dreams,
> Raising a World of gayer Tint and Grace;
> O'er which were shadowy cast Elysian Gleams,
> That play'd, in waving Lights, from Place to Place,
> And shed a roseate Smile on Nature's Face.
>
> (I. xliv)

Here we have a remote reflection of the northern lights which Thomson had described so brilliantly in his lines on Lapland (*Winter*, 859-64), but the stanza goes on to compare Morpheus

---

[28] See Notes to *The Castle of Indolence*, Appendix A.
[29] *PL*, IV. 682; V. 547-48. Cf. also *FQ* I. xii. 39.
[30] See further I.xlvi and discussion below,

with Titian, and we are again in the world of the picturesque painters.

As Canto I rises to the height of the dream-vision, the insidious evil that may lurk behind or within pleasure and beauty is only remotely suggested, and its effects are suspended. In the art-sequence the lurking evil is overlooked or submerged, we may say, by the prevailing harmony of art and nature which appears both in the art which the poet practises and the art which the poet describes. For the nonce this harmony provides an escape both from the moral struggle within and the material and social struggle without. The whole situation is explored with greater philosophical range by Spenser. He has other gardens beside the Bower of Blisse; the Garden of Adonis is a true expression of the organic life of nature (*FQ* III. vi. 29 ff.), and in the Garden of Venus art harmoniously supplements nature:

> For all that Nature by her Mother Wit
> Could frame in Earth, and form of Substance base,
> Was there; and all that Nature did omit,
> Art (playing second Nature's Part) supplied it.
>
> (*FQ* IV. x. 21. 6-9)

In *Muiopotmos,* however, the beauties yielded by the concert of nature and art may be carried to excess:

> To the gay Gardens, his unstaid Desire
> Him wholly carried, to refresh his Sprights;
> There lavish Nature, in her best Attire,
> Pours forth sweet Odors, and alluring Sights;
> And Art with her contending, doth aspire
> T' excel the natural, with made Delights:
> And all that fair or pleasant may be found,
> In riotous Excess doth there abound.
>
> (163-68)

Moreover, a specious art appears in the glaring tapestries of the House of Busirane, in which gold lurks like the tempter serpent (*FQ* III. xi. 28). And the beauties of the Bower of Blisse are suffused with a lavishness or excess that accords with the sensual temptations in which the action culminates. It is not entirely correct to say that the Bower is viciously artificial, that nature is here completely superseded by art—the contention of the two produces new beauties:

29

> One would have thought (so cunningly the rude
> And scorned Parts were mingled with the fine)
> That Nature had for Wantonness ensu'd
> Art, and that Art at Nature did repine;
> So striving each th' other to undermine,
> Each did the other's Work more beautify;
> So differing both in Wills, agreed in fine:
> So all agreed through sweet Diversity,
> This Garden to adorn with all variety.
>
> (*FQ* II. xii. 59)

The last two lines of this stanza could be adjusted to Thomson's milieu, but not Spenser's description of the "spacious Plain"

> With all the Ornaments of *Flora's* Pride,
> Wherewith her Mother Art, as half in scorn
> Of niggard Nature, like a pompous Bride
> Did deck her, and too lavishly adorn,
> When forth from Virgin Bower she comes in th' early Morn.
>
> (*FQ* II. xii. 50. 5-9)

The meretricious imitation of nature by art in scenes of temptation would naturally appear in eighteenth century Spenserian pieces, as in Gilbert West's *Canto of the Fairy Queen* (1739), when the damsels allure the Red Cross Knight:

> But all was false Pretence, and hollow Show,
> False as the Flow'rs, which to their Breasts they ty'd,
> Or those which seemed on their Cheeks to glow
> For both were false, and not by Nature dy'd.

With Thomson in this poem art always extends, duplicates, and interchanges with nature (cf. I. xiv. 9; lvii. 9). The friendly rivalry between art and nature enriches life:

> With Nature his creating Pencil vy'd,
> With Nature joyous at the mimic Strife.
>
> (II. xiii)

> As nearer to his Farm you made Approach,
> He polish'd Nature with a finer Hand:
> Yet on her Beauties durst not Art incroach;
> 'Tis Art's alone these Beauties to expand.
>
> (II. xxviii)

Spenser associates elaboration and excess in art with lavishness and plenitude in nature. With Thomson too it is always "boon Nature," but for him in this poem nature is a rich and varied field in which to exercise discrimination and refinement, not a cosmic scene of lavish profusion.

Shenstone, whose ideal of a choice retreat may seem to resemble Thomson's, and who conceived of indolence as a refined and somewhat melancholy retirement (see his "Ode to Indolence") differs from Thomson on this same point of the opposition of nature and art. He presents the contrast elaborately in his "Rural Elegance," setting up a "Palace of Art" in opposition to his retreat, not, like Thomson, within the retreat.

And sure there seem, of human kind,
 Some born to shun the solemn strife;
Some for amusive tasks design'd,
 To soothe the certain ills of life;
Grace its lone vales with many a budding rose,
 New founts of bliss disclose,
Call forth refreshing shades, and decorate repose.

From plains and woodlands; from the view
 Of rural nature's blooming face,
 Smit with the glare of rank and place,
 To courts the sons of fancy flew;
There long had art ordain'd a rival seat;
 There had she lavish'd all her care
 To form a scene more dazling fair,
And call'd them from their green retreat
 To share her proud controul;
Had giv'n the robe with grace to flow,
Had taught exotic gems to glow;
 And emulous of nature's pow'r,
 Mimick'd the plume, the leaf, the flow'r;
Chang'd the complexion's native hue,
Moulded each rustic limb anew,
 And warp'd the very soul!

Awhile her magic strikes the novel eye,
 Awhile the faery forms delight;
 And now aloof we seem to fly
On purple pinions thro' a purer sky,
 Where all is wonderous, all is bright:
 Now landed on some spangled shore
 Awhile each dazled maniac roves
 By saphire lakes, thro' em'rald groves:
 Paternal acres please no more;
Adieu the simple, the sincere delight—
 Th' habitual scene of hill and dale;

31

The rural herds, the vernal gale,
The tangled vetch's purple bloom,
The fragrance of the bean's perfume,
Be theirs alone who cultivate the soil,
And drink the cup of thirst, and eat the bread of toil.

But soon the pageant fades away!
'Tis nature only bears perpetual sway.
We pierce the counterfeit delight,
Fatigu'd with splendor's irksome beams.
Fancy again demands the sight
Of native groves, and wonted streams.
Pants for the scenes that charm'd her youthful eyes,
Where truth maintains her court, and banishes disguise.[31]

All goes so naturally in Thomson's treatment of art that it comes as something of a shock to realize that the enchanter has his part in the music of the Aeolian harp, which

breath'd such Soul-dissolving Airs,
As did, alas! with soft Perdition please:
Entangled deep in its enchanting Snares,
The listening Heart forgot all Duties and all Cares.
(I. xxxix)

The raising and distancing of the tempest by the joint action of demons and wizard (I. xliii), as we have already remarked, falls in with the aesthetic distancing of the arts, though it has a faintly ominous effect. The visions that challenge the genius of the poet are sent by "guileful Angel-seeming Sprights" (I. xlv).

They were in Sooth a most enchanting Train,
Even feigning Virtue; skilful to unite
With Evil Good, and strew with Pleasure Pain.
(I. xlvi)

This note of warning, however, has not been insistently sounded in the descriptions themselves. The warning can come only from the poet himself, even though the vision and the illusion are his. But he cannot get ahead of his story and anticipate the action of the Knight of Arts and Industry; he must therefore become a commentator and moralist in his own right. As an artist, he still wishes to maintain the continuity of the vision, and so, instead of abandoning the dream and precipitating disenchantment and punishment, he is impelled to give his vision

---

[31] Shenstone, *Works* (1764), I, 112-13.

moral content. Behind the dream stands the insidious enchanter; threatening more remotely are the demons who bring
horror and despair (I. xlvi. 4-9). "Guardian Spirits," "Angels
of Fancy and of Love," are then invoked against these demons
—spirits who may

> Evoke the sacred Shades of *Greece* and *Rome*,
> And let them Virtue with a Look impart!
> (I. xlvii)

The theme of *Liberty* appears for a moment within the dream.
But more particularly the beneficent spirits are to restore to
the dreamer his better self, the memory of long-lost friends
(I. xlvii. 7-9), and above all the recollection of childhood innocence in communion with Nature (I. xlviii). The implication
is that this Wordsworthian regeneration may save the victim
of Indolence, the hedonist in the Castle, and thus become an
inward counter- or anti-enchantment, a virtuous alternative to
illusion. But the private and subjective history, moving clearly
in the direction of Wordsworth, cannot easily be made to run
concurrently with the social or public history, the framing allegory. The Knight of Arts and Industry has still to do his
work in Canto II. Thomson realizes that he has got ahead too
fast, chooses to treat this important development as a digression,
and brings the great sequence to an abrupt conclusion:

> But, fondly wandering wide,
> My Muse, resume the Task that yet doth thee abide.
> (I. xlviii)

vi

Thus far we have considered two dream-visions which con-
centrate the characteristic effects of Canto I—the early stanzas
developed from the landscape, and a second sequence (xxxvi-
xlviii) which we may call the vision of the arts. Between the two
is a sequence growing out of the social side of the allegorical
action, the entrance of the throng into the Castle, the gathering
in the court, and the proclamation made to "the Sons of Indolence." Other aspects of this social situation are to be considered later; at this point we should note the recurrence of
the theme of enchantment and reverie, so that we are still led
from vision to vision. The effect of the song of the enchanter
(I. ix-xix), initiating the action of the group, is given in a stanza
which shows a subtle blending of Spenser and Milton:

He ceas'd. But still their trembling Ears retain'd
The deep Vibrations of his witching Song;
That, by a Kind of Magic Power, constrain'd
To enter in, pell-mell, the listening Throng.
Heaps pour'd on Heaps, and yet they slip'd along
In silent Ease: as when beneath the Beam
Of Summer-Moons, the distant Woods among,
Or by some Flood all silver'd with the Gleam,
The soft-embodied Fays through airy Portal stream.
(I. xx)

The opening reminds us that the lay of Thomson's enchanter
derives not only from Phaedria's song, already noted, but from
the "love Lay" sung in Spenser's Bower of Blisse:

He ceast, and then 'gan all the Quire of Birds
Their diverse Notes t' attune unto his Lay,
As in approvance of his pleasing words.
(*FQ* II. xii. 76. 1-3)

The rest of the stanza comes from the entrance of Milton's
devils into Pandemonium, an "aery crowd" who "swarm'd and
were straiten'd," in "narrow room throng numberless," and
are compared to

Faery Elves,
Whose midnight Revels, by a Forest side
Or Fountain some belated Peasant sees,
Or dreams he sees, while over-head the Moon
Sits Arbitress, and nearer to the Earth
Wheels her pale course.
(*PL* I. 781-86)

Thomson had already imitated this passage directly in *Summer:*

Onward they pass, o'er many a panting Height,
And Valley sunk, and unfrequented; where
At Fall of Eve the Fairy People throng,
In various Game, and Revelry to pass
The Summer-Night, as Village-Stories tell.
(1671-75)

After the proclamation to the Sons of Indolence, the crowd in
the courtyard disperses and disappears so suddenly that it may
be said to vanish, like the ring of fairies from the vision of
Milton's bemused peasant.

34

Strait of these endless Numbers, swarming round,
As thick as idle Motes in sunny Ray,
Not one eftsoons in View was to be found,
But every Man stroll'd off his own glad Way.
Wide o'er this ample Court's blank Area,
With all the Lodges that thereto pertain'd,
No living Creature could be seen to stray;
While Solitude, and perfect Silence reign'd:
So that to think you dreamt you almost was constrain'd.

(I. xxix)

The first two lines are directly from another familiar passage
in Milton:

As thick and numberless
As the gay motes that people the Sun-Beams. . . .
(*Il Penseroso*, 5-6)

The swarming numbers link back to the earlier stanza; they
are now transferred to broad daylight and a more commonplace social scene, with an "ample Court" and "Lodges," which
are nevertheless given over to solitude and silence as if by
magic. And the dream motif is immediately repeated in the
most famous stanza in Thomson's poem, perhaps the most famous Spenserian stanza since Spenser himself:

As when a Shepherd of the *Hebrid-Isles*,
Plac'd far amid the melancholy Main,
(Whether it be, lone Fancy him beguiles;
Or that aerial Beings sometimes deign
To stand, embodied, to our Senses plain)
Sees on the naked Hill, or Valley low,
The whilst in Ocean *Phoebus* dips his Wain,
A vast Assembly moving to and fro:
Then all at once in Air dissolves the wondrous Show.

(I. xxx)

The opening cadences and the situation of the shepherd at sun-
down echo the beginning of a stanza in Spenser:

As gentle Shepherd in sweet Even-tide,
When ruddy *Phoebus* 'gins to welk in West,
High on a Hill, his Flock to vewen wide—
(*FQ* I. i. 23. 1-3)

but instead of Spenser's realistically presented feeding flock and
"Cloud of combrous Gnats" Thomson develops a romantic

35

vision within the perspective of hill and ocean. This second culminating imaginary landscape stands in parallel to the earlier vision in I. v. In both passages shadowy forms move to and fro in a perspective of hill, valley, and surrounding or distant sea; the dreamer *Idless* of the earlier stanza becomes the shepherd; the shepherd in turn plays the same role in the epic simile as does Milton's "belated peasant" who sees or dreams he sees an "aery crowd." The lines on the Hebrides in *Autumn*, 871 ff., show how, under the influence of Martin Martin's travel narratives, "shepherd" and "Hebrid" would be associated for Thomson;[32] and also draw their geographical sweep and power from "the stormy *Hebrides*" of *Lycidas*, 156-58. In *Autumn* the lines on the Hebridean shepherd and his flocks and herds are immediately followed by a general prospect of Scotland, beginning

> And here a while the Muse,
> High-hovering o'er the broad cerulean Scene,
> Sees CALEDONIA, in romantic View.
>
> (878-80)

For such a prospect Thomson now substitutes the shepherd's vision, which may be colored by Scottish folklore, though not, as far as I can see, by Martin's reports. Milton, Martin, and Thomson's own prospect of Caledonia now give way to a more truly "romantic View," presented in a single epic simile.

Where can the poet go from here? What can follow the climactic vision? He asks these questions in his own way:

> Ye Gods of Quiet, and of Sleep profound!
> Whose soft Dominion o'er this Castle sways,
> And all the widely-silent Places round,
> Forgive me, if my trembling Pen displays
> What never yet was sung in mortal Lays.
> But how shall I attempt such arduous String?
> I who have spent my Nights, and nightly Days,
> In this Soul-deadening Place, loose-loitering?
> Ah! how shall I for This uprear my moulted Wing?
>
> (I. xxxi)

In the first five lines Thomson echoes directly the words of Virgil, asking the gods of the Lower World for their favor so that he may describe the secrets of their realm:

---

[32] *Background of Seasons*, pp. 132-33; *Britannia*, 88-89 and n.

36

Di, quibus imperium est animarum, umbraeque silentes,
et Chaos, et Phlegethon, loca nocte tacentia late,
sit mihi fas audita loqui; sit numine vestro
pandere res alta terra et caligine mersas!

(Aeneid, VI. 264-67)

Thomson has opened the portals of another world, but in order
to develop this theme, inspired by Indolence in one sense, he
exhorts himself to throw off the spell of Indolence in another
sense. The poet plays a double role, and in the stanza just
quoted he has shifted from one to the other; he can for a stanza
be the visionary seer, as William Collins at certain moments
was, conscious of inevitable frustration even at the moment of
his inspiration; but he is also the writer of relatively long poems
that aspire to weight and importance; to show that he denies
Indolence in a more pedestrian sense he must work in established forms, and we pass in the next stanza from *The Castle
of Indolence* to prospective dramas and patriotic poems:

Come on, my Muse, nor stoop to low Despair,
Thou Imp of *Jove,* touch'd by celestial Fire!
Thou yet shalt sing of War, and Actions fair,
Which the bold Sons of BRITAIN will inspire;
Of antient Bards thou yet shalt sweep the Lyre;
Thou yet shalt tread in Tragic Pall the Stage,
Paint Love's enchanting Woes, the Heroe's Ire,
The Sage's Calm, the Patriot's noble Rage,
Dashing Corruption down through every worthless Age.

(I. xxxii)

Thomson here adapts Spenser's invocation to his Muse:

Now, O thou sacred Muse, most learned Dame,
Fair Imp of *Phoebus,* and his aged Bride,
The Nurse of Time, and everlasting Fame,
That warlike Hands ennoblest with immortal Name.

(FQ I.xi. 5. 6-9)

The emphasis is somewhat different in Spenser, who is asking
the Muse to confer inspiration in a gentler form, to defer her
martial rage:

Fair Goddess, lay that furious Fit aside,
Till I of Wars and bloody *Mars* do sing,
And *Briton* Fields with *Sarazin* Blood bedy'd.

(FQ I. xi. 7. 1-3)

Both Spenser and Thomson have in mind at this point the parallel passage in the *Shepherds' Calendar,* which in the manner of pastoral poetry looks forward to future epic:

> Abandon then the base and viler Clown,
> Lift up thy self out of the lowly Dust;
> And sing of bloody *Mars,* of Wars, of Giusts— ...
>
> (October, 37-39)

And Thomson for his part echoes later lines in the same piece:

> How I could rear the Muse on stately Stage,
> And teach her tread aloft in Buskin fine,
> With queint *Bellona* in her Equipage.
>
> (112-14)

Thomson's transition in stanzas xxxi-xxxii may be compared with that in stanzas xlv-xlviii, where as we have noted, he passes from the immediately or ultimately evil effects of Indolence, to guardian spirits who inspire virtue and revive purifying childhood memories. In the latter transition Thomson approaches the Wordsworthian ideal of combining romantic and ethical vision; within the vision the inspiring spirits become beneficent. The shift in stanzas xxxi-xxxii is different; in escaping from Indolence the poet changes his theme and moves in the direction of the campaign of the Knight in Canto II. So far as the lines may be taken as referring to Thomson's plans for future work they point in a general way to Canto II and to the dramas which exalt liberty and patriotism, but it is impossible to be sure of their chronological relationship to *Agamemnon, Edward and Eleonora,* and *Coriolanus.*

On the aesthetic side, Indolence is connected with an imaginative spontaneity which can at times produce high poetic concentration. On the ethical side Indolence promotes relaxed benevolence—though here to be sure we are following the insidious words of the enchanter—and substitutes "soft Gales of Passion" for violent and selfish impulses. At this point we are not far from the shadowy central figure of *The Seasons,* the contemplative enthusiast and benevolist. When treated lightly, however, such a figure may sink to mere geniality. We here return to the casual origin of the poem, its social setting, and the associated idea that the Spenserian style is particularly suited for "raillery" or burlesque. A middle way thus develops which is neither broadly ludicrous nor highly elevated. As has been noted, the Spenserian medium admits easy modulation, and the various levels of style shade into one another. But the easy middle style is the hardest of all to combine with formal allegory. In this context the extreme evils of Indolence and the chivalric enterprise of the Knight of Arts and Industry are alike incongruous; the Knight comes from another world, and if he had suddenly appeared among the group in the Castle he might have been addressed in the words used by Ferret to Sir Launcelot Greaves at the beginning of Smollett's story: "What! you set up for a modern Don Quixote?—The scheme is rather too stale and extravagant."

The company in the Castle forms a group such as might be found in many an eighteenth century country-house. It is after all only slightly less sedate than the kind of retirement esteemed in eighteenth century life and literature, the life described, for example, in Thomson's own account of a visit to Lyttelton's Hagley Park: "Nor is the Society here inferior to the Scene. It is gentle, animated, pleasing. Nothing passes but what either tends to amuse the Imagination, improve the Head, or better the Heart. This is the truly happy Life, this Union of Retirement and choice Society: it gives an Idea of that which the Patriarchal or Golden Age is supposed to have been; when every Family was a little State by itself, governed by the mild Laws of Reason, Benevolence, and Love."[33]

Writing in praise of the domestic life to Mrs. Robertson, Thomson refers to "the gay wretches of the age, the joyless inmates of Bachelor's Hall."[34] We are told that "Bachelor's Hall" was "a house on Richmond Hill; so called, from being occupied during the summer season by a society of gentlemen from London,"[35] and here we possibly have a counterpart in real life of the gathering place in Canto I. A related local reference may be "the *Hall of Smoak*" (I. lxx), perhaps a neighboring coffeehouse where an associated group gathered. Thomson invests "Bachelor's Hall" with ideal charms along with a genial bohemianism and a disregard for the minor proprieties and regularities—a liberty that falls short of li-

---

[33] *LD*, p. 166. Thomson to Elizabeth Young, August 29, 1743. This passage, it should be remembered, is connected with the appropriate landscape setting. With the reference to the Golden Age, cf. 1. xxxvii.

[34] *Ibid.*, pp. 144-45.

[35] David Stewart Erskine, Earl of Buchan, *Essays on the Lives and Writings of Fletcher of Saltoun and the Poet Thomson* (1792), p. 276 n.

centiousness. Yet life in the Castle has something in common with life in Rabelais' Abbey of Thélème. The proclamation "Ye Sons of INDOLENCE, do what you will" (I. xxviii), is the cardinal rule of Rabelais: "In all their rule and strictest tie of their order there was but this one clause to be observed, DO WHAT THOU WILT."[36] A few stanzas later Thomson elaborates the borrowing:

> For why? There was but One great Rule for All;
> To-wit, That each should work his own Desire,
> And eat, drink, study, sleep, as it may fall.
> (I. xxxv)

As Rabelais says in the passage just cited: "All their life was spent not in laws, statutes, or rules, but according to their own free will and pleasure. They rose out of their beds when they thought good; they did eat, drink, labour, sleep, when they had a mind to it, and were disposed for it." Of course Thomson's company does not lead a brilliant Renaissance court life, with all spontaneously agreeing, as in Rabelais, to pursue the same diversions. From Rabelais' elaborate chapter on costume (I, lvi) Thomson may have been prompted to expand a hint in Spenser's description of "Pleasure's porter," at the entrance to the Bower of Blisse:

> His looser Garment to the ground did fall,
> And flew about his Heels in wanton wise,
> Not fit for speedy Pace, or manly Exercise.
> (FQ II. xii. 46. 7-9)

Thomson's porter, with his staff, derives from this figure, and is also called "comely," though he is made gross and sleepy, and given a little page, like Falstaff. But his principal duty is to provide "great Store of Caps, of Slippers, and of Gowns" (I. xxvi), the familiar undress of the period, in which Thomson's inmates, less fashionable than Rabelais' cavaliers, saunter up and down. In the porch of Spenser's Bower there was also a "comely dame" called Excesse—

> Clad in fair Weeds, but foul disordered,
> And Garments loose, that seem'd unmeet for Womanhed.
> (FQ II. xii. 55. 8-9)

---

[36] Trans. Urquhart-Motteux, 1, lvii.

Yet Thomson avoids the suggestion of sexual license in such a passage. Somewhat similarly, we may say that there is as much Rabelaisian exaggeration as Spenserian luxury in the furnishings of Thomson's halls—

> where, who can tell
> What Elegance and Grandeur wide expand
> The Pride of *Turkey* and of *Persia* Land?
> Soft Quilts on Quilts, on Carpets Carpets spread,
> And Couches stretch around in seemly Band;
> And endless Pillows rise to prop the Head;
> So that each spacious Room was one full-swelling Bed.
>
> (I. xxxiii)

The chamber in the Castle Joyeous whose tapestries Thomson knew is further described in this way by Spenser:

> So was that Chamber clad in goodly wise,
> And round about it many Beds were dight,
> As whilome was the antique Worldez Guise,
> Some for untimely Ease, some for Delight,
> As pleased them to use, that use it might:
> And all was full of Damzels, and of Squires,
> Dauncing and revelling both day and night,
> And swimming deep in sensual Desires,
> And *Cupid* still emongst them kindled lustful Fires.
>
> (*FQ* III. i. 39)

Thomson devotes his beds to innocent repose. Spenser still predominates, and it is unnecessary to make an extensive claim for the influence of Rabelais here, evident though it is, but it is worth noticing that both the Abbey of Thélème and the Castle of Indolence are virtually free of the grosser aspects of sex, and Rabelais may have helped to strengthen Thomson's emphasis on choice and lavish material comforts and innocent diversions within a framework of Spenserian enchantment.

This middle level, or light burlesque, very prominent in Canto I, can be distinguished from the more imaginative flights into the world of "Drowsy-hed" and also from the moralizing program. At the same time, it usually stops short of the extravagantly burlesque. Spenser had given his imitators abundant precedent for including expressions, situations, and episodes which might produce a quaint or grotesque effect for the modern reader. The exact Elizabethan connotation of a word or phrase is of course hard to estimate, but later imitators would

41

take some of Spenser's lines as an invitation to playful home-
liness and broad humorous effects, e.g.,

> Below her Ham her Weed did somewhat train—
> (*FQ* II. iii. 27. 1)

> Like foolish Flies about an Honey-Crock—
> (*FQ* V. ii. 33. 3)

the description of the child who cannot be quieted by his nurse,

> But kicks, and squalls, and shrieks for fell Despight;
> Now scratching her, and her loose Locks misusing—
> (*FQ* V. vi. 14. 5-6)

or the episode in which the knights defeated by Radigund are
forced to do housework—

> To spin, to card, to sew, to wash, to wring. . . .
> (*FQ* V. iv. 31. 6)

A principal point about eighteenth century Spenserian imitation is that the reader's expectations may be complex and
uncertain. He may be in quick succession expecting the high
and getting the low, expecting the low and getting the high,
expecting the abstract and getting the concrete and *vice versa.*
Pope's "The Alley," too short to show any wide range of effects,
gives us Spenserian stanzas which approximate the circumstantial realism of Swift's "Description of the Morning"; Shenstone's *The School-Mistress* playfully elevates ordinary circumstances without a touch of allegory, and is pretty consistently
mock-heroic. Thomson, trying to write a full-scale Spenserian
allegory and a playful study in Spenserian style at the same
time, gets into difficulties with his complex program, but at-
tains happy effects, especially in Canto I, because he takes advantage of the opportunity to develop a flexible style which
can move easily without too rigid a commitment in any one
direction.

A close study of the modulations and transitions of Canto I
is unnecessary, and would entail a reading stanza by stanza; but
a few illustrations may be given, to show the various ways in
which realistic detail is handled here. A favorite theme is the
luxury of silence and repose, which inspires exquisite phrasing:

> But whate'er smack'd of Noyance, or Unrest,
> Was far far off expell'd from this delicious Nest.
> (I. vi)

But when we are told that the doors

> knew no shrill alarming Bell,
> Ne cursed Knocker ply'd by Villain's Hand—
>
> (I. xxxiii)

the same theme is translated into terms of eighteenth century society; the footman of a person of quality would demand attention by giving a thundrous double knock. "At every Door, hark! how they thundering call" (I. liii and note). A stanza in the enchanter's song elaborates the same topic:

> No Cocks, with me, to rustic Labour call,
> From Village on to Village sounding clear;
> To tardy Swain no shrill-voic'd Matrons squall;
> No Dogs, no Babes, no Wives, to stun your Ear;
> No Hammers thump; no horrid Blacksmith sear,
> Ne noisy Tradesman your sweet Slumbers start,
> With Sounds that are a Misery to hear:
> But all is calm, as would delight the Heart
> Of *Sybarite* of old, all Nature, and all Art.
>
> (I. xiv)

This passage was inspired by Spenser's long account of Sir Scudamour's sleepless night in the blacksmith shop of Care (*FQ* IV. v. 33 ff.), the perfect antitype of Thomson's enchanted realm of peace, and Thomson cannot surpass Spenser here in humorous realism:

> And evermore, when he to sleep did think,
> The Hammer's sound his Senses did molest;
> And evermore, when he began to wink,
> The Bellows Noise disturb'd his quiet Rest,
> Ne suffred Sleep to settle in his Breast:
> And all the Night the Dogs did bark and howl
> About the House, at scent of Stranger Guest:
> And now the crowing Cock, and now the Owl
> Loud shrieking, him afflicted, to the very Soul.
>
> (*FQ* IV. v. 41)

The light and easy elevation of the theme at the end of Thomson's stanza comes directly or indirectly from Athenaeus: "The Sybarites were also the first to forbid noise-producing crafts from being established within the city, such as blacksmiths, carpenters, and the like, their object being to have their sleep undisturbed in any way; it was not permitted even to keep a rooster inside the city."[37]

Thus much of the charm of Canto I comes from the fact that the transitions and shadings of tone are various and unpredictable, with an underlying control that avoids the gross and the extravagant. The stanza on harsh noises is rounded off with the Sybaritic touch. The torpor of the porter at the gate represents the comic side of the Morpheus tradition, and his little page, as we have noticed, is like Falstaff's, but the situation is lightly sketched, and limited to three stanzas (I. xxiv-xxvi). Similarly, Thomson touches only lightly on the sensual side of sex, as in the reference to the maiden "in some Losel's hot Embrace" (I. xxiii), or the remote allusion to "th' Arabian Heav'n" (I. xlv). There are no descriptions of damsels bathing and sleeping, as in Spenser's palaces and gardens, and readers who remember the Damon and Musidora episode in *Summer* will be thankful for this. As for the pleasures of the table, Thomson seeks for the rich without the palpable or realistic, and resorts to the romantic tradition:

> And every-where huge cover'd Tables stood,
> With Wines high-flavour'd and rich Viands crown'd;
> Whatever sprightly Juice, or tasteful Food,
> On the green Bosom of this Earth are found,
> And all old Ocean genders in his Round:
> Some Hand unseen These silently display'd,
> Even undemanded by a Sign or Sound;
> You need but wish, and, instantly obey'd,
> Fair-rang'd the Dishes rose, and thick the Glasses play'd.
>
> (I. xxxiv)

Here Thomson parts company with the simple country life praised by Virgil and Horace. Into his adaptation of the passage at the end of the second Georgic he had put the lines:

> What tho', from utmost Land and Sea purvey'd,
> For him each rarer tributary Life
> Bleeds not, and his insatiate Table heaps
> With Luxury, and Death? What tho' his Bowl
> Flames not with costly Juice?
>
> (*Autumn*, 1246-50)

---

[37] *Deipnosophistae,* trans. C. B. Gulick (Loeb Classical Library), xii, 518.

But at this point in *The Castle of Indolence* we are at a sump-
tuous table like the one set by Tasso's enchantress Armida for
the Christian knights whom she beguiles:

> Apprestar sù l'herbetta, ov'è più densa
> L'ombra, e vicino al suon de l'acque chiare
> Fece di sculti vasi altera mensa,
> E ricca di vivande elette, e care.
> Era quì ciò, ch'ogni stagion dispensa:
> Ciò che dona la terra, ò manda il mare;
> Ciò che l'arte condisce, e cento belle
> Servivano al convito accorte ancelle.
> (*Gerusalemme Liberata*, X. lxiv)

This stanza is thus translated by Fairfax:

> Under the Curtain of the green-wood Shade,
> Beside the Brook, upon the velvet Grass,
> In massy Vessels of pure Silver made,
> A Banquet rich and costly furnish'd was:
> All Beasts, all Birds beguil'd by Fowlers Trade,
> All Fish were there, in Floods or Seas that pass,
>   All Dainties made by Art; and at the Table
>   An hundred Virgins serv'd, for Husbands able.

It seems probable that Thomson was led from Acrasia's Bower
of Blisse to one of Spenser's principal models, the alluring
Armida of Tasso. Armida elsewhere sets a banquet for Rinaldo
(*Gerusalemme Liberata*, XV. lviii), a passage also used by
Spenser. Here the lines

> Quivi di cibi preciosa, e cara
> Apprestata è una mensa in su le rive—

appear thus in Fairfax:

> There on a Table was all dainty Food
> That Sea, that Earth, or liquid Air could give.

Since this passage in Fairfax had already been imitated by West
in his *Canto of the Fairy Queen,* it was evidently familiar to
eighteenth century Spenserians:

> There when they landed were, them ran to greet
> A Bevy bright of Damsels gent and gay,
> Who with soft Smiles, and Salutation sweet,
> And courteous Violence would force them stay,
> And rest them in their Bow'r not far away;

Their Bow'r that most luxuriously was dight
With all the Dainties of Air, Earth, and Sea,
All that mote please the Taste, and charm and Sight,
The Pleasure of the Board, and Charm of Beauty bright.

For the temptation banquet of *Paradise Regained* (II. 340-47) Milton follows the stanza in Fairfax quoted in full above. Thomson no doubt knew all these passages, from Tasso on,[38] but he does not give us Milton's elaborate bill of fare, suggesting the grossness of plenitude. In Milton too, as in Tasso, alluring damsels help to offer the food, and eventually, as in Virgil, harpies with sounding wings sweep it away. Meanwhile the whole show is held up to scorn—"Thy Pompous Delicacies I contemn." Thomson substitutes for all this a facile and silent magic; the emphasis is on the ease and delicacy of the service rather than on the sumptuousness of the banquet, and there is nothing obviously gross or ominous.

It is not until the Mirror of Vanity passage (I. xlix ff.) that eighteenth century society reappears. The "huge crystal magic Globe" in which the inhabitants of the Castle view the outer world is of course from Merlin's "world of Glass" or "glassy Globe" (*FQ* III. ii. 18 ff.). Thomson's mirror reveals, instead of the absent lovers of romance, the futile activities of "Idly-busy Men." Like the inscription on the gate of Rabelais' Abbey it reminds us of what is excluded—misers, spendthrifts, those variously involved in the feverish activities of a world dominated by the love of pleasure, gain, and fame. The vision of the great world as it appears from a country retreat, favorably presented in *L'Allegro* (117 ff.), had appeared in an unfavorable light in *Winter* (630 ff.), and now from the vantage point of the Castle takes an exclusively satiric turn.

In returning from this view of the vanities of the world to his special theme (I. lvi), Thomson has some difficulty in keeping up the fiction of residence in the Castle. Indolence is widespread, from statesmen to gipsies. He could "unmask" many a man who seems to be heavily involved in serious concerns, but whose activity really amounts to nothing. All these could be counted among "the Thousands dwelling here"; they exemplify the vanity of life, active though they seem to be. This tran-

---

[38] Thomson's knowledge of Italian is indicated by the considerable number of Italian books in his library, among them the *Gerusalemme Liberata*, Padua, 1737 (Sale Catalogue, No. 153).

46

sitional passage confuses or at least combines futility and indolence.

The catalogue of Thomson's friends, the original incentive
to the poem, shows the range of effects characteristic of Canto I
and also the ambiguity of the theme—indolence inspires now
praise and now reproach. As has been suggested, we have one-
stanza portraits, with a strong element of humor and caricature,
which may represent early work, notably the stanzas on the
sloven (I. lxi) and on Patrick Murdoch (I. lxix). But it is obvious that the sketches of Quin, Lyttelton, and the obese and
indolent poet himself (since this last was substantially written
by Lyttelton) come after 1740. And the stanzas on Paterson
(I. lvii-lix) represent a full development of the major theme
of Canto I, and rise to a climax in the last of the great reverie
passages:

> Oft as he travers'd the Cerulean Field,
> And mark'd the Clouds that drove before the Wind,
> Ten thousand glorious Systems would he build,
> Ten thousand great Ideas fill'd his Mind;
> But with the Clouds they fled, and left no Tract behind.
>
> (I. lix)

The daydream can be poetry, as we have seen in the stanzas on
the dark wood, the vanishing throng, and the shepherd of the
Hebrides, but here it is connected with the theme of wasted
and buried talents, and Thomson goes as far as he can in working out a connection between the praise and the dispraise of
Indolence:

> As soot this Man could sing as Morning-Lark,
> And teach the noblest Morals of the Heart:
> But These his Talents were ybury'd stark;
> Of the fine Stores he Nothing would impart,
> Which or boon Nature gave, or Nature-painting Art.
>
> (I. lvii)

Stock personal jokes of the coterie continue to be put on record, as in the stanzas on Quin's temporary retirement (I. lxvii),
Thomson's reluctance to compose poetry (I. lxviii), the youthful exuberance of Forbes (I. lxii-lxiv), and Armstrong's spleen
(I. lx). The original jest about laziness recurs in ingeniously
varied forms. The portrait of Lyttelton is entirely complimentary and deferential, and the invitation to retire to a lodge

in Hagley Park when he shall at last be tired of politics is in key with the praise of Indolence in an elevated sense (I. lxv-lxvi). Then follows a stanza on some local characters who apparently gather in a Richmond coffeehouse (I. lxx), and two less effective stanzas on fashionable ladies who waste their time, and who of course are subject to the vapours (I. lxxi-lxxii). Thus the ill effects of Indolence come to the fore again.

The transition to the allegory is rather abrupt: "Now must I mark the Villainy we found" (I. lxxiii). Indolence leads to disease and misery, and eventually the inmates of Thomson's Castle are relegated to a dungeon which corresponds to the place assigned to the victims of Acrasia:

> Whom then she does transform to monstrous Hues,
> And horribly mishapes with ugly Sights,
> Captiv'd eternally in iron Mews;
> And darksome Dens, where *Titan* his Face never shews.
> (*FQ* II. v. 27. 6-9)

The place is called in Thomson's poem a "dark Den, where Sickness toss'd alway" (I. lxxiv), and later a "Lazar-House" (II. lxix). At this point Dr. John Armstrong contributed four stanzas for the conclusion of Canto I based on the catalogue of diseases in Milton's "Lazar-house," *PL* XI. 477-95. A heavier hand makes itself felt in these stanzas; in the description of Lethargy, Hydropsy, Hypochondria or Spleen, Ague, Gout, or Apoplexy we have a harsh grotesque which goes beyond the limits Thomson usually observes, even though contemporary medicine might connect all these diseases with the endlessly varied phases and developments of Vapours, Spleen, and Hypochondria. It should be noted, however, that Cantos I and II have abrupt and grotesque endings deliberately devised as part of the Spenserian plan.

vii

The opening stanza of Canto II again illustrates the ambiguity of Indolence;

> Escap'd the Castle of the Sire of Sin,
> Ah! where shall I so sweet a Dwelling find?
> For all around, without, and all within,
> Nothing save what delightful was and kind,
> Of Goodness savouring and a tender Mind,
> E'er rose to View. But now another Strain,

Of doleful Note, alas! remains behind:
I now must sing of Pleasure turn'd to Pain,
And of the false Enchanter INDOLENCE complain.

There is a Miltonic echo here—"I now must change those notes
to tragic" (*PL* IX. 5-6). In the dominant strain of Canto I Indolence was treated as paradisiacal, and the overthrow of the
Castle is therefore in some respects analogous to the Fall and
its consequences. Yet the Castle is a "false Eden" like Acrasia's
Bower,[39] and its overthrow is a triumph of virtue, a noble
achievement of the Knight of Arts and Industry.

Meanwhile, does the poet himself really need to be saved,
and if so, how can he save himself? The question has already
arisen in connection with the climactic visions of Canto I. It
would seem that true inspiration and virtuous pleasure might
be attainable within the delightful surroundings of the Castle;
it requires no revolution or conversion for the poet to say as
he passes from Canto I to Canto II:

I care not, Fortune, what you me deny:
You cannot rob me of free Nature's Grace;
You cannot shut the Windows of the Sky,
Through which *Aurora* shews her brightening Face:
You cannot bar my constant Feet to trace
The Woods and Lawns, by living Stream, at Eve:
Let Health my Nerves and finer Fibres brace,
And I their Toys to the *great Children* leave;
Of Fancy, Reason, Virtue, nought can me bereave.
                                        (II. iii)

This fine and important stanza does in effect reconcile the
nature cult of philosophic retirement, already celebrated in
Canto I, with the theme of the poet at work on his entire
project. But there must now be a transition from the celebration of the delights of reverie to celebration of the active
life, though, with varying emphasis, "Fancy, Reason, Virtue"
are involved in both alike. The poet has already said that he
aspires to celebrate both (I. xxxi-xxxii) in imitating Spenser's
invocation to his epic Muse (see above, pp. 37-38). But there is
now a change in meter and tone which corresponds to the
altered purpose to be realized in Canto II. Professor Dobrée
has pointed out, quoting this stanza, that the style now re-

---

[39] See Harry Berger, Jr., *The Allegorical Temper* (New Haven, 1957), p. 236.

sponds to the new strenuousness, that there is here "a new note, a different pace, of which one would not have thought Thomson capable; the verse has forgotten sublimity but has a vigour and an ease, almost one would say a lordly Byronic assumption of careless power, not it is true sustained, but never far away."[40] Thomson shows that he has mastered both the slowly evolving periodic stanza and the stanza which moves more sharply and vigorously with the single line or clause as the unit. The difficulty is that the changes which modulate the poet's style, sometimes very successfully, are too subtle and suggestive for the heavy allegorical mechanism based on the program of Whig panegyric to which the poet is committed in Canto II. He must rise from "the Bed of Sloth" to sing the prowess of the Knight of Arts and Industry, the offspring of the rough hunter Selvaggio and Dame Poverty, a pedigree suggested by, though not exactly parallel to, Spenser's story of Satyrane's birth (*FQ* I. vi. 20 ff.). Thomson's hero initiates and spreads the arts of civilization and brings them to Britain in a progress like that of *Liberty* and of Industry at the beginning of Thomson's *Autumn*. The course of empire passes from Egypt, Greece, and Rome to Britain.

Even in this progress we note that the ambiguity continues; the development of agriculture yields delights virtually identical with the refined pleasures of Indolence.

> Fair Queen of Arts! from Heaven itself who came,
> When *Eden* flourish'd in unspotted Fame:
> And still with Her sweet Innocence we find,
> And tender Peace, and Joys without a Name,
> That, while they rapture, tranquillize the Mind;
> Nature and Art at once, Delight and Use combin'd.
>
> (II. xix)

The withdrawal of the Knight to a farm in "Deva's Vale" represents an attempt to make the best of the two worlds opposed in the two cantos:

> Nor, from his deep Retirement, banish'd was
> Th' amusing Cares of Rural Industry.
>
> (II. xxvii)

---

[40] Bonamy Dobrée, *English Literature in the Early Eighteenth Century 1700-1740* (Oxford, 1959), p. 498.

The Knight has much to do with creating the landscapes he enjoys. A few lines in this passage resemble Thomson's account of the strenuous and progressive policies of Peter the Great. Compare the cadences and phrasing of the following lines:

> Then Cities rise amid th' illumin'd Waste;
> O'er joyless Desarts smiles the rural Reign;
> Far-distant Flood to Flood is social join'd.
> (Winter, 973-75)

> New Scenes arise, new Landskips strike the Eye,
> And all th' enliven'd Country beautify:
> Gay Plains extend where Marshes slept before:
> O'er recent Meads th' exulting Streamlets fly.
> Dark frowning Heaths grow bright with *Ceres'* Store,
> And woods imbrown the Steep, or wave along the Shore.
> (II. xxvii)

This is the Augustan compromise, we may say, reconciling rural pleasure and social purpose, with landscape gardening as the representative art. The double role of the poet, be he Thomson or Shenstone, is closely analogous. Here, as so often, Addison lays down the program clearly:

But why may not a whole Estate be thrown into a kind of Garden by frequent Plantations, that may turn as much to the Profit, as the Pleasure of the Owner? A Marsh overgrown with Willows, or a Mountain shaded with Oaks, are not only more beautiful, but more beneficial, than when they lie bare and unadorned. Fields of Corn make a pleasant Prospect, and if the Walks were a little taken care of that lie between them, if the natural Embroidery of the Meadows were helpt and improved by some small Additions of Art, and the several Rows of Hedges set off by Trees and Flowers that the Soil was capable of receiving, a Man might make a pretty Landskip of his own Possessions.[41]

In other words, a gentleman may follow the program of Canto II and still have many of the more legitimate enjoyments of Canto I. The Knight's way of life is that of the man of affairs who has interests both in the city and the country.

But with the campaign against corruption that calls the Knight from his retirement, these refined pleasures drop out of the poem. The Knight and the Bard who attends him commend the same hard quest for honor which is exemplified and

---

[41] *Spectator*, No. 414. See also *Background of Seasons*, p. 45.

praised by Spenser's Belphoebe (*FQ* II. iii. 40-41). John Hughes had remarked that the song of *"Idleness"* in Spenser, Phaedria's song, stands in contrast to the speech of Belphoebe.[42] Counterbalancing the song of the enchanter in Canto I we now have the song of the Bard, which opens with a last brief statement of Thomson's religious philosophy, and a last adaptation of one of his favorite passages in Virgil, the "mens agitat molem" of Anchises:

> What is TH' ADOR'D SUPREME PERFECTION, say?
> What, but eternal never-resting Soul,
> Almighty Power, and all-directing Day;
> By whom each Atom stirs, the Planets roll;
> Who fills, surrounds, informs, and agitates the Whole?
> (II. xlvii)[43]

The hymn repeats Thomson's favorite idea of spiritual progress or the return to God along the chain of being (II. xlviii), exhorts men either to the quest of glory or to the wholesome life of the toiling swain (II. liv-lix), and ends with an appeal to the

> Heirs of Eternity! yborn to rise
> Through endless States of Being, still more near
> To Bliss approaching, and Perfection clear.
> (II. lxiii)

For those who resolve, the way is easy. As the Knight had said:

> Those Men, those wretched Men! who *will* be Slaves,
> Must drink a bitter wrathful Cup of Woe:
> But some there be, thy Song, as from their Graves,
> Shall raise. Thrice happy he! who without Rigour saves.
> (II. xxxiv)

> Grace be to Those who can, and will, repent;
> But Penance long, and dreary, to the Slave,
> Who must in Floods of Fire his gross foul Spirit lave.
> (II. xxxix)

One scholar has used the last passage to support the theory that in later life, especially during the period when he was completing this poem, Thomson turned from easy optimism to a

---

[42] Spenser, *Works* (1715), I, lxxix-lxxx.
[43] *Aeneid*, VI. 724 ff. Cf. *Spring*, 854-55, "pervades,/Adjusts, sustains, and agitates the Whole"; *Newton*, 143, "fills, sustains, and actuates the Whole;" "A Hymn on the Seasons," 1730 text, 116, "sustains, and animates the whole;" *Edward and Eleonora*, I, iii. "pervades, sustains,/Surrounds and fills this universal Frame."

more somber and profound view of the human situation, a rapprochement with Christian orthodoxy.[44] The poem as a whole, however, will not bear this interpretation. At the other extreme Professor Fairchild, testing the poets for orthodoxy, can find that *The Castle of Indolence* exhibits in "not only pre-romantic but pre-Victorian" style an optimistic cult of action, a "sentimentalized Protestant energy" worthy of Rabbi Ben Ezra himself.[45] We may note here a minor instance of the same kind of complication and critical difficulty that arises from the elaboration of Christian imagery at the conclusion of the Second Part of *Faust*.

For the reader of the poem, however, the primary difficulty must be the integrity of the poetic vision rather than the soundness of the doctrine. Thomson's real purpose is to present contrasting visions in a Spenserian antithesis of beauty over against ugliness and deformity—a "Palace of Art" or "Earthly Paradise" in contrast to a "Vision of Sin." His poetry admits easily the kind of action or movement that we find in *The Seasons* in characteristic passages presenting the shifting scenes of earth or sky, or the penetration of nature by a subtle vital spirit. His appropriation of the quasi-dramatic part of Spenser's allegory is derivative and mechanical, at best only a framework for his finer effects. Moreover, he stakes his moral and religious teaching largely on the direct adaptation of the Bower of Blisse episode, whereas Spenser has other knights and innumerable other scenes and episodes to convey various aspects of his doctrine. The achievement of Guyon in destroying the Bower of Blisse is not an entirely appropriate symbol for the triumphs of arts and industry. As Professor Arthos has pointed out, Guyon is not so active as Spenser's other knights; his opponent was not a devil or a rival, but an enchanter. "So for [him] there were mostly the vistas of his senses to resist, and his journey became not so much a marching against enemies as a transport through a series of dreams."[46] But Thomson's champion in Canto II has not been transported through the dreams of Canto I. There is no one in particular who experiences both the delights of Indolence and the penalties that follow, as the isolated

---

[44] "Nature's Volume Broad-Displayed," (London) *Times Literary Supplement*, August 28, 1948, p. 487.

[45] Hoxie N. Fairchild, *Religious Trends in English Poetry*, I (1939), 532-34.

[46] John Arthos, *On the Poetry of Spenser and the Form of Romances* (1956), p. 186.

soul in Tennyson's "Palace of Art" comes to have sleeping or waking visions of horror.

Thomson's borrowings from the Bower of Blisse need hardly be set forth in detail.[47] In Spenser travelers are enticed by the Porter and by the damsel Excesse, who offers a cup of liquor, before Acrasia herself, the "fair witch," casts her spell over the infatuated victim. There are no alluring damsels in Thomson. He keeps the Porter as a realistic and semi-comic figure; the spell of Thomson's enchanted castle is exercised only by the wizard himself, who, as we have seen, derives from Spenser's Archimago. Guyon uses a net, like the one Vulcan used to entrap Mars and Venus, in order to bind Acrasia and her lover Verdant; similarly Thomson's Knight uses "the Net of Woe" twisted by the Fates (II. xxxii, xliii), as a means of capturing the enchanter without being weakened by his magic touch. In Spenser, Acrasia is then bound in chains of adamant, Verdant being dismissed with some good advice; the wild beasts into which Acrasia's victims had been transformed by her Circean spell had previously been subdued by the palmer's staff and are then restored to human form by the same staff. In Thomson some of the sons of Indolence are converted by the Bard's song, but most of them angrily resist, whereupon the Knight by means of a wand of "anti-magic Power" transforms the beautiful landscape into a dreary and foul scene (II. lxvii). This is then elaborated into an Inferno which owes many of its details to the Cave of Despair in Spenser:

> And here and there, on Trees by Lightning scath'd,
> Unhappy Wights who loathed Life yhung;
> Or, in fresh Gore and recent Murder bath'd,
> They weltering lay; or else, infuriate flung
> Into the gloomy Flood, while Ravens sung
> The funeral Dirge, they down the Torrent rowl'd:
> These, by distemper'd Blood to Madness stung,
> Had doom'd themselves; whence oft, when Night controul'd
> The World, returning hither their sad Spirits howl'd.
>
> (II. lxviii)

Spenser's cave is

> like a greedy Grave,
> That still for Carion Carcasses doth crave.

---

[47] A full account is given by Gustav Cohen, *Thomson's Castle of Indolence eine Nachahmung von Spenser's Faerie Queene*, Bonn, 1899.

The owl sounds his "baleful Note,"
And all about it wandring Ghosts did wail and howl.

(FQ I. ix. 33. 4-5, 9)

> And all about, old Stocks and Stubs of Trees,
> Whereon nor Fruit, nor Leaf was ever seen,
> Did hang upon the ragged rocky Knees;
> On which had many Wretches hanged been,
> Whose Carcasses were scattered on the Green,
> And thrown about the Clifts.

(I. ix. 34. 1-6)

Within the cave is a corpse

> All wallow'd in his own yet luke-warm Blood,
> That from his Wound yet welled fresh, alas!

(I. ix. 36. 6-7)

Thomson's adaptation of these stark horrors, without imaginative penumbra, is intended to be but does not actually serve as a counter-picture to the seductive delights of Canto I.[48]

The Knight's disenchanting stroke brings light and relief to the dark catacombs of the Lazar House described at the end of Canto I, and conjures up as anti-type a "goodly Hospital" where the penitent get relief, suggested in a general way by the hospital in Spenser's House of Holiness (FQ I. x. 36 ff.), and also in line with the current praise of philanthropic public works (Liberty, V. 647 ff.). But Thomson is evidently more interested in continuing his graphic report of damnation. The lost souls find themselves in a burning desert strewn with "Gibbets, Bones, and Carcasses" (II. lxxvii, with some details drawn from the description of the desert sandstorm in Summer, 961 ff.), or they find themselves in "a joyless Land of Bogs," or a region of piercing cold (II. lxxviii). There is a slightly sketched landscape of this kind in Spenser:

> A foggy Mist had cover'd all the Land;
> And underneath their Feet, all scatter'd lay
> Dead Skulls, and Bones of Men whose Life had gone astray.

(FQ I. iv. 36. 7-9)

---

[48] Imitation of the Cave of Despair was a device easily available to contemporary allegorizing poets, whether avowedly Spenserian or not. Cf. William Thompson, Sickness (1745), I. 434-46. John Upton's New Canto of Spencer's Fairy Queen (1747) transfers details of the Cave of Despair to his opening description of "the lonesome Cot" in which Archimage prepares his spells.

The general adaptation here of *Paradise Lost* (II. 587-628) need not be indicated in detail. For the dreary Arctic region there is also a borrowing from the *Georgics*, III. 279, 354-56. Within this landscape appear two elaborately described allegorical figures, Beggary and Scorn, driving the damned from one extreme to the other. And there is a final adaptation of Spenser when the "ungodly Fry" are compared to a herd of swine driven through the notoriously muddy high street of Brentford.

> Said *Guyon:* See the Mind of beastly Man,
> That hath so soon forgot the Excellence
> Of his Creation, when he Life began,
> That now he chuseth, with vile difference,
> To be a Beast, and lack Intelligence.
> To whom the Palmer thus: The Dunghil Kind
> Delights in Filth and foul Incontinence;
> Let *Grill* be *Grill,* and have his hoggish Mind,
> But let us hence depart, whilst Weather serves, and Wind.
>
> (*FQ* II. xii. 87)

The enchanter is only the approximate equivalent of Circe, and there has been no magic man-beast metamorphosis, but Thomson repeats the motif of the "hoggish Mind" by means of the epic simile. His herd of swine also connects with the story of the legion of devils driven into the Gadarene swine, and particularly with Milton's use of this story at the end of *Paradise Regained* (IV. 628-30). His final stanza is also indebted to Pope's "The Alley" for the dominant sound of the grunting hogs; and his reference to the prosaic town of Brentford, just across the river from Richmond, may have been suggested by Pope's unheroic catalogue of places along the Thames from Deptford to Windsor. By a last stroke of Spenserian grotesque, as harsh as the conclusion furnished by Armstrong for Canto I, Thomson returns from visionary and allegorical flights to the topical and occasional themes with which he started, and gives his canto an ending as abrupt as Spenser's.

viii

Thomson's bookseller friend Andrew Millar entered the copy of *The Castle of Indolence* at Stationers' Hall on May 6, 1748, and the poem was published the next day (*General Advertiser*). The price, given in the advertisements but not on the title-page, was three shillings. News of the forthcoming publication had evidently been circulated among Thomson's Scottish friends, for on March 22, 1748, David Fordyce had written from Aberdeen to Dr. Doddridge, "I dare say you will be glad to hear that Thomson's 'Castle of Indolence,' which has lain so long indolent, is in the press."[49]

A brief description of the first edition follows:

Title-page: Reproduced below, p. 71.

Collation: [ ]², B-L⁴,[ ]¹.

Contents: Title-leaf, verso blank, [i-ii]; advertisement, explanation of obsolete words, [iii-iv]; text, [1]-81. B¹ is a cancel. In some copies the leaf with advertisement and explanation follows the text, and in some a leaf of advertisements is added.

The second edition was published on September 22, 1748 *(Daily Advertiser)*.

Title-page: Reproduced below, p. 73.

Collation: [ ]³, B-F⁸, [ ]¹.

Contents: Title-leaf, verso blank, [i-ii]; advertisement, explanation of obsolete words, [iii]-v, [vi] blank; text, [1]-81. Page 75 is misnumbered 77. Page 29 was misnumbered 19; this was corrected. Later, the misspelling "Thompson" on the title-page was corrected, *"Catherine-street"* in the imprint became *"Catharine-street,"* and, probably at the same time, an advertisement of books published by Millar was printed on the verso of the last leaf. The later title-page is reproduced on page 75 below. At about the end of 1748 or the beginning of 1749 the remaining copies of this edition were bound up as part of Volume III of the edition of Thomson's Works which Millar was offering for sale, and *The Castle of Indolence* does not thereafter appear as a separate item in Millar's list. Since then, separate publication of the poem in any form has been rare indeed; I can name only Thomas James Mathias' translation into *ottava rima, Il Castello dell' Ozio* (Naples, 1826), and Alec M. Hardie's inadequately annotated edition (Hong Kong, 1956).

Another contemporary edition, with the imprint "London: Printed in the Year MDCCXLVIII," is evidently a piracy, probably printed in Edinburgh. There are copies in the British Museum, at the University of Chicago, and at the University of Michigan. This edition was used as copy text in R. S. Crane's *Collection of English Poems 1660-1800* (1932). It follows the

---

[49] Philip Doddridge, *Correspondence and Diary* (1831), V, 57.

text of the first edition closely, including details of spelling and punctuation, except that it uniformly begins nouns with lower-case letters. The Dublin reprint, "Dublin: Printed for George and Alexander Ewing, and Richard James, Booksellers, in *Dame-Street*. MDCCXLVIII," also follows the text of the first edition closely.[50]

Thomson died on August 27, 1748. Since the second edition appeared less than a month later, the natural presumption might be that this was the last edition under the author's control, and that it would therefore qualify as the copy text. Professor William B. Todd, in the closest study of the subject that has yet been made, reaches the conclusion that "the second is essentially the definitive edition," but is disposed to "deny the implied conclusion that it was attended by the author."[51] He is fully aware of the fact that all posthumous editions of Thomson may be under suspicion of having been corrupted by Lyttelton, whose nefarious operations with the text of *The Seasons* are well known.[52] It is therefore particularly striking that Todd has succeeded in demonstrating that Lyttelton did not meddle materially with the second edition of *The Castle of Indolence*. Lyttelton was certainly responsible for the text of the *Castle* in Volume II of the 1750 *Works:* he dropped stanzas lv and lvi of Canto II, and made other changes; at the same time, however, he followed the readings of the first edition, not the second. If he had been responsible for the changes in the second edition, he would naturally have incorporated them in his "improvements" of 1750. To this extent, at least, the text of the second edition escapes suspicion. Todd acutely points out that only one important revision is common both to the second edition and to the 1750 text—the change in I. lxxv. 6 from

And here a moping Mystery did sit

to

And moping here did Hypochondria sit.

---

[50] For further bibliographical particulars, see R. W. Chapman, "*The Castle of Indolence*," *RES*, III (1927), 456; William B. Todd, "The 1748 Editions of *The Castle of Indolence*," *The Book Collector*, I (1952), 192-93.

[51] "The Text of *The Castle of Indolence*," *English Studies*, XXXIV (1953), 117-21.

[52] See John Edwin Wells, "Thomson's *Seasons* 'Corrected and Amended,'" *JEGP*, XLII (1943), 104-14.

It should be noted that this line occurs in one of the stanzas contributed by Dr. John Armstrong. These stanzas were considerably revised for insertion in Thomson's poem (see notes to I. lxxiv-lxxvii). Except for this one line, all the revisions made in Armstrong's stanzas are fully incorporated in the first edition, and remain unchanged in the second. The revised form of this line, the substitution of "Hypochondria" for "Mystery," was closely connected with the revision of the second line following, which originally read in Armstrong,

> She call'd herself the Hypochondriack Fit,

and reads in both editions of Thomson,

> Who vexed was full oft with ugly Fit.

Presumably the two revisions were made at the same time. It seems likely that by oversight the unrevised reading "moping Mystery" found its way into the first edition, and that Thomson simply put into the second edition a change that had already been made. It also seems clear that Lyttelton was privy to the changes in Armstrong's lines, which form a special group and were probably made *en bloc*, as a transaction earlier than and separate from Thomson's revisions for the second edition.

The verbal changes in the second edition can therefore be accepted. As to other details, the ideal copy text for our purposes would be Thomson's manuscript in its final form. It would be desirable to know how far the mechanical details in the two editions reflect the author's practice and to what extent they were determined by the printer.[53] Though we have no holograph manuscript of Thomson's poem, these questions are not quite unanswerable. An examination of Thomson's autograph corrections in the famous interleaved copy in the British Museum (Pressmark C. 28. e. 17), made about 1743 in preparation for the edition of 1744, shows that the poet paid close attention to the details of punctuation, spelling, and the use of capitals and italics, and that he kept pretty consistently to certain distinctive spellings. The printer Woodfall in 1744 followed Thomson's corrections closely. We cannot of course say just how faithfully the printer of *The Castle of Indolence* fol-

---

[53] For a brief but suggestive and helpful discussion of the relation of printers' and authors' practices in this period, see B. H. Bronson, "Printing as an Index of Taste in Eighteenth Century England," *Bulletin of the New York Public Library*, LXII (1958).

lowed copy in all details; but when we compare usages in the two editions of *The Castle* and in the 1744 and 1746 editions of *The Seasons,* they are on the whole so consistent that we can be fairly sure that they represent Thomson's practice. Examples of forms characteristic of (not of course exclusively peculiar to) Thomson are: *Nought, etherial, Ether, chear, Cott, antient, spreds, Gulph, croud, strait* (in the sense of *straightway*). It may be remarked that Spenserian imitation does not modify Thomson's practice in such points as these. Both editions of *The Castle* show Thomson's habitual capitalization of adjectives (e.g., *Rural Reign, Cerulean Field*) under certain conditions. Italics and small capitals are used in *The Castle* and the last two editions of *The Seasons* on the same general principles: small capitals are used for proper names of the first order of importance, and for key terms generally; italics are used for proper names of secondary importance, and for quoted or emphasized words or phrases. The second edition of *The Castle* shows somewhat heavier punctuation than the first, and in this respect is in line with the last two editions of *The Seasons.*

Under these circumstances, mechanical differences between the two editions do not seem to be of major significance, but the text is of such importance that I have recorded all variants. I have preferred the readings of the second edition unless there was some special reason for choosing the first. The verbal changes in the second edition, as the textual notes will show, are of more significance for Canto I than for Canto II.

ix

The Castle of Indolence pleased the taste of contemporary readers and virtually without exception won their enthusiastic approval. Dr. Thomas Birch, that industrious reporter of literary events, wrote to the Earl of Cork and Orrery on September 30, 1748, a month after Thomson's death: "His last poem, *The Castle of Indolence,* in *Spenser's* style and metre, is, I think worth your Lordsp's perusal, being allowed to be the most intelligible, correct, regular and spiritted of all his performances."[54] In the month of publication Philip Yorke, later Lord Hardwicke, had written to Birch: "I have Thomsons Poem & like it, but think the 1st Book has most of Spencer. Do you

---

[54] *Orrery Papers* (1903), II, 43, in the Houghton Library, Harvard University.

know all the Characters? They are well drawn."[55] On June 5, Thomas Gray remarked in a letter to Wharton, "There is a Poem by Thomson, the Castle of Indolence, with some good Stanzas."[56] We may infer that Gray shared the preferences of Yorke and later readers for the best stanzas of Canto I.

The first full appreciation came from Henry Fielding, in the "Proceedings at the Court of Criticism" dated June 2 and published in the *Jacobite's Journal* June 4:

The Court delivered the following Opinion concerning the *Castle of Indolence,* lately published by Mr. *Thomson:* "This is a noble allegorical Poem, and truly breathes the Spirit of that Author which it professes to imitate.

"The Description of the Castle is truly poetical, and contains every Image which can be drawn from Nature, suitable to the Occasion. The Author hath, with wonderful Art, brought together all the Inducements to Slumber; and at the same time hath taken sufficient Care that they shall have no Effect on his Reader.

"No less Genius appears in the Wizard's Speech. The *Epicurean* System is here enforced with Arguments of such seeming Solidity, that we cannot wonder if it captivated the Hearers. Their Entrance into the Castle is finely described in the 28th Stanza, and illustrated with a beautiful Simile.

"The Inside of the Castle is described with wonderful Power of Fancy. The Subjects of the Paintings are happily chose, and in the exact Spirit of the Antients. The Music likewise is adapted with much Knowledge and Judgment.

"Nothing can be imagined with more Propriety than the Amusements of this Place. The Crystal Globe, in which all the Inhabitants of the Earth are represented, is really a Master-piece, and would have shined in *Homer, Virgil,* or *Milton;* nor is the Execution here unequal to so noble a Hint.

"I shall pass over those Parts where the Author hath chosen to pay a Compliment to some of his Friends; tho' I cannot help saying that these are extremely delicate; and what is contained in the 65th and 66th Stanzas, I know to be extremely just; nor less so is, I believe, the Author's Description of himself, tho' the Character is certainly amiable.

"The Prosopopeia, with which the first Stanza concludes, is a fine Allegory, and contains an excellent Moral; and the Introduction of the Diseases into the Castle by secret Treachery, is one of

---

[55] Letter of May 24, 1748. British Museum, Addit. MS. 35, 397, f. 106ᵛ.

[56] *Correspondence,* ed. Paget Toynbee and Leonard Whibley (Oxford, 1935), I, 307.

those nice Touches which, tho' they principally constitute a great Writer, pass often unobserved by the Generality of Readers.

"The Poet's Lamentation at the Beginning of the 2d Stanza; the Generation of the Knight of Arts and Industry; his Education and Accomplishments; his Introduction into *Britain,* and Establishment here; the Mischief wrought by Indolence; the Description of the Page; the Sally; the Conversation between the Knight and his Bard; the Attempts of the Wizard; the Bard's Song; the Destruction of the Castle, with the different Fates of those who have suffered under different Degrees of the Enchantment of Indolence; the Erection of the Hospital by the Charities descending from Heaven; and lastly, the Descriptions of Beggary and Scorn, form the principal Incidents of the 2d Stanza; nor is there one of all these which doth not deserve great Commendation.

"Upon the whole, there is much Merit in this Performance; and I do order, that the Thanks of the Court be forthwith signified to Mr. *Thomson,* the Author, for his excellent Composition.["]

The Castle of Indolence was a special favorite with Lady Hertford, William Shenstone, and their circle of correspondents. On May 15 Lady Hertford wrote to Lady Luxborough: "I conclude yᵘ will read Mʳ Thomsons Castle of Indolence wᶜʰ is after the manner of Spenser, but I think he does not always keep so close to his Stile as the Author of the School Mistress, whose Name I never knew till yᵘ were so good to inform me of it. . . . to return to the Castle of Indolence, I believe it will afford yᵘ some Entertainment, there are many pretty Paintings in it, but I think the Wizards Song deserves a preferrence

He needs no Muse who dictates from his Heart."[57]

But Shenstone, who was revising *The School-Mistress* for Dodsley's *Collection* just at this time, did not buy and read *The Castle* immediately, because he thought the quarto form made it "unbindable." He was keenly interested in the poem, however, and had formed clear views about it already: "I long to see his Book. My Schoolmistress, I suppose, is much more in Spenser's way than any one wou'd chuse to write in that writes quite *gravely:* in which Case The Dialect & stanza of Spenser is hardly preferable to modern Heroic. I look upon my Poem as somewhat more grave than Pope's Alley, & a good deal less

[57] British Museum, Addit. MS, 23, 728, f. 25ᵛ. Printed in *Select Letters between the Late Duchess of Somerset, Lady Luxborough . . . and Others,* ed. Thomas Hull (1778), I, 68-69.

y^n Mr. Thomson's Castle etc."[58] Meanwhile, at the instance of his correspondent Richard Jago, Shenstone was quite ready to apply Thomson's allegory to himself: "You speak of my dwelling in a Castle of Indolence, and I verily believe I *do*. There is something like enchantment in my present inactivity."[59] By September 25 he had read and approved the poem—in the quarto edition after all, though the octavo edition had now appeared. "It is I think a very pretty Poem, & also a good *Imitation* of *Spenser*; which latter Circumstance is ye more remarkable, as Mr. Thomson's Diction was not reckon'd ye most *simple*. I own I read it wth partiality of y^e *Author*, as I had seen & lik'd y^e *Man*."[60] As was his wont, Shenstone repeated the comment on diction a little later: "Who would have thought that Thomson could have so well imitated a person remarkable for simplicity both of sentiment and phrase."[61] In other words, readers who thought they knew Thomson found the *Castle* a delightful surprise, a brilliant performance in a kind which they were already prepared to accept. Lady Luxborough, writing to Shenstone on October 16, alludes to his verses on Thomson's death and his urn to Thomson's memory, and echoes Lady Hertford and Shenstone himself in her comments on the poem: "His Castle of Indolence I have read at last, and admire several parts of it. He makes the Wizard's Song most engaging: but, as Lady Hertford observes, it is no wonder; for

He needs no Muse who dictates from the Heart;

and Thomson's heart was ever devoted to that Archimage. Do not copy him too nearly in that; it would be cruel to your friends, if, like him,

—your ditty sweet
You loathed much to write, nor cared to repeat."

Other passages in this letter show how the poem was running in her mind. "The eldest son of Archimage [Mr. Outing], and the little round fat oily Man of God [Parson Hull], talk of making you a visit the week that is now coming in." On Shenstone's plans for a "Show-Box" or camera obscura for displaying

---

[58] William Shenstone, *Letters*, ed. Marjorie Williams (Oxford, 1939), pp. 144-45. To Lady Luxborough, June 1, 1748.

[59] *Letters*, p. 165. To Richard Jago, September 11.

[60] *Letters*, p. 170. To Lady Luxborough.

[61] *Letters*, p. 177. To Jago, November 13.

views, she comments: "It would be a good amusement in the Wizard's Castle; for by this means it would give no trouble to bring all the beautiful gardens and palaces of the world to your view, as his chrystal globe by turning shewed him the various turns of man. For my part, I propose to have at my Castle of Barrells Aeolus's Harp; a music which will never cease here as long as the winds maintain their power."[62] Shenstone's reply on November 9 adds another point to the comments being relayed back and forth: "I think he shou'd by no means anticipate y[e] Diseases & Inconveniences of Indolence at y[e] End of his *first* Canto. You know there is a large Display of them in y[e] *second*, where they wou'd have appear'd more strikingly had he not touch'd upon 'em before."[63]

Thus many eighteenth century readers could be found to agree with the contemporary comment that *The Castle of Indolence* "is one of those imitations that, in many respects, equals the original."[64] The later course of the poem in the stream of romantic English verse cannot be traced here, but James Beattie's *Minstrel* is a notable example of the diffusion of its influence among later writers of Spenserian verse. The early parts of Beattie's poem show a conscious effort to elaborate the landscapes, sound effects, and genre pictures of Thomson's Canto I.[65] The general plan of *The Minstrel* is a remaking of *The Castle of Indolence* as a progress poem; Edwin in his career passes from carefree communion with nature and the pleasures of the imagination to an initiation into philosophy and an active life. To the Spenserian stanza as written by the romantic generation Thomson no doubt made his contribution, largely by way of Beattie. Scott, using the stanza in playful mood, acknowledges an affiliation in the Introduction to *Harold*

---

[62] *Letters Written by the Late Right Honourable Lady Luxborough to William Shenstone, Esq.* (1775), pp. 56-59.

[63] *Letters*, pp. 174-75. Shenstone says the same thing in the letter to Jago, November 13, *Letters*, p. 177. Lady Luxborough passes this comment on to Lady Hertford on November 14 (Alnwick Castle, Percy Family Letters and Papers, XXX, 199-200; printed by Helen S. Hughes, *MP*, XXV [1928], 465-66).

[64] *The Art of Poetry on a New Plan* (London: John Newbery, 1762), II, 25.

[65] Without undertaking full illustration, we may note Beattie's upland and romantic views, *Minstrel*, I. xix-xxi; his tasteless elaboration of the "endless Numbers" and "vast Assembly" of Thomson's I. xxix-xxx as a fairy pageant, *Minstrel*, I. xxxiii-xxxv; the expansion of the stanza on Chanticleer, I. xxxvi, from a hint in Thomson; the more successful stanzas on "the melodies of morn," I. xxxviii-xxxix.

the Dauntless, when he speaks of trivial books written to dispel ennui:

> And not of such the strain my Thomson sung,
> Delicious dreams inspiring by his note.
> What time to Indolence his harp he strung;—
> O, might my lay be ranked that happier list among!

Such lines express the spontaneous personal fondness for Canto I which can be variously discovered or inferred, for example, in Hazlitt, Hunt, Byron, and Campbell.

Thomson's personal sketches had a special influence, and inspired Wordsworth's stanzas "Written in my Pocket-Copy of Thomson's Castle of Indolence," dated May 9-11, 1802. This is no fragmentary *jeu d'esprit,* but a poetical adaptation of aspects of the personalities of Wordsworth and Coleridge to Thomson's vision of the delightful way of life in the Castle. There is a special connection with the stanzas associated with Paterson. Somewhat later, John Keats and Charles Armitage Brown exchanged Spenserian stanzas evidently suggested by Thomson's portraits; Keats' line on Brown have the jocose tone of Thomson's stanza on Murdoch.[66]

Perhaps the most memorable literary response to the dream-world of Canto I is Tennyson's "The Lotos-Eaters," especially the Spenserian stanzas which open the poem. For a full appreciation of Tennyson's effects the reader must follow his use of the repeated and echoing word to extend and retard the line in Thomson's manner—

> The murmuring Main was heard, and scarcely heard, to flow.
> Along the cliff to fall and pause and fall did seem.
> Give us long rest or death, dark death, or dreamful ease.—

his enrichment of Thomson's imaginary landscape, and his elaboration of the themes of melancholy, lassitude, and insidious enchantment. But as a response to Thomson's entire poem "The Palace of Art" is even more significant. The Palace is the Castle, and Tennyson greatly elaborates its architecture and decoration, using lavish imagery where Thomson had contented himself with brief strokes and hints. For example, under the influence of collegiate architecture, Thomson's one court with its fountain becomes four courts:

---

[66] *Letters of John Keats,* ed. Hyder E. Rollins (Cambridge, Mass., 1958), II, 89-90. John Keats to the George Keatses, April 16, 1819.

> In each a squared lawn, wherefrom
> The golden gorge of dragons spouted forth
> A flood of fountain-foam.

And the fountains in turn are linked with the surrounding landscape:

> From those four jets four currents in one swell
> Across the mountains streamed below
> In misty folds, that floating as they fell
> Lit up a torrent-bow.

Tennyson extends Thomson's iconic theme, the widening of imaginative range by the contemplation of works of art within the secure retreat; the "great rooms" are "hung with arras" presenting a wide variety of landscape, and there are paintings on wall and ceiling, and all human history in mosaic. As in Thomson, this aesthetic pageant is distinguished from a detached and hostile view of the active world; but here, it is interesting to observe, Tennyson uses the Spenser-Thomson swine-image to express the contempt felt by the soul which holds aloof:

> O Godlike isolation which art mine,
> I can but count thee perfect gain,
> What time I watch the darkening droves of swine
> That range on yonder plain.

> In filthy sloughs they roll a prurient skin,
> They graze and wallow, breed and sleep;
> And oft some brainless devil enters in,
> And drives them to the deep.

But before long she is plunged into the inferno which awaits aesthetic isolation. At this point of course Whig panegyric has been replaced by a more subjective social gospel, and the machinery of Spenserian allegory has been cast aside, yet we may think of Thomson's Lazar House as we read of the soul

> Shut up as in a crumbling tomb, girt round
> With blackness as a solid wall.

Tennyson uses imaginative horror imagery and his power of creating imaginary landscape to attain a balance between the two movements of aesthetic delight and moral despair which Thomson never attained in his two cantos, yet the underlying relationship between the two poems is unmistakable.

It is appropriate that the last significant imitation of Thomson's Spenserian stanzas should be by the nineteenth century James Thomson ("B.V."). The later Thomson's poem, "The Lord of the Castle of Indolence" (1859), is one of the most distinguished of the imitations which use the formula of the description of an inmate of the Castle, and achieves a fine distillation of the theme of the higher Indolence in the original Canto I, clear of all suggestions of evil or impending despair. The stanza which Thomson himself quotes in his later essay on "Indolence" may stand as representative:

> Look, as within some fair and princely hall
> The marble statue of a God may rest,
> Admired in silent reverence by all;
> Soothing the weary brain and anguished breast,
> By life's sore burthens all-too-much oppressed,
> With visions of tranquillity supreme;
> So, self-sufficing, grand and bland and blest,
> He dwelt enthroned, and who so gazed did seem
> Endowed with death-calm life in long unwistful dream.[67]

THE CASTLE OF INDOLENCE

Note on the Critical Apparatus

A   First edition, quarto, 1748
B   Second edition, octavo, 1748
1750 *Works*, Vol. II, 1750
1762 *Works*, Vol. I, 1762

---

[67] *Essays and Phantasies* (1881), p. 152. "B.V." 's friend Bertram Dobell in turn imitated this imitation in companion pieces, *The Dreamer of the Castle of Indolence* (the title-poem of a slender volume published in 1915) and "The Châtelaine of the Castle of Indolence."

THE CASTLE OF INDOLENCE

ADVERTISEMENT

This Poem being writ in the Manner of Spenser, *the obsolete Words, and a Simplicity of Diction in some of the Lines, which borders on the Ludicrous, were necessary to make the Imitation more perfect. And the Stile of that admirable Poet, as well as the Measure in which he wrote, are as it were appropriated by Custom to all Allegorical Poems writ in our Language; just as in French the Stile of* Marot *who lived under* Francis I. *has been used in Tales, and familiar Epistles, by the politest Writers of the Age of* Louis XIV.

[Thomson's] "Explanation of the obsolete Words used in this Poem"

Archimage—*The chief, or greatest of Magicians or Enchanters.*
Atween—*between.*

Bale—*Sorrow, Trouble, Misfortune.*
Benempt—*named.*
Blazon—*Painting, Displaying.*

Carol—*to sing Songs of Joy.*
Certes—*certainly.*

Eath—*easy.*
Eftsoons—*immediately, often, afterwards.*

Gear or Geer—*Furniture, Equipage, Dress.*
Glaive—*Sword.* (Fr.)

Han—*have.*
Hight—*is named, called.*
Idless—*Idleness.*
Imp—*Child, or Offspring; from the* Saxon *Impan, to graft or plant.*

Kest—*for cast.*

Lad—*for led.*
Lea—*a Piece of Land, or Meadow.*
Libbard—*Leopard.*

Lig—*to lie.*
Losel—*a loose idle Fellow.*
Louting—*Bowing, Bending.*

Mell—*mingle.*
Moe—*more.*
Moil—*to labour.*
Muchel or Mochel—*much, great.*

Nathless—*nevertheless.*
Ne—*nor.*
Needments—*Necessaries.*
Noursling—*a Nurse, or what is nursed.*
Noyance—*Harm.*

Perdie— (Fr. *par Dieu*) *an old Oath.*

Prick'd thro' the Forest—*rode thro' the Forest.*

Sear—*dry, burnt-up.*
Sheen—*bright, shining.*
Sicker—*sure, surely.*
Soot—*sweet, or sweetly.*
Sooth—*true, or truth.*
Stound—*Misfortune, Pang.*
Sweltry—*Sultry, consuming with Heat.*
Swink—*to labour.*

68

Transmew'd—*transform'd.*

Vild—*vile.*

Unkempt— (Lat. *incomptus*) *unadorn'd.*

Whilom—*ere-while, formerly.*
Wis, for Wist—*to know, think, understand.*
Ween—*to think, be of Opinion.*
Weet—*to know; to weet, to wit.*
Wonne [Woonne *A*]— (a Noun) *Dwelling.*

N.B. *The Letter* Y *is frequently placed in the Beginning of a Word, by* Spenser, *to lengthen it a Syllable.*

Yborn—*born.*
Yblent, or blent—*blended, mingled.*
Yclad—*clad.*
Ycleped—*called, named.*
Yfere—*together.*
Ymolten—*melted.*
Yode— (*Preter Tense of* Yede) *went.*

69

THE CASTLE OF INDOLENCE

Canto I

The Castle hight of Indolence,
And its false Luxury;
Where for a little Time, alas!
We liv'd right jollily.

i

O Mortal Man, who livest here by Toil,
Do not complain of this thy hard Estate;
That like an Emmet thou must ever moil,
Is a sad Sentence of an ancient Date:
And, certes, there is for it Reason great;
For, though sometimes it makes thee weep and wail,
And curse thy Stars, and early drudge and late,
Withouten That would come an heavier Bale,
Loose Life, unruly Passions, and Diseases pale.

ii

In lowly Dale, fast by a River's Side,
With woody Hill o'er Hill encompass'd round,
A most enchanting Wizard did abide,
Than whom a Fiend more fell is no-where found.
It was, I ween, a lovely Spot of Ground;
And there a Season atween June and May,
Half prankt with Spring, with Summer half imbrown'd,
A listless Climate made, where, Sooth to say,
No living Wight could work, ne cared even for Play.

iii

Was nought around but Images of Rest:
Sleep-soothing Groves, and quiet Lawns between;
And flowery Beds that slumbrous Influence kest,
From Poppies breath'd; and Beds of pleasant Green,
Where never yet was creeping Creature seen.
Mean time unnumber'd glittering Streamlets play'd,
And hurled every-where their Waters sheen;
That, as they bicker'd through the sunny Glade,
Though restless still themselves, a lulling Murmur made.

Argument 1 Indolence] *Indolence* A
i 7 Stars] Star *A*
ii 4 no-where] no where *A*
iii 1 nought] Nought *B*

THE

C A S T L E

O F

INDOLENCE:

A N

ALLEGORICAL POEM.

Written in

IMITATION *of* SPENSER.

By

J A M E S   T H O M S O N.

L O N D O N:

Printed for A. MILLAR, over againſt *Catherine-ſtreet,*
in the *Strand.*

M DCC XLVIII.

Title-page, *The Castle of Indolence,* first edition

iv

Join'd to the Prattle of the purling Rills,
Were heard the lowing Herds along the Vale,
And Flocks loud-bleating from the distant Hills,
And vacant Shepherds piping in the Dale;
And now and then sweet Philomel would wail,
Or Stock-Doves plain amid the Forest deep,
That drowsy rustled to the sighing Gale;
And still a Coil the Grashopper did keep:
Yet all these Sounds yblent inclined all to Sleep.

v

Full in the Passage of the Vale, above,
A sable, silent, solemn Forest stood;
Where nought but shadowy Forms were seen to move,
As *Idless* fancy'd in her dreaming Mood.
And up the Hills, on either Side, a Wood
Of blackening Pines, ay waving to and fro,
Sent forth a sleepy Horror through the Blood;
And where this Valley winded out, below,
The murmuring Main was heard, and scarcely heard, to flow.

vi

A pleasing Land of Drowsy-hed it was:
Of Dreams that wave before the half-shut Eye;
And of gay Castles in the Clouds that pass,
For ever flushing round a Summer-Sky:
There eke the soft Delights, that witchingly
Instil a wanton Sweetness through the Breast,
And the calm Pleasures always hover'd nigh;
But whate'er smack'd of Noyance, or Unrest,
Was far far off expell'd from this delicious Nest.

vii

The Landskip such, inspiring perfect Ease,
Where INDOLENCE (for so the Wizard hight)
Close-hid his Castle mid embowering Trees,
That half shut out the Beams of *Phoebus* bright,
And made a Kind of checker'd Day and Night.

vi 1 Drowsy-hed] Drowsyhed *B*
vii 4 *Phoebus*] Phoebus *A*

THE

CASTLE

OF

INDOLENCE.

AN

ALLEGORICAL POEM.

Written in

IMITATION *of* SPENSER.

By

JAMES THOMPSON.

The SECOND EDITION.

LONDON:

Printed for A. MILLAR, over-againſt *Catherine-ſtreet,* in the *Strand.*

M DCC XLVIII.   [Price 1 ſ. 6 d.]

Title-page, *The Castle of Indolence,* second edition, earlier impression

Mean while, unceasing at the massy Gate,
Beneath a spacious Palm, the wicked Wight
Was plac'd; and to his Lute, of cruel Fate,
And Labour harsh, complain'd, lamenting Man's Estate.

viii

Thither continual Pilgrims crouded still,
From all the Roads of Earth that pass there by:
For, as they chaunc'd to breathe on neighbouring Hill,
The Freshness of this Valley smote their Eye,
And drew them ever and anon more nigh,
Till clustering round th' Enchanter false they hung,
Ymolten with his Syren Melody;
While o'er th' enfeebling Lute his Hand he flung,
And to the trembling Chord these tempting Verses sung:

ix

"Behold! ye Pilgrims of this Earth, behold!
See all but Man with unearn'd Pleasure gay.
See her bright Robes the Butterfly unfold,
Broke from her wintry Tomb in Prime of May.
What youthful Bride can equal her Array?
Who can with Her for easy Pleasure vie?
From Mead to Mead with gentle Wing to stray,
From Flower to Flower on balmy Gales to fly,
Is all she has to do beneath the radiant Sky.

x

"Behold the merry Minstrels of the Morn,
The swarming Songsters of the careless Grove,
Ten thousand Throats! that, from the flowering Thorn,
Hymn their good GOD, and carol sweet of Love.
Such grateful kindly Raptures them emove:
They neither plough, nor sow; ne, fit for Flail,
E'er to the Barn the nodding Sheaves they drove;
Yet theirs each Harvest dancing in the Gale,
Whatever crowns the Hill, or smiles along the Vale.

xi

"Outcast of Nature, Man! the wretched Thrall
Of bitter-dropping Sweat, of sweltry Pain,

viii 6 Till] 'Till *A*   9 Chord] Chords *A*

THE

CASTLE

OF

INDOLENCE.

AN

ALLEGORICAL POEM.

Written in

IMITATION *of* SPENSER.

By

JAMES THOMSON.

The SECOND EDITION.

LONDON:

Printed for A. MILLAR, over-againſt *Catharine-ſtreet,* in the *Strand.*

M DCC XLVIII. [Price 1 ſ. 6 d.]

Title-page, *The Castle of Indolence,* second edition, later impression

75

Of Cares that eat away thy Heart with Gall,
And of the Vices, an inhuman Train,
That all proceed from savage Thirst of Gain:
For when hard-hearted *Interest* first began
To poison Earth, *Astraea* left the Plain;
Guile, Violence, and Murder seiz'd on Man;
And, for soft milky Streams, with Blood the Rivers ran.

xii

"Come, ye, who still the cumbrous Load of Life
Push hard up Hill; but as the farthest Steep
You trust to gain, and put an End to Strife,
Down thunders back the Stone with mighty Sweep,
And hurls your Labours to the Valley deep,
For-ever vain: come, and, withouten Fee,
I in Oblivion will your Sorrows steep,
Your Cares, your Toils, will steep you in a Sea
Of full Delight: O come, ye weary Wights, to me!

xiii

"With me, you need not rise at early Dawn,
To pass the joyless Day in various Stounds:
Or, louting low, on upstart Fortune fawn,
And sell fair Honour for some paltry Pounds;
Or through the City take your dirty Rounds,
To cheat, and dun, and lye, and Visit pay,
Now flattering base, now giving secret Wounds;
Or proul in Courts of Law for human Prey,
In venal Senate thieve, or rob on broad High-way.

xiv

"No Cocks, with me, to rustic Labour call,
From Village on to Village sounding clear;
To tardy Swain no shrill-voic'd Matrons squall;
No Dogs, no Babes, no Wives, to stun your Ear;
No Hammers thump; no horrid Blacksmith sear,
Ne noisy Tradesman your sweet Slumbers start,
With Sounds that are a Misery to hear:
But all is calm, as would delight the Heart
Of *Sybarite* of old, all Nature, and all Art.

XV

"Here nought but Candour reigns, indulgent Ease,
Good-natur'd Lounging, Sauntering up and down:
They who are pleas'd themselves must always please;
On Others' Ways they never squint a Frown,
Nor heed what haps in Hamlet or in Town.
Thus, from the Source of tender Indolence,
With milky Blood the Heart is overflown,
Is sooth'd and sweeten'd by the social Sense;
For Interest, Envy, Pride, and Strife are banish'd hence.

xvi

"What, what, is Virtue, but Repose of Mind?
A pure ethereal Calm! that knows no Storm;
Above the Reach of wild Ambition's Wind,
Above those Passions that this World deform,
And torture Man, a proud malignant Worm!
But here, instead, soft Gales of Passion play,
And gently stir the Heart, thereby to form
A quicker Sense of Joy; as Breezes stray
Across th' enliven'd Skies, and make them still more gay.

xvii

"The Best of Men have ever lov'd Repose:
They hate to mingle in the filthy Fray;
Where the Soul sowrs, and gradual Rancour grows,
Imbitter'd more from peevish Day to Day.
Even Those whom Fame has lent her fairest Ray,
The most renown'd of worthy Wights of Yore,
From a base World at last have stolen away:
So SCIPIO, to the soft *Cumaean* Shore
Retiring, tasted Joy he never knew before.

xviii

"But if a little Exercise you chuse,
Some Zest for Ease, 'tis not forbidden here.
Amid the Groves you may indulge the Muse,
Or tend the Blooms, and deck the vernal Year;
Or softly stealing, with your watry Gear,
Along the Brooks, the crimson-spotted Fry

You may delude: The whilst, amus'd, you hear
Now the hoarse Stream, and now the Zephyr's Sigh,
Attuned to the Birds, and woodland Melody.

xix

"O grievous Folly! to heap up Estate,
Losing the Days you see beneath the Sun;
When, sudden, comes blind unrelenting Fate,
And gives th'untasted Portion you have won,
With ruthless Toil, and many a Wretch undone,
To Those who mock you gone to *Pluto's* Reign,
There with sad Ghosts to pine, and Shadows dun:
But sure it is of Vanities most vain,
To toil for what you here untoiling may obtain."

xx

He ceas'd. But still their trembling Ears retain'd
The deep Vibrations of his witching Song;
That, by a Kind of Magic Power, constrain'd
To enter in, pell-mell, the listening Throng.
Heaps pour'd on Heaps, and yet they slip'd along
In silent Ease: as when beneath the Beam
Of Summer-Moons, the distant Woods among,
Or by some Flood all silver'd with the Gleam,
The soft-embodied Fays through airy Portal stream.

xxi

By the smooth Demon so it order'd was,
And here his baneful Bounty first began:
Though some there were who would not further pass,
And his alluring Baits suspected han.
The Wise distrust the too fair-spoken Man.
Yet through the Gate they cast a wishful Eye:
Not to move on, perdie, is all they can;
For do their very Best they cannot fly,
But often each Way look, and often sorely sigh.

xxii

When this the watchful wicked Wizard saw,
With sudden Spring he leap'd upon them strait;

xviii 8 Zephyr's] Zephir's *A   Thomson probably wrote* Zephir's; *see, for example, LD, p. 176*

And soon as touch'd by his unhallow'd Paw,
They found themselves within the cursed Gate;
Full hard to be repass'd, like That of Fate.
Not stronger were of old the Giant-Crew,
Who sought to pull high *Jove* from regal State;
Though feeble Wretch he seem'd, of sallow Hue:
Certes, who bides his Grasp, will that Encounter rue.

xxiii

For whomsoe'er the Villain takes in Hand,
Their Joints unknit, their Sinews melt apace;
As lithe they grow as any Willow-Wand,
And of their vanish'd Force remains no Trace:
So when a Maiden fair, of modest Grace,
In all her buxom blooming May of Charms,
Is seized in some Losel's hot Embrace,
She waxeth very weakly as she warms,
Then sighing yields Her up to Love's delicious Harms.

xxiv

Wak'd by the Croud, slow from his Bench arose
A comely full-spred Porter, swoln with Sleep:
His calm, broad, thoughtless Aspect breath'd Repose;
And in sweet Torpor he was plunged deep,
Ne could himself from ceaseless Yawning keep;
While o'er his Eyes the drowsy Liquor ran,
Through which his half-wak'd Soul would faintly peep.
Then taking his black Staff he call'd his Man,
And rous'd himself as much as rouse himself he can.

xxv

The Lad leap'd lightly at his Master's Call.
He was, to weet, a little roguish Page,
Save Sleep and Play who minded nought at all,
Like most the untaught Striplings of his Age;
This Boy he kept each Band to disengage,
Garters and Buckles, Task for him unfit,
But ill-becoming his grave Personage,
And which his portly Paunch would not permit.
So this same limber Page to All performed It.

xxii 9 Grasp,] Grasp *B*

xxvi

Mean time the Master-Porter wide display'd
Great Store of Caps, of Slippers, and of Gowns;
Wherewith he Those who enter'd in, array'd;
Loose, as the Breeze that plays along the Downs,
And waves the Summer-Woods when Evening frowns.
O fair Undress, best Dress! it checks no Vein,
But every flowing Limb in Pleasure drowns,
And heightens Ease with Grace. This done, right fain,
Sir Porter sat him down, and turn'd to Sleep again.

xxvii

Thus easy-rob'd, they to the Fountain sped,
That in the Middle of the Court up-threw
A Stream, high-spouting from its liquid Bed,
And falling back again in drizzly Dew;
There Each deep Draughts, as deep he thirsted, drew.
It was a Fountain of *Nepenthe* rare:
Whence, as Dan HOMER sings, huge Pleasaunce grew,
And sweet Oblivion of vile earthly Care;
Fair gladsome waking Thoughts, and joyous Dreams more fair.

xxviii

This Rite perform'd, All inly pleas'd and still,
Withouten Trump, was Proclamation made.
"Ye Sons of INDOLENCE, do what you will;
And wander where you list, through Hall or Glade:
Be no Man's Pleasure for another's staid;
Let Each as likes him best his Hours employ,
And curs'd be he who minds his Neighbour's Trade!
Here dwells kind Ease, and unreproving Joy:
He little merits Bliss who Others can annoy."

xxix

Strait of these endless Numbers, swarming round,
As thick as idle Motes in sunny Ray,
Not one eftsoons in View was to be found,

xxvi 3 in,] in *B*

xxviii 2 Trump] Tromp *A*
    8 Ease,] Ease *A*
    9 annoy."] annoy. *A*

But every Man stroll'd off his own glad Way.
Wide o'er this ample Court's blank Area,
With all the Lodges that thereto pertain'd,
No living Creature could be seen to stray;
While Solitude, and perfect Silence reign'd:
So that to think you dreamt you almost was constrain'd.

xxx

As when a Shepherd of the *Hebrid-Isles,*
Plac'd far amid the melancholy Main,
(Whether it be, lone Fancy him beguiles;
Or that aerial Beings sometimes deign
To stand, embodied, to our Senses plain)
Sees on the naked Hill, or Valley low,
The whilst in Ocean *Phoebus* dips his Wain,
A vast Assembly moving to and fro:
Then all at once in Air dissolves the wondrous Show.

xxxi

Ye Gods of Quiet, and of Sleep profound!
Whose soft Dominion o'er this Castle sways,
And all the widely-silent Places round,
Forgive me, if my trembling Pen displays
What never yet was sung in mortal Lays.
But how shall I attempt such arduous String?
I who have spent my Nights, and nightly Days,
In this Soul-deadening Place, loose-loitering?
Ah! how shall I for This uprear my moulted Wing?

xxxii

Come on, my Muse, nor stoop to low Despair,
Thou Imp of *Jove,* touch'd by celestial Fire!
Thou yet shalt sing of War, and Actions fair,
Which the bold Sons of BRITAIN will inspire;
Of antient Bards thou yet shalt sweep the Lyre;
Thou yet shalt tread in Tragic Pall the Stage,
Paint Love's enchanting Woes, the Heroe's Ire,
The Sage's Calm, the Patriot's noble Rage,
Dashing Corruption down through every worthless Age.

xxx 3 be,] be *A*
xxxi 7 Nights,] Nights *A*
    9 This] this *A*
xxxii 5 antient] ancient *A*

xxxiii

The Doors, that knew no shrill alarming Bell,
Ne cursed Knocker ply'd by Villain's Hand,
Self-open'd into Halls, where, who can tell
What Elegance and Grandeur wide expand
The Pride of *Turkey* and of *Persia* Land?
Soft Quilts on Quilts, on Carpets Carpets spread,
And Couches stretch around in seemly Band;
And endless Pillows rise to prop the Head;
So that each spacious Room was one full-swelling Bed.

xxxiv

And every-where huge cover'd Tables stood,
With Wines high-flavour'd and rich Viands crown'd;
Whatever sprightly Juice, or tasteful Food,
On the green Bosom of this Earth are found.
And all old Ocean genders in his Round:
Some Hand unseen These silently display'd,
Even undemanded by a Sign or Sound;
You need but wish, and, instantly obey'd,
Fair-rang'd the Dishes rose, and thick the Glasses play'd.

xxxv

Here Freedom reign'd, without the least Alloy;
Nor Gossip's Tale, nor ancient Maiden's Gall,
Nor saintly Spleen durst murmur at our Joy,
And with envenom'd Tongue our Pleasures pall.
For why? There was but One great Rule for All;
To-wit, That each should work his own Desire,
And eat, drink, study, sleep, as it may fall,
Or melt the Time in Love, or wake the Lyre,
And carol what, unbid, the Muses might inspire.

xxxvi

The Rooms with costly Tapestry were hung,
Where was inwoven many a gentle Tale;
Such as of old the Rural Poets sung,

xxxiv 1 every-where] every where *A*
    3 Juice,] Juice *A*   Food,] Food *A*
    7 undemanded] undemanded, *A*
xxxv 6 To-wit] To wit *A*   xxxvi 3 Rural] rural *A*

Or of *Arcadian* or *Sicilian* Vale:
Reclining Lovers, in the lonely Dale,
Pour'd forth at large the sweetly-tortur'd Heart;
Or, looking tender Passion, swell'd the Gale,
And taught charm'd Echo to resound their Smart;
While Flocks, Woods, Streams, around, Repose and Peace impart.

xxxvii

Those pleas'd the most, where, by a cunning Hand,
Depeinten was the Patriarchal Age;
What Time Dan *Abraham* left the *Chaldee* Land,
And pastur'd on from verdant Stage to Stage,
Where Fields and Fountains fresh could best engage.
Toil was not then. Of nothing took they Heed,
But with wild Beasts the silvan War to wage,
And o'er vast Plains their Herds and Flocks to feed:
Blest Sons of Nature they! True Golden Age indeed!

xxxviii

Sometimes the Pencil, in cool airy Halls,
Bade the gay Bloom of Vernal Landskips rise,
Or Autumn's vary'd Shades imbrown the Walls:
Now the black Tempest strikes the astonished Eyes;
Now down the Steep the flashing Torrent flies;
The trembling Sun now plays o'er Ocean blue,
And now rude Mountains frown amid the Skies;
Whate'er *Lorrain* light-touch'd with softening Hue,
Or savage *Rosa* dash'd, or learned *Poussin* drew.

xxxix

Each Sound too here to Languishment inclin'd,
Lull'd the weak Bosom, and induced Ease.
Aerial Music in the warbling Wind,
At Distance rising oft, by small Degrees,
Nearer and nearer came, till o'er the Trees

xxxvii 2 Depeinten] Depainted *A*
xxxviii 3 vary'd] varied *A*
xxxix 3 Aerial] Aereal *B*

It hung, and breath'd such Soul-dissolving Airs,
As did, alas! with soft Perdition please:
Entangled deep in its enchanting Snares,
The listening Heart forgot all Duties and all Cares.

xl

A certain Music, never known before,
Here sooth'd the pensive melancholy Mind;
Full easily obtain'd. Behoves no more,
But sidelong, to the gently-waving Wind,
To lay the well-tun'd Instrument reclin'd;
From which, with airy flying Fingers light,
Beyond each mortal Touch the most refin'd,
The God of Winds drew Sounds of deep Delight:
Whence, with just Cause, *The Harp of Aeolus* it hight.

xli

Ah me! what Hand can touch the Strings so fine?
Who up the lofty Diapasan roll
Such sweet, such sad, such solemn Airs divine,
Then let them down again into the Soul?
Now rising Love they fan'd; now pleasing Dole
They breath'd, in tender Musings, through the Heart;
And now a graver sacred Strain they stole,
As when Seraphic Hands an Hymn impart:
Wild warbling Nature all, above the Reach of Art!

xlii

Such the gay Splendor, the luxurious State,
Of *Caliphs* old, who on the *Tygris'* Shore,
In mighty *Bagdat*, populous and great,
Held their bright Court, where was of Ladies store;
And Verse, Love, Music still the Garland wore:
When Sleep was coy, the Bard, in Waiting there,
Chear'd the lone Midnight with the Muse's Lore;
Composing Music bade his Dreams be fair,
And Music lent new Gladness to the Morning Air.

8 enchanting] inchanting *B*
xl 1 Music] Musick *A*
   2 sooth'd] lull'd *A*

xliii

Near the Pavilions where we slept, still ran
Soft-tinkling Streams, and dashing Waters fell,
And sobbing Breezes sigh'd, and oft began
(So work'd the Wizard) wintry Storms to swell,
As Heaven and Earth they would together mell:
At Doors and Windows, threatening, seem'd to call
The Demons of the Tempest, growling fell,
Yet the least Entrance found they none at all;
Whence sweeter grew our Sleep, secure in massy Hall.

xliv

And hither *Morpheus* sent his kindest Dreams,
Raising a World of gayer Tinct and Grace;
O'er which were shadowy cast Elysian Gleams,
That play'd, in waving Lights, from Place to Place,
And shed a roseate Smile on Nature's Face.
Not *Titian's* Pencil e'er could so array,
So fleece with Clouds the pure Etherial Space;
Ne could it e'er such melting Forms display,
As loose on flowery Beds all languishingly lay.

xlv

No, fair Illusions! artful Phantoms, no!
My Muse will not attempt your Fairy-Land:
She has no Colours that like you can glow;
To catch your vivid Scenes too gross her Hand.
But sure it is, was ne'er a subtler Band
Than these same guileful Angel-seeming Sprights,
Who thus in Dreams, voluptuous, soft, and bland,
Pour'd all th' *Arabian Heav'n* upon our Nights,
And bless'd them oft besides with more refin'd Delights.

xlvi

They were in Sooth a most enchanting Train,
Even feigning Virtue; skilful to unite
With Evil Good, and strew with Pleasure Pain.
But for those Fiends, whom Blood and Broils delight;
Who hurl the Wretch, as if to Hell outright,

xliv 7 Etherial] Ethereal *B*
xlv 8 *Heav'n*] *Heaven A*

Down down black Gulphs, where sullen Waters sleep,
Or hold him clambering all the fearful Night
On beetling Cliffs, or pent in Ruins deep:
They, till due Time should serve, were bid far hence to keep.

xlvii

Ye Guardian Spirits, to whom Man is dear,
From these foul Demons shield the Midnight Gloom!
Angels of Fancy and of Love, be near,
And o'er the Wilds of Sleep diffuse a Bloom;
Evoke the sacred Shades of *Greece* and *Rome,*
And let them Virtue with a Look impart!
But chief, a while o lend us from the Tomb
Those long-lost Friends for whom in Love we smart,
And fill with pious Awe and Joy-mixt Woe the Heart!

xlviii

Or are you sportive—Bid the Morn of Youth
Rise to new Light, and beam afresh the Days
Of Innocence, Simplicity, and Truth;
To Cares estrang'd, and Manhood's thorny Ways.
What Transport! To retrace our boyish Plays,
Our easy Bliss, when each Thing Joy supply'd:
The Woods, the Mountains, and the warbling Maze
Of the wild Brooks—But, fondly wandering wide,
My Muse, resume the Task that yet doth thee abide.

xlix

One great Amusement of our Houshold was,
In a huge crystal magic Globe to spy,
Still as you turn'd it, all Things that do pass
Upon this Ant-Hill Earth; where constantly
Of Idly-busy Men the restless Fry
Run bustling to and fro with foolish Haste,
In search of Pleasures vain, that from them fly;
Or which, obtain'd, the Caitiffs dare not taste:
When nothing is enjoy'd, can there be greater Waste?

xlvii 4 Wilds] Blank *A*   Bloom;] Bloom! *A*
    9 Heart!] Heart. *A*
xlix 5 Idly-busy] idly-busy *A*
    6 to] too *A*
    7 vain,] vain *A*   fly;] fly, *A*
    8 which, obtain'd,] which obtain'd *A*

l

Of Vanity the Mirror This was call'd.
Here you a Muckworm of the Town might see,
At his dull Desk, amid his Legers stall'd,
Eat up with carking Care and Penurie;
Most like to Carcase parch'd on Gallow-Tree.
A Penny saved is a Penny got:
Firm to this scoundrel Maxim keepeth he,
Ne of its Rigour will he bate a Jot,
Till it has quench'd his Fire, and banished his Pot.

li

Strait from the Filth of this low Grub, behold!
Comes fluttering forth a gaudy spendthrift Heir,
All glossy gay, enamel'd all with Gold,
The silly Tenant of the Summer-Air.
In Folly lost, of Nothing takes he Care;
Pimps, Lawyers, Stewards, Harlots, Flatterers vile,
And thieving Tradesmen him among them share:
His Father's Ghost from Limbo-Lake, the while,
Sees This, which more Damnation does upon him pile.

lii

This Globe pourtray'd the Race of learned Men,
Still at their Books, and turning o'er the Page,
Forwards and backwards: oft they snatch the Pen,
As if inspir'd, and in a *Thespian* Rage;
Then write, and blot, as would your Ruth engage.
Why, Authors, all this Scrawl and Scribbling sore?
To lose the present, gain the future Age,
Praised to be when you can hear no more,
And much enrich'd with Fame when useless worldly Store.

liii

Then would a splendid City rise to View,
With Carts, and Cars, and Coaches roaring all:
Wide-pour'd abroad, behold the prowling Crew;

lii 3 Forwards and backwards] Backwards and forwards *A*
lii 6 Authors] Auhors *A*
liii 3 abroad,] abroad *A*

See! how they dash along from Wall to Wall;
At every Door, hark! how they thundering call.
Good Lord! what can this giddy Rout excite?
Why? Each on Each to prey, by Guile or Gall;
With Flattery These, with Slander Those to blight,
And make new tiresome Parties for the coming Night.

liv

The puzzling Sons of Party next appear'd,
In dark Cabals and nightly Juntos met;
And now they whisper'd close, now shrugging rear'd
Th' important Shoulder; then, as if to get
New Light, their twinkling Eyes were inward set:
No sooner *Lucifer* recalls Affairs,
Than forth they various rush in mighty Fret;
When, lo! push'd up to Power, and crown'd their Cares,
In comes another Set, and kicketh them down Stairs.

lv

But what most shew'd the Vanity of Life,
Was to behold the Nations all on Fire,
In cruel Broils engag'd, and deadly Strife;
Most Christian Kings, inflam'd by black Desire,
With Honourable Ruffians in their Hire,
Cause War to rage, and Blood around to pour:
Of this sad Work when Each begins to tire,
They sit them down just where they were before,
Till for new Scenes of Woe Peace shall their Force restore.

lvi

To number up the Thousands dwelling here,
An useless were, and eke an endless Task:
From Kings, and Those who at the Helm appear,
To Gipsies brown, in Summer-Glades who bask.
Yea, many a Man perdie I could unmask,
Whose Desk and Table make a solemn Show,

6 eager] giddy *A*
7 Why? On each other with fell Tooth to fall; *A*
8 A Neighbour's Fortune, Fame, or Peace, to blight, *A*
liv 3 now shrugging] new shrugging *A*
 5 set:] set. *A*
lvi 3 Those] those *B*
 4 brown,] brown *A*
 5 Yea,] Yea *A*

With Tape-ty'd Trash, and Suits of Fools that ask
For Place or Pension, laid in decent Row;
But These I passen by, with nameless Numbers moe.

lvii

Of all the gentle Tenants of the Place,
There was a Man of special grave Remark:
A certain tender Gloom o'erspred his Face,
Pensive not sad, in Thought involv'd not dark,
As soot this Man could sing as Morning-Lark,
And teach the noblest Morals of the Heart:
But These his Talents were ybury'd stark;
Of the fine Stores he Nothing would impart,
Which or boon Nature gave, or Nature-painting Art.

lviii

To Noontide Shades incontinent he ran,
Where purls the Brook with Sleep-inviting Sound;
Or when Dan *Sol* to slope his Wheels began,
Amid the Broom he bask'd him on the Ground,
Where the wild Thyme and Camomil are found:
There would he linger, till the latest Ray
Of Light sat quivering on the Welkin's Bound:
Then homeward through the twilight Shadows stray,
Sauntring and slow. So had he passed many a Day.

lix

Yet not in thoughtless Slumber were they past:
For oft the heavenly Fire, that lay conceal'd
Emongst the sleeping Embers, mounted fast,
And all its native Light anew reveal'd;
Oft as he travers'd the Cerulean Field,
And mark'd the Clouds that drove before the Wind,
Ten thousand glorious Systems would he build,
Ten thousand great Ideas fill'd his Mind;
But with the Clouds they fled, and left no Tract behind.

lvii 3 o'erspred] o'erspread *A*
 5 soot] soote *B Cf. "Explanation of obsolete Words"*
 7 quivering] trembling *A*
lix 3 Emongst] Beneath *A*
 9 Tract *A, 1750*] Trace *B*] track *Pirated ed. 1748*

lx

With him was sometimes join'd, in silent Walk,
(Profoundly silent, for they never spoke)
One shyer still, who quite detested Talk:
Oft, stung by Spleen, at once away he broke,
To Groves of Pine, and brown o'ershadowing Oak;
There, inly thrill'd, he wander'd all alone,
And on himself his pensive Fury wroke,
Ne ever utter'd Word, save when first shone
The glittering Star of Eve—"Thank Heaven! the Day is done."

lxi

Here lurk'd a Wretch, who had not crept abroad
For forty Years, ne Face of Mortal seen;
In Chamber brooding like a loathly Toad,
And sure his Linen was not very clean;
Through secret Loop-hole, that had practis'd been
Near to his Bed, his Dinner vile he took;
Unkempt, and rough, of squalid Face and Mien,
Our Castle's Shame! whence, from his filthy Nook,
We drove the Villain out for fitter Lair to look.

lxii

One Day there chaunc'd into these Halls to rove
A joyous Youth, who took you at first Sight;
Him the wild Wave of Pleasure hither drove,
Before the sprightly Tempest tossing light:
Certes, he was a most engaging Wight,
Of social Glee, and Wit humane though keen,
Turning the Night to Day and Day to Night;
For him the merry Bells had rung, I ween,
If in this Nook of Quiet Bells had ever been.

lxiii

But not even Pleasure to Excess is good,
What most elates then sinks the Soul as low;
When Spring-Tide Joy pours in with copious Flood,

lx 5 brown] broad *A*
lxi 4 Linen] Linnen *A*
  5 Loop-hole] Loop-Hole *A*
  7 Mien] Mein *A*
  8 Shame] shame *A*

The higher still the' exulting Billows flow,
The farther back again they flagging go,
And leave us groveling on the dreary Shore:
Taught by this Son of Joy, we found it so;
Who, whilst he staid, kept in a gay Uproar
Our madden'd Castle all, th' Abode of Sleep no more.

lxiv

As when in Prime of June a burnish'd Fly,
Sprung from the Meads, o'er which he sweeps along,
Chear'd by the breathing Bloom, and vital Sky,
Tunes up amid these airy Halls his Song,
Soothing at first the gay reposing Throng:
And oft he sips their Bowl; or, nearly drown'd,
He, thence recovering, drives their Beds among,
And scares their tender Sleep, with Trump profound;
Then out again he flies, to wing his mazy Round.

lxv

Another Guest there was, of Sense refin'd,
Who felt each Worth, for every Worth he had;
Serene yet warm, humane yet firm his Mind,
As little touch'd as any Man's with Bad:
Him through their inmost Walks the Muses lad,
To him the sacred Love of Nature lent,
And sometimes would he make our Valley glad;
Whenas we found he would not here be pent,
To him the better Sort this friendly Message sent.

lxvi

"Come, dwell with us! true Son of Virtue, come!
But if, alas! we cannot Thee persuade,
To lie content beneath our peaceful Dome,
Ne ever more to quit our quiet Glade;
Yet when at last thy Toils, but ill apaid,
Shall dead thy Fire, and damp its Heavenly Spark,
Thou wilt be glad to seek the Rural Shade,
There to indulge the Muse, and Nature mark:
We then a Lodge for Thee will rear in HAGLEY-PARK."

lxiv 3 Bloom,] Bloom *A*
    6 or,] or *A*
lxvi 7 Rural] rural *A*

lxvii

Here whilom ligg'd th' Esopus of the Age;
But call'd by Fame, in Soul ypricked deep,
A noble Pride restor'd him to the Stage,
And rous'd him like a Gyant from his Sleep.
Even from his Slumbers we Advantage reap:
With double Force th' astonish'd Scene he wakes,
Yet quits not Nature's Bounds. He knows to keep
Each due Decorum: Now the Heart he shakes,
And now with well-urg'd Sense th' enlighten'd Judgment takes.

lxviii

A Bard here dwelt, more fat than Bard beseems;
Who void of Envy, Guile, and Lust of Gain,
On Virtue still, and Nature's pleasing Themes,
Pour'd forth his unpremeditated Strain,
The World forsaking with a calm Disdain:
Here laugh'd he careless in his easy Seat,
Here quaff'd encircled with the joyous Train;
Oft moralizing sage; his Ditty sweet
He loathed much to write, ne cared to repeat.

lxix

Full oft by Holy Feet our Ground was trod,
Of Clerks good Plenty here you mote espy.
A little, round, fat, oily Man of God,
Was one I chiefly mark'd among the Fry:
He had a roguish Twinkle in his Eye,
And shone all glistening with ungodly Dew,
If a tight Damsel chaunc'd to trippen by;
Which when observ'd, he shrunk into his Mew,
And strait would recollect his Piety anew.

lxx

Nor be forgot a Tribe, who minded Nought
(Old Inmates of the Place) but State-Affairs:
They look'd, perdie, as if they deeply thought;

lxvii 6 astonish'd] enliven'd *A*
lxix 6 glistening] glittering *A*
    9 strait] straight *B*

And on their Brow sat every Nation's Cares.
The World by them is parcel'd out in Shares,
When in the *Hall of Smoak* they Congress hold,
And the sage Berry sun-burnt *Mocha* bears
Has clear'd their inward Eye: then, smoak-enroll'd,
Their Oracles break forth, mysterious as of old.

lxxi

Here languid Beauty kept her pale-fac'd Court:
Bevies of dainty Dames, of high Degree,
From every Quarter hither made Resort;
Where, from gross mortal Care and Business free,
They lay, pour'd out in Ease and Luxury.
Or should they a vain Shew of Work assume,
Alas! and well-a-day! what can it be?
To knot, to twist, to range the vernal Bloom;
But far is cast the Distaff, Spinning-Wheel, and Loom.

lxxii

Their only Labour was to kill the Time;
And Labour dire it is, and weary Woe.
They sit, they loll, turn o'er some idle Rhyme;
Then, rising sudden, to the Glass they go,
Or saunter forth, with tottering Step and slow:
This soon too rude an Exercise they find;
Strait on the Couch their Limbs again they throw,
Where Hours on Hours they sighing lie reclin'd,
And court the vapoury God soft-breathing in the Wind.

lxxiii

Now must I mark the Villainy we found,
But ah! too late, as shall eftsoons be shewn.
A Place here was, deep, dreary, under Ground;
Where still our Inmates, when unpleasing grown,
Diseas'd, and loathsome, privily were thrown.
Far from the Light of Heaven, they languish'd there,
Unpity'd uttering many a bitter Groan;
For of these Wretches taken was no Care:
Fierce Fiends, and Hags of Hell, their only Nurses were.

lxx 9 forth,] forth *A*

lxxiv

Alas! the Change! from Scenes of Joy and Rest,
To this dark Den, where Sickness toss'd alway.
Here *Lethargy*, with deadly Sleep opprest,
Stretch'd on his Back a mighty Lubbard lay,
Heaving his Sides, and snored Night and Day;
To stir him from his Traunce it was not eath,
And his half-open'd Eyne he shut strait way:
He led, I wot, the softest Way to Death,
And taught withouten Pain and Strife to yield the Breath.

lxxv

Of Limbs enormous, but withal unsound,
Soft-swoln and pale, here lay the *Hydropsy:*
Unwieldly Man! with Belly monstrous round,
For ever fed with watery Supply;
For still he drank, and yet he still was dry.
And moping here did *Hypochondria* sit,
Mother of Spleen, in Robes of various Dye,
Who vexed was full oft with ugly Fit;
And some Her frantic deem'd, and some Her deem'd a Wit.

lxxvi

A Lady proud she was, of ancient Blood,
Yet oft her Fear her Pride made crouchen low:
She felt, or fancy'd in her fluttering Mood,

lxxiv-lxxvii *The version of these stanzas in John Armstrong's* Miscellanies
(1770), I, 164, is presumably the text originally contributed by Armstrong for
The Castle of Indolence. *Divergent readings in this version are marked* Armstrong *in the following notes.*

lxxiv 1-2 *Armstrong:* Full many a fiend did haunt this house of rest,
               And made of passive wights an easy prey.
   7 strait way] straightway *Armstrong*
   8 led, I wot,] led I ween *Armstrong*

lxxv 2 *Hydropsy*] Hydropsie *Armstrong*
   3 Man!] man, *Armstrong*
   6 And here a moping Mystery did sit *Armstrong A 1750*
   8-9 *Armstrong:* She call'd herself the Hypochondriack Fit,
               And frantick seem'd to some, to others seem'd a wit.

lxxvi 1-2 *Armstrong:* A lady was she whimsical and proud,
               Yet oft thro' fear her pride would crouchen low

All the Diseases which the Spittles know,
And sought all Physic which the Shops bestow.
And still new Leaches and new Drugs would try,
Her Humour ever wavering to and fro;
For sometimes she would laugh, and sometimes cry,
Then sudden waxed wroth; and all she knew not why.

lxxvii

Fast by her Side a listless Maiden pin'd,
With aching Head, and squeamish Heart-Burnings;
Pale, bloated, cold, she seem'd to hate Mankind,
Yet lov'd in Secret all forbidden Things.
And here the *Tertian* shakes his chilling Wings;
The sleepless *Gout* here counts the crowing Cocks,
A Wolf now gnaws him, now a Serpent stings;
Whilst *Apoplexy* cramm'd Intemperance knocks
Down to the Ground at once, as Butcher felleth Ox.

CANTO II

The Knight of Arts and Industry,
And his Atchievements fair;
That, by this Castle's Overthrow,
Secur'd, and crowned were.

i

Escap'd the Castle of the Sire of Sin,
Ah! where shall I so sweet a Dwelling find?
For all around, without, and all within,

lxxvi 4 which the Spittles] that the Spitals *Armstrong*
    5 Physic which] physick that *Armstrong*
    7 'Twas hard to hit her humour high or low *Armstrong*
    9 wroth;] wroth, *A*
        Then sudden waxed wroth] Sometimes would waxen wroth *Armstrong*
lxxvii 1 Maiden] virgin *Armstrong*
    4 Yet] But *Armstrong*
    5 shakes] shook *Armstrong*
lxxvii 6-9 *Armstrong:*
        And here the Gout, half tyger half a snake,
        Rag'd with an hundred teeth, an hundred stings;
        These and a thousand furies much did shake
        Those weary realms, and kept ease-loving men awake.
Argument 1 *Arts*] *Art B*
i 3 around,] around *A*

Nothing save what delightful was and kind,
Of Goodness savouring and a tender Mind,
E'er rose to View. But now another Strain,
Of doleful Note, alas! remains behind:
I now must sing of Pleasure turn'd to Pain,
And of the false Enchanter INDOLENCE complain.

ii

Is there no Patron to protect the Muse,
And fence for Her *Parnassus'* barren Soil?
To every Labour its Reward accrues,
And they are sure of Bread who swink and moil;
But a fell Tribe th' *Aonian Hive* despoil,
As ruthless Wasps oft rob the painful Bee:
Thus while the Laws not guard that noblest Toil,
Ne for the Muses other Meed decree,
They praised are alone, and starve right merrily.

iii

I care not, Fortune, what you me deny:
You cannot rob me of free Nature's Grace;
You cannot shut the Windows of the Sky,
Through which *Aurora* shews her brightening Face:
You cannot bar my constant Feet to trace
The Woods and Lawns, by living Stream, at Eve:
Let Health my Nerves and finer Fibres brace,
And I their Toys to the *great Children* leave;
Of Fancy, Reason, Virtue, nought can me bereave.

iv

Come then, my Muse, and raise a bolder Song;
Come, lig no more upon the Bed of Sloth,
Dragging the lazy languid Line along,
Fond to begin, but still to finish loth,
Thy half-writ Scrolls all eaten by the Moth:
Arise, and sing that generous Imp of Fame,

9 Enchanter] Inchanter *A*
ii 2 Her] her *B*
  7 Toil,] Toil *B*
iii 4 Face:] Face; *A*
iv 4 begin,] begin *A*

Who, with the Sons of Softness nobly wroth,
To sweep away this Human Lumber came,
Or in a chosen Few to rouse the slumbering Flame.

v

In *Fairy-Land* there liv'd a Knight of old,
Of Feature stern, *Selvaggio* well yclep'd,
A rough unpolish'd Man, robust and bold,
But wondrous poor: he neither sow'd nor reap'd,
Ne Stores in Summer for cold Winter heap'd;
In Hunting all his Days away he wore;
Now scorch'd by June, now in November steep'd,
Now pinch'd by biting January sore,
He still in Woods pursu'd the Libbard and the Boar.

vi

As he one Morning, long before the Dawn,
Prick'd through the Forest to dislodge his Prey,
Deep in the winding Bosom of a Lawn,
With Wood wild-fring'd, he mark'd a Taper's Ray,
That from the beating Rain, and wintry Fray,
Did to a lonely Cott his Steps decoy:
There, up to earn the Needments of the Day,
He found Dame *Poverty,* nor fair nor coy:
Her he compress'd, and fill'd Her with a lusty Boy.

vii

Amid the green-wood Shade this Boy was bred,
And grew at last a Knight of muchel Fame,
Of active Mind and vigorous Lustyhed,
THE KNIGHT OF ARTS AND INDUSTRY by Name.
Earth was his Bed, the Boughs his Roof did frame;
He knew no Beverage but the flowing Stream;
His tasteful well-earn'd Food the silvan Game,
Or the brown Fruit with which the Wood-Lands teem:
The same to him glad Summer, or the Winter breme.

viii

So pass'd his youthly Morning, void of Care,
Wild as the Colts that through the Commons run:

vii 9 Summer,] Summer *A*

For him no tender Parents troubled were,
He of the Forest seem'd to be the Son,
And certes had been utterly undone;
But that *Minerva* Pity of him took,
With all the Gods that love the Rural Wonne,
That teach to tame the Soil and rule the Crook;
Ne did the sacred Nine disdain a gentle Look.

ix

Of fertile Genius him they nurtur'd well,
In every Science, and in every Art,
By which Mankind the thoughtless Brutes excel,
That can or Use, or Joy, or Grace impart,
Disclosing all the Powers of Head and Heart.
Ne were the goodly Exercises spar'd,
That brace the Nerves, or make the Limbs alert,
And mix elastic Force with Firmness hard:
Was never Knight on Ground mote be with him compar'd.

x

Sometimes, with early Morn, he mounted gay
The Hunter-steed, exulting o'er the Dale,
And drew the roseat Breath of orient Day;
Sometimes, retiring to the secret Vale,
Yclad in Steel, and bright with burnish'd Mail,
He strain'd the Bow, or toss'd the sounding Spear,
Or darting on the Goal outstrip'd the Gale,
Or wheel'd the Chariot in its Mid-Career,
Or strenuous wrestled hard with many a tough Compeer.

xi

At other Times he pry'd through Nature's Store,
Whate'er she in th' Etherial Round contains,
Whate'er she hides beneath her verdant Floor,
The vegetable and the mineral Reigns;
Or else he scann'd the *Globe,* those small Domains,
Where restless Mortals such a Turmoil keep,
Its Seas, its Floods, its Mountains, and its Plains;
But more he search'd the Mind, and rous'd from Sleep
Those moral Seeds whence we heroic Actions reap.

ix 2 Science,] Science *A*
x 5 Steel,] Steel *A*

xii

Nor would he scorn to stoop from high Pursuits
Of heavenly Truth, and practise what she taught.
Vain is the Tree of Knowledge without Fruits.
Sometimes in Hand the Spade or Plough he caught,
Forth-calling all with which boon Earth is fraught;
Sometimes he ply'd the strong mechanic Tool,
Or rear'd the Fabric from the finest Draught;
And oft he put himself to *Neptune's* School,
Fighting with Winds and Waves on the vext Ocean Pool.

xiii

To solace then these rougher Toils, he try'd
To touch the kindling Canvass into Life;
With Nature his creating Pencil vy'd,
With Nature joyous at the mimic Strife:
Or, to such Shapes as grac'd *Pygmalion's* Wife,
He hew'd the Marble; or, with vary'd Fire,
He rous'd the Trumpet, and the martial Fife,
Or bad the Lute sweet Tenderness inspire,
Or Verses fram'd that well might wake *Apollo's* Lyre.

xiv

Accomplish'd thus he from the Woods issu'd,
Full of great Aims, and bent on bold Emprize;
The Work, which long he in his Breast had brew'd,
Now to perform he ardent did devise;
To-wit, a barbarous World to civilize.
Earth was till Then a boundless Forest wild;
Nought to be seen but savage Wood, and Skies;
No Cities nourish'd Arts, no Culture smil'd,
No Government, no Laws, no gentle Manners mild.

xv

A rugged Wight, the Worst of Brutes, was Man:
On his own wretched Kind he, ruthless, prey'd;
The Strongest still the Weakest over-ran;
In every Country mighty Robbers sway'd,

xii 7 Fabric] Fabrick *A*
xiii 7 Trumpet,] Trumpet *A*

And Guile and ruffian Force were all their Trade.
Life was not Life, but Rapine, Want, and Woe;
Which this brave Knight, in noble Anger, made
To swear, he would the rascal Rout o'erthrow,
For, by the Powers Divine, it should no more be so!

xvi

It would exceed the Purport of my Song,
To say how this *best Sun,* from orient Climes,
Came beaming Life and Beauty all along,
Before him chasing Indolence and Crimes.
Still as he pass'd, the Nations he sublimes,
And calls forth Arts and Virtue with his Ray:
Then *Egypt, Greece,* and *Rome* their Golden Times,
Successive, had; but now in Ruins grey
They lie, to slavish Sloth and Tyranny a Prey.

xvii

To crown his Toils, SIR INDUSTRY then spred
The swelling Sail, and made for BRITAIN's Coast.
A Sylvan Life till then the Natives led,
In the brown Shades and green-wood Forest lost,
All careless rambling where it lik'd them most:
Their Wealth the Wild-Deer bouncing through the Glade;
They lodg'd at large, and liv'd at Nature's Cost;
Save Spear, and Bow, withouten other Aid,
Yet not the *Roman* Steel their naked Breast dismay'd.

xviii

He lik'd the Soil, he lik'd the clement Skies,
He lik'd the verdant Hills and flowery Plains.
Be This my great, my chosen Isle (he cries)
This, whilst my Labours LIBERTY sustains,
This Queen of Ocean all Assault disdains.
Nor lik'd he less the Genius of the Land,
To Freedom apt and persevering Pains,
Mild to obey, and generous to command,
Temper'd by forming HEAVEN with kindest firmest Hand.

xvii 6 through] thro' *B*
xviii 3 great,] great *A*

xix

Here, by Degrees, his Master-Work arose,
Whatever Arts and Industry can frame:
Whatever finish'd Agriculture knows,
Fair Queen of Arts! from Heaven itself who came,
When *Eden* flourish'd in unspotted Fame:
And still with Her sweet Innocence we find,
And tender Peace, and Joys without a Name,
That, while they rapture, tranquillize the Mind;
Nature and Art at once, Delight and Use combin'd.

xx

Then Towns he quicken'd by mechanic Arts,
And bade the fervent City glow with Toil;
Bade social Commerce raise renowned Marts,
Join Land to Land, and marry Soil to Soil,
Unite the Poles, and without bloody Spoil
Bring home of either *Ind* the gorgeous Stores;
Or, should Despotic Rage the World embroil,
Bade Tyrants tremble on remotest Shores,
While o'er th' encircling Deep BRITANNIA's Thunder roars.

xxi

The drooping Muses then he westward call'd,
From the fam'd City by *Propontis* Sea,
What Time the *Turk* th' enfeebled *Grecian* thrall'd;
Thence from their cloister'd Walks he set them free:
And brought them to another *Castalie:*
Where *Isis* many a famous Noursling breeds;
Or where old *Cam* soft-paces o'er the Lea,
In pensive Mood, and tunes his *Doric* Reeds,
The whilst his Flocks at large the lonely Shepherd feeds.

xxii

Yet the fine Arts were what he finish'd least.
For why? They are the Quintessence of All,
The Growth of labouring Time, and slow increast;
Unless, as seldom chances, it should fall,
That mighty Patrons the coy Sisters call
Up to the Sun-shine of uncumber'd Ease,

xxi 4 free:] free, *A*

Where no rude Care the mounting Thought may thrall,
And where they nothing have to do but please:
Ah! gracious God! thou know'st they ask no other Fees.

xxiii

But now, alas! we live too late in Time:
Our Patrons now even grudge that little Claim,
Except to such as sleek the soothing Rhyme;
And yet, forsooth, they wear MAECENAS' Name,
Poor Sons of puft-up Vanity, not Fame!
Unbroken Spirits, chear! still, still remains
Th' *Eternal Patron*, LIBERTY; whose Flame,
While she protects, inspires the noblest Strains.
The best, and sweetest far, are Toil-created Gains.

xxiv

Whenas the Knight had fram'd, in BRITAIN-LAND,
A matchless Form of glorious Government;
In which the sovereign Laws alone command,
Laws stablish'd by the public free Consent,
Whose Majesty is to the Sceptre lent:
When this great Plan, with each dependent Art,
Was settled firm, and to his Heart's Content,
Then sought he from the toilsome Scene to part,
And let Life's vacant Eve breathe Quiet through the Heart.

xxv

For This he chose a Farm in *Deva's* Vale,
Where his long Alleys peep'd upon the Main.
In this calm Seat he drew the healthful Gale,
Commix'd the Chief, the Patriot, and the Swain,
The happy Monarch of his Sylvan Train!
Here, sided by the Guardians of the Fold,
He walk'd his Rounds, and chear'd his blest Domain;
His Days, the Days of unstain'd Nature, roll'd,
Replete with Peace and Joy, like Patriarch's of old.

xxvi

Witness, ye lowing Herds, who lent him Milk;
Witness, ye Flocks, whose woolly Vestments far

xxv 9 old.] old, *B*

Exceed soft *India's* Cotton, or her silk;
Witness, with Autumn charg'd, the nodding Car,
That homeward came beneath sweet Evening's Star,
Or of September-Moons the Radiance mild.
O hide thy Head, abominable War!
Of Crimes and ruffian Idleness the Child!
From Heaven this Life ysprung, from Hell thy Glories vild!

xxvii

Nor, from his deep Retirement, banish'd was
Th' amusing Cares of Rural Industry.
Still, as with grateful Change the Seasons pass,
New Scenes arise, new Landskips strike the Eye,
And all th' enliven'd Country beautify:
Gay Plains extend where Marshes slept before;
O'er recent Meads th' exulting Streamlets fly;
Dark frowning Heaths grow bright with *Ceres'* Store,
And Woods imbrown the Steep, or wave along the Shore.

xxviii

As nearer to his Farm you made Approach,
He polish'd Nature with a finer Hand:
Yet on her Beauties durst not Art incroach;
'Tis Art's alone these Beauties to expand.
In graceful Dance immingled, o'er the Land,
Pan, Pales, Flora, and *Pomona* play'd:
Even here, sometimes, the rude wild Common fand
An happy Place; where free, and unafraid,
Amid the flowering Brakes each coyer Creature stray'd.

xxix

But in prime Vigour what can last for ay?
That soul-enfeebling Wizard INDOLENCE,
I whilom sung, wrought in his Works decay:
Spred far and wide was his curs'd Influence;
Of Public Virtue much he dull'd the Sense,
Even much of Private; eat our Spirit out,
And fed our rank luxurious Vices: whence
The Land was overlaid with many a Lout;
Not, as old Fame reports, wise, generous, bold, and stout.

xxvi 6 September-Moons] september-Moons *A B*
xxvii 8 *Ceres'* Store] Ceres' store *A*

XXX

A Rage of Pleasure madden'd every Breast,
Down to the lowest Lees the Ferment ran:
To his licentious Wish Each must be blest,
With Joy be fever'd; snatch it as he can.
Thus *Vice* the Standard rear'd; her Arrier-Ban
Corruption call'd, and loud she gave the Word.
"Mind, mind yourselves! Why should the vulgar Man,
The Lacquey be more virtuous than his Lord?
Enjoy this Span of Life! 'tis all the Gods afford."

xxxi

The Tidings reach'd to Where in quiet Hall,
The good old Knight enjoy'd well-earn'd Repose.
"Come, come, Sir Knight! thy Children on thee call;
Come, save us yet, ere Ruin round us close!
The Demon INDOLENCE thy Toils o'erthrows."
On This the noble Colour stain'd his Cheeks,
Indignant, glowing through the whitening Snows
Of venerable Eld; his Eye full-speaks
His ardent Soul, and from his Couch at once he breaks.

xxxii

"I will, (he cry'd) so help me, God! destroy
That Villain Archimage!"—His Page then strait
He to him call'd, a fiery-footed Boy,
Benempt *Dispatch*. "My Steed be at the Gate;
My Bard attend; quick, bring the Net of Fate."
This Net was twisted by the Sisters Three;
Which when once cast o'er harden'd Wretch, too late
Repentance comes: Replevy cannot be
From the strong iron Grasp of vengeful Destiny.

xxxiii

He came, the Bard, a little Druid-Wight,
Of wither'd Aspect; but his Eye was keen,
With Sweetness mix'd. In Russet brown bedight,
As is his Sister of the Copses green,
He crept along, unpromising of Mien.

xxxi 6 This] this *B*
xxxii 1-2 *A omits quotation-marks*

Gross he who judges so. His Soul was fair,
Bright as the Children of yon Azure sheen.
True Comeliness, which nothing can impair,
Dwells in the Mind: all else is Vanity and Glare.

xxxiv

"Come! (quoth the Knight) a Voice has reach'd mine Ear,
The Demon INDOLENCE threats Overthrow
To All that to Mankind is good and dear:
Come, PHILOMELUS! let us instant go,
O'erturn his Bowers, and lay his Castle low!
Those Men, those wretched Men! who *will* be Slaves,
Must drink a bitter wrathful Cup of Woe:
But some there be, thy Song, as from their Graves,
Shall raise. Thrice happy he! who without Rigour saves."

xxxv

Issuing forth, the Knight bestrode his Steed
Of ardent Bay, and on whose Front a Star
Shone blazing bright: Sprung from the generous Breed
That whirl of active Day the rapid Car,
He pranc'd along, disdaining Gate or Bar.
Meantime, the Bard on milk-white Palfrey rode;
An honest sober Beast, that did not mar
His Meditations, but full softly trode:
And much they moraliz'd as thus yfere they yode.

xxxvi

They talked of Virtue, and of Human Bliss.
What else so fit for Man to settle well?
And still their long Researches met in This,
This *Truth of Truths,* which nothing can refel:
"From Virtue's Fount the purest Joys out-well,
Sweet Rills of Thought that chear the conscious Soul;
While Vice pours forth the troubled Streams of Hell,
The which, howe'er disguis'd, at last with Dole
Will through the tortur'd Breast their fiery Torrent roll."

xxxiii 7 sheen.] sheen, *B*
xxxv 1 Steed] Steed, *A*

xxxvii

At length it dawn'd, that fatal Valley gay,
O'er which high wood-crown'd Hills their Summits rear.
On the cool Height awhile our Palmers stay,
And spite even of themselves their Senses chear;
Then to the Wizard's Wonne their Steps they steer.
Like a green Isle, it broad beneath them spred,
With Gardens round, and wandering Currents clear,
And tufted Groves to shade the Meadow-Bed,
Sweet Airs and Song; and without Hurry all seem'd glad.

xxxviii

"As God shall judge me, Knight, we must forgive
(The half-enraptur'd PHILOMELUS cry'd)
The frail good Man deluded here to live,
And in these Groves his musing Fancy hide.
Ah, Nought is pure! It cannot be deny'd,
That Virtue still some Tincture has of Vice,
And Vice of Virtue. What should then betide,
But that our Charity be not too nice?
Come, let us Those we can to real Bliss entice."

xxxix

"Ay, sicker, (quoth the Knight) all Flesh is frail,
To pleasant Sin and joyous Dalliance bent;
But let not brutish Vice of This avail,
And think to scape deserved Punishment.
Justice were cruel weakly to relent;
From *Mercy's* Self she got her sacred Glaive:
Grace be to Those who can, and will, repent;
But Penance long, and dreary, to the Slave,
Who must in Floods of Fire his gross foul Spirit lave."

xl

Thus, holding high Discourse, they came to Where
The cursed Carle was at his wonted Trade;

xxxvii 9 Hurry] Hurrry *A*
xxxviii 9 entice."] entice. *A B*
xxxix 7 Those] those *B*
xxxix 9 lave."] lave. *A B*

Still tempting heedless Men into his Snare,
In witching Wise, as I before have said.
But when he saw, in goodly Geer array'd,
The grave majestic Knight approaching nigh,
And by his Side the Bard so sage and staid,
His Countenance fell; yet oft his anxious Eye
Mark'd them, like wily Fox who roosted Cock doth spy.

xli

Nathless, with feign'd Respect, he bade give back
The Rabble-Rout, and welcom'd them full kind;
Struck with the noble Twain, they were not slack
His Orders to obey, and fall behind.
Then he resum'd his Song; and, unconfin'd,
Pour'd all his Music, ran through all his Strings:
With magic Dust their Eyne he tries to blind,
And Virtue's tender Airs o'er Weakness flings.
What Pity base his Song who so divinely sings!

xlii

Elate in Thought, he counted them his own,
They listen'd so intent with fix'd Delight:
But they instead, as if transmew'd to Stone,
Marvel'd he could, with such sweet Art, unite
The Lights and Shades of Manners, Wrong and Right.
Mean time, the silly Croud the Charm devour,
Wide-pressing to the Gate. Swift, on the Knight
He darted fierce, to drag him to his Bower,
Who back'ning shun'd his Touch; for well he knew its Power.

xliii

As in throng'd Amphitheatre, of old,
The wary *Retiarius* trap'd his Foe:
Even so the Knight, returning on him bold,
At once involv'd him in the *Net of Woe,*
Whereof I Mention made not long ago.

xlii 9 back'ning . . . Touch;] backning . . . Touch, *A*
xliii 2 Foe:] Foe; *A*

Enrag'd at first, he scorn'd so weak a Jail,
And leap'd, and flew, and flounced to and fro;
But when he found that nothing could avail,
He sat him felly down, and gnaw'd his bitter Nail.

xliv

Alarm'd, th' inferior Demons of the Place
Rais'd rueful Shrieks and hideous Yells around;
Black ruptur'd Clouds deform'd the Welkin's Face,
And from beneath was heard a wailing Sound,
As of Infernal Sprights in Cavern bound;
A solemn Sadness every Creature strook,
And Lightnings flash'd, and Horror rock'd the Ground:
Huge Crouds on Crouds out-pour'd, with blemish'd Look,
As if on Time's last Verge this Frame of Things had shook.

xlv

Soon as the short-liv'd Tempest was yspent,
Steam'd from the Jaws of vext Avernus' Hole,
And hush'd the Hubbub of the Rabblement,
SIR INDUSTRY the first calm Moment stole.
"There must, (he cry'd) amid so vast a Shoal,
Be Some who are not tainted at the Heart,
Not poison'd quite by this same Villain's Bowl:
Come then, my Bard, thy heavenly Fire impart;
Touch Soul with Soul, till forth the latent Spirit start."

xliii 6 Enrag'd] Inrag'd *A*
*Laing MS. II, 330, University of Edinburgh Library, has the following stanza
and note in Thomson's hand, first printed by J. E. Wells, N&Q, CLXXV (1938),
420-21:*
    As when, in Vengeance of his pilfer'd cheese
    An angry Cambrian has ensnared a Rat;
    With rising Morn, th' astonish'd Felon sees
    His Foes around, man, woman, dog, and cat:
    He in his wiry Prison first lies squat;
    Till, rous'd, he gnaws it with fell Fury keen;
    But what, lewd Wretch! avails thy Rage? Ah! what?
    Thou in the Toils of Fate art caught, I ween:
Happy for thee! had Cheese and Luxury ne'er been.
    In the Castle of Indolence, when the demon of Indolence is caught
    in a net by the Knight of Arts and Industry. Stanza xliii
    changed thus [quotes two lines, "As in throngd amphitheatre," etc.]

xliv 5 Infernal] infernal *B*
xlv 9 start."] start. *A B*

xlvi

The Bard obey'd; and taking from his Side,
Where it in seemly Sort depending hung,
His *British* Harp, its speaking Strings he try'd,
The which with skilful Touch he deftly strung,
Till tinkling in clear Symphony they rung.
Then, as he felt the Muses come along,
Light o'er the Chords his raptur'd Hand he flung,
And play'd a Prelude to his rising Song:
The whilst, like Midnight mute, ten Thousands round him throng.

xlvii

Thus, ardent, burst his Strain. "Ye hapless Race,
Dire-labouring here to smother Reason's Ray,
That lights our Maker's Image in our Face,
And gives us wide o'er Earth unquestion'd Sway;
What is TH' ADOR'D SUPREME PERFECTION, say?
What, but eternal never-resting Soul,
Almighty Power, and all-directing Day;
By whom each Atom stirs, the Planets roll;
Who fills, surrounds, informs, and agitates the Whole?

xlviii

"Come, to the beaming GOD your Hearts unfold!
Draw from its Fountain Life! 'Tis thence, alone,
We can excel. Up from unfeeling Mold,
To seraphs burning round th' ALMIGHTY's Throne,
Life rising still on Life, in higher Tone,
Perfection forms, and with Perfection Bliss.
In Universal Nature This clear shewn,
Not needeth Proof; To prove it were, I wis,
To prove the beauteous World excels the brute Abyss.

xlix

"Is not the Field, with lively Culture green,
A Sight more joyous than the dead Morass?
Do not the Skies, with active Ether clean,

xlviii 8 Proof;] Proof: *A*

And fan'd by sprightly Zephyrs, far surpass
The foul November-Fogs, and slumbrous Mass,
With which sad Nature veils her drooping Face?
Does not the Mountain-Stream, as clear as Glass,
Gay-dancing on, the putrid Pool disgrace?
The same in All holds true, but chief in Human Race.

l

"It was not by vile Loitering in Ease,
That GREECE obtain'd the brighter Palm of Art,
That soft yet ardent ATHENS learn'd to please,
To keen the Wit, and to sublime the Heart,
In all supreme! compleat in every Part!
It was not thence majestic ROME arose,
And o'er the Nations shook her conquering Dart:
For Sluggard's Brow the Laurel never grows;
Renown is not the Child of indolent Repose.

li

"Had unambitious Mortals minded Nought,
But in loose Joy their Time to wear away;
Had they alone the Lap of Dalliance sought,
Pleas'd on her Pillow their dull Heads to lay;
Rude Nature's State had been our State To-day;
No Cities e'er their towery Fronts had rais'd,
No Arts had made us opulent and gay;
With Brother-Brutes the Human Race had graz'd;
None e'er had soar'd to Fame, None honour'd been, None
    prais'd.

lii

"Great HOMER's Song had never fir'd the Breast
To Thirst of Glory, and heroic Deeds;
Sweet MARO's Muse, sunk in inglorious Rest,
Had silent slept amid the *Mincian* Reeds:
The Wits of modern Time had told their Beads,

xlix 4 Zephyrs] Zephirs *A (See above, I, xviii 8.)*
    5 Mass,] Mass; *B*
    7 Glass,] Glass; *B*
    9 All] all *B*
l 5 compleat] complete *B*
lii 1 Breast] Breast, *A*

And monkish Legends been their only Strains;
Our MILTON's *Eden* had lain wrapt in Weeds,
Our SHAKESPEAR stroll'd and laugh'd with *Warwick* Swains,
Ne had my Master SPENSER charm'd his *Mulla's* Plains.

liii

"Dumb too had been the sage Historic Muse,
And perish'd all the Sons of antient Fame;
Those starry Lights of Virtue, that diffuse
Through the dark Depth of Time their vivid Flame,
Had all been lost with Such as have no Name.
Who then had scorn'd his Ease for others' Good?
Who then had toil'd rapacious Men to tame?
Who in the Public Breach devoted stood,
And for his Country's Cause been prodigal of Blood?

liv

"But should to Fame your Hearts impervious be,
If right I read, you Pleasure All require:
Then hear how best may be obtain'd this Fee,
How best enjoy'd this Nature's wide Desire.
Toil, and be glad! Let Industry inspire
Into your quicken'd Limbs her buoyant Breath!
Who does not act is dead; absorpt intire
In miry Sloth, no Pride, no Joy he hath:
O Leaden-hearted Men, to be in Love with Death!

lv

"Better the toiling Swain, oh happier far!
Perhaps the happiest of the Sons of Men!
Who vigorous plies the Plough, the Team, or Car;
Who houghs the Field, or ditches in the Glen,
Delves in his Garden, or secures his Pen:
The Tooth of Avarice poisons not his Peace;
He tosses not in Sloth's abhorred Den;
From Vanity he has a full Release;
And, rich in Nature's Wealth, he thinks not of Increase.

liii 5 all] All *A*   6 others'] other's *B*
liv 8 Pride,] Pride *A*
lv-lvi *omitted 1750 1762*

lvi

"Good Lord! how keen are his Sensations all!
His Bread is sweeter than the Glutton's Cates;
The Wines of *France* upon the Palate pall,
Compar'd with What his simple Soul elates,
The native Cup whose Flavour Thirst creates;
At one deep Draught of Sleep he takes the Night;
And for that Heart-felt Joy which Nothing mates,
Of the pure nuptial Bed the chaste Delight,
The Losel is to him a miserable Wight.

lvii

"But what avail the largest Gifts of HEAVEN,
When sickening Health and Spirits go amiss?
How tasteless then Whatever can be given?
Health is the vital Principle of Bliss,
And Exercise of Health. In Proof of This,
Behold the Wretch, who slugs his Life away,
Soon swallow'd in Disease's sad Abyss;
While he whom Toil has brac'd, or manly Play,
Has light as Air each Limb, each Thought as clear as Day.

lviii

"O who can speak the vigorous Joys of Health!
Unclogg'd the Body, unobscur'd the Mind:
The Morning rises gay; with pleasing Stealth,
The temperate Evening falls serene and kind.
In Health the wiser Brutes true Gladness find.
See! how the Younglings frisk along the Meads,
As May comes on, and wakes the balmy Wind;
Rampant with Life, their Joy all Joy exceeds:
Yet what save high-strung Health this dancing Pleasaunce
breeds?

lix

"But here, instead, is foster'd every Ill,
Which or distemper'd Minds or Bodies know.
Come then, my kindred Spirits! do not spill
Your Talents here. This Place is but a Shew,

lviii 3 rises] raises *A*

Whose Charms delude you to the Den of Woe;
Come, follow me, I will direct you right,
Where Pleasure's Roses, void of Serpents, grow,
Sincere as sweet; come, follow this good Knight,
And you will bless the Day that brought him to your Sight.

lx

"Some he will lead to Courts, and Some to Camps;
To Senates Some, and public sage Debates,
Where, by the solemn Gleam of Midnight-Lamps,
The World is pois'd, and manag'd mighty States;
To high Discovery Some, that new-creates
The Face of Earth; Some to the thriving Mart;
Some to the Rural Reign, and softer Fates;
To the sweet Muses Some, who raise the Heart:
All Glory shall be yours, all Nature, and all Art!

lxi

"There are, I see, who listen to my Lay,
Who wretched sigh for Virtue, but despair.
All may be done, (methinks I hear them say)
Even Death despis'd by generous Actions fair;
All, but for Those who to these Bowers repair,
Their every Power dissolv'd in Luxury,
To quit of torpid Sluggishness the Lair,
And from the powerful Arms of Sloth get free.
'Tis rising from the Dead—Alas!—It cannot be!

lxii

"Would you then learn to dissipate the Band
Of these huge threatning Difficulties dire,
That in the weak Man's Way like Lions stand,
His Soul appall, and damp his rising Fire?
Resolve! resolve! and to be Men aspire!
Exert that noblest Privilege, alone,
Here to Mankind indulg'd: controul Desire;
Let Godlike Reason, from her sovereign Throne,
Speak the commanding Word—*I will!*— and it is done.

lix 5 Woe;] Woe: *A*
lxii 2 threatning] threat'ning *B*
  6 Privilege] Priviledge *A Thomson probably wrote*
Priviledge; *see, for example, LD,* pp. 152, 169

lxiii

"Heavens! can you then thus waste, in shameful wise,
Your few important Days of Trial here?
Heirs of Eternity! yborn to rise
Through endless States of Being, still more near
To Bliss approaching, and Perfection clear,
Can you renounce a Fortune so sublime,
Such glorious Hopes, your backward Steps to steer,
And roll, with vilest Brutes, through Mud and Slime?
No! No!—Your Heaven-touch'd Hearts disdain the piteous
Crime!"

lxiv

"Enough! enough! they cry'd"—Strait, from the Croud,
The better Sort on Wings of Transport fly.
As when amid the lifeless Summits proud
Of *Alpine* Cliffs, where to the gelid Sky
Snows pil'd on Snows in wintry Torpor lie,
The Rays divine of vernal *Phoebus* play;
Th' awaken'd Heaps, in Streamlets from on high,
Rous'd into Action, lively leap away,
Glad-warbling through the Vales, in their new Being gay.

lxv

Not less the Life, the vivid Joy serene,
That lighted up these new-created Men,
Than That which wings th' exulting Spirit clean,
When, just deliver'd from this fleshly Den,
It soaring seeks its native Skies agen.
How light its Essence! how unclogg'd its Powers!
Beyond the Blazon of my mortal Pen:
Even so we glad forsook these sinful Bowers,
Even such enraptur'd Life, such Energy was ours.

lxvi

But far the greater Part, with Rage inflam'd,
Dire-mutter'd Curses, and blasphem'd high Jove.
"Ye Sons of Hate! (They bitterly exclaim'd)
What brought you to this Seat of Peace and Love?

lxiii 2 Trial] Tryal *A*

While with kind Nature, here amid the Grove,
We pass'd the harmless Sabbath of our Time,
What to disturb it could, fell Men, emove
Your barbarous Hearts? Is Happiness a Crime?
Then do the Fiends of Hell rule in yon Heaven sublime."

lxvii

"Ye impious Wretches! (quoth the Knight in Wrath)
Your Happiness behold!"—Then strait a Wand
He wav'd, an anti-magic Power that hath,
Truth from illusive Falshood to command.
Sudden, the Landskip sinks on every Hand;
The pure quick Streams are marshy Puddles found;
On baleful Heaths the Groves all blacken'd stand;
And, o'er the weedy foul abhorred Ground,
Snakes, Adders, Toads, each loathly Creature crawls around.

lxviii

And here and there, on Trees by Lightning scath'd,
Unhappy Wights who loathed Life yhung;
Or, in fresh Gore and recent Murder bath'd,
They weltering lay; or else, infuriate flung
Into the gloomy Flood, while Ravens sung
The funeral Dirge, they down the Torrent rowl'd:
These, by distemper'd Blood to Madness stung,
Had doom'd themselves; whence oft, when Night controul'd
The World, returning hither their sad Spirits howl'd.

lxix

Meantime a moving Scene was open laid.
That Lazar-House, I whilom in my Lay
Depeinten have, its Horrors deep-display'd,
And gave unnumber'd Wretches to the Day,
Who tossing there in squalid Misery lay.
Soon as of sacred Light th' unwonted Smile
Pour'd on these living Catacombs its Ray,
Through the drear Caverns stretching many a Mile,
The Sick up-rais'd their Heads, and dropp'd their Woes awhile.

lxvi 9 sublime."] sublime. *A B*
lxvii 1 Knight] Knight, *B*

lxx

"O Heaven! (they cry'd) and do we once more see
Yon blessed Sun, and this green Earth so fair?
Are we from noisome Damps of Pest-House free?
And drink our Souls the sweet ethereal Air?
O Thou! or Knight, or God! who holdest there
That Fiend, oh keep him in eternal Chains!
But what for us, the Children of Despair,
Brought to the Brink of Hell, what Hope remains?
Repentance does itself but aggravate our Pains."

lxxi

The gentle Knight, who saw their rueful Case,
Let fall adown his silver Beard some Tears.
"Certes (quoth he) it is not even in Grace,
T' undo the Past, and eke your broken Years:
Nathless, to nobler Worlds Repentance rears,
With humble Hope, her Eye; to Her is given
A Power the truly contrite Heart that chears;
She quells the Brand by which the Rocks are riven;
She more than merely softens, she rejoices HEAVEN.

lxxii

"Then patient bear the Sufferings you have earn'd,
And by these Sufferings purify the Mind;
Let Wisdom be by past Misconduct learn'd:
Or pious die, with Penitence resign'd;
And to a Life more happy and refin'd,
Doubt not, you shall, new Creatures, yet arise.
Till Then, you may expect in me to find
One who will wipe your Sorrow from your Eyes,
One who will soothe your Pangs, and wing you to the Skies."

lxxiii

They silent heard, and pour'd their Thanks in Tears.
"For you (resum'd the Knight with sterner Tone)
Whose hard dry Hearts th' obdurate Demon sears,
That Villain's Gifts will cost you many a Groan;

lxxiii 2 Knight] Knight, *B*

116

James Thomson
Portrait by William Aikman, 1725-26
Huntington Library

JAMES THOMSON
Portrait by John Patoun, 1746
Scottish National Portrait Gallery

In dolorous Mansion long you must bemoan
His fatal Charms, and weep your Stains away;
Till, soft and pure as Infant-Goodness grown,
You feel a perfect Change: then, who can say,
What Grace may yet shine forth in Heaven's eternal Day?"

lxxiv

This said, his powerful Wand he wav'd anew:
Instant, a glorious Angel-Train descends,
The Charities, to-wit, of rosy Hue;
Sweet Love their Looks a gentle Radiance lends,
And with seraphic Flame Compassion blends.
At once, delighted, to their Charge they fly:
When lo! a goodly Hospital ascends;
In which they bade each human Aid be nigh,
That could the Sick-Bed smoothe of that unhappy Fry.

lxxv

It was a worthy edifying Sight,
And gives to Human-Kind *peculiar* Grace,
To see kind Hands attending Day and Night,
With tender Ministry, from Place to Place.
Some prop the Head; some, from the pallid Face,
Wipe off the faint cold Dews weak Nature sheds;
Some reach the healing Draught: the whilst, to chase
The Fear supreme, around their soften'd Beds,
Some holy Man by Prayer all opening Heaven dispreds.

lxxvi

Attended by a glad acclaiming Train
Of those he rescu'd had from gaping Hell,
Then turn'd the Knight; and, to his Hall again
Soft-pacing, sought of Peace the mossy Cell;
Yet down his Cheeks the Gems of Pity fell,
To see the helpless Wretches that remain'd,
There left through Delves and Deserts dire to yell;
Amaz'd, their Looks with pale Dismay were stain'd,
And spreading wide their Hands they meek Repentance feign'd.

117

lxxvii

But ah! their scorned Day of Grace was past:
For (Horrible to tell!) a Desert wild
Before them stretch'd, bare, comfortless, and vast;
With Gibbets, Bones, and Carcases defil'd.
There nor trim Field, nor lively Culture smil'd;
Nor waving Shade was seen, nor Fountain fair;
But Sands abrupt on Sands lay loosely pil'd,
Through which they floundering toil'd with painful Care,
Whilst *Phoebus* smote them sore, and fir'd the cloudless Air.

lxxviii

Then, varying to a joyless Land of Bogs,
The sadden'd Country a grey Waste appear'd;
Where Nought but putrid Streams and noisome Fogs
For ever hung on drizzly *Auster's* Beard;
Or else the Ground by piercing *Caurus* sear'd,
Was jagg'd with Frost, or heap'd with glazed Snow:
Through these Extremes a ceaseless Round they steer'd,
By cruel Fiends still hurry'd to and fro,
Gaunt *Beggary*, and *Scorn*, with many Hell-Hounds moe.

lxxix

The First was with base dunghill Rags yclad,
Tainting the Gale, in which they flutter'd light;
Of morbid Hue his Features, sunk, and sad;
His hollow Eyne shook forth a sickly Light;
And o'er his lank Jaw-Bone, in piteous Plight,
His black rough Beard was matted rank and vile;
Direful to see! an Heart-appalling Sight!
Meantime foul Scurf and Blotches him defile;
And Dogs, where-e'er he went, still barked all the While.

lxxx

The other was a fell despightful Fiend:
Hell holds none worse in baleful Bower below;
By Pride, and Wit, and Rage, and Rancour, keen'd;
Of Man alike, if good or bad, the Foe:

lxxvi 1 Train] Train, *A*
    4 Cell;] Cell: *A*
lxxix 8 defile;] defile! *B*

With Nose up-turn'd, he always made a Shew
As if he smelt some nauseous Scent; his Eye
Was cold, and keen, like blast from boreal Snow;
And Taunts he casten forth most bitterly.
Such were the Twain that off drove this ungodly Fry.

lxxxi

Even so through *Brentford* Town, a Town of Mud,
An Herd of bristly Swine is prick'd along;
The filthy Beasts, that never chew the Cud,
Still grunt, and squeak, and sing their troublous Song,
And oft they plunge themselves the Mire among:
But ay the ruthless Driver goads them on,
And ay of barking Dogs the bitter Throng
Makes them renew their unmelodious Moan;
Ne ever find they Rest from their unresting Fone.

Hymn on Solitude

INTRODUCTION

The "Hymn on Solitude" is the earliest of Thomson's important short poems, and a landmark in the development of the Miltonic lyric, sharing honors in this regard with Dyer's "Grongar Hill." These pieces mark the point of connection between the imitation of *L'Allegro* and *Il Penseroso* and the development of the descriptive and allegorical ode by Collins and the Wartons in the 1740's.[1] We can follow the "Hymn on Solitude" from its earliest form to a final version which can probably be dated in the last year of Thomson's life. Thomson included a transcript in his letter to Mallet, July 10, 1725 *(A)*; another version is preserved in Lady Hertford's manuscript miscellany (begun March 5, 1725-26), and printed by Helen S. Hughes *(B)*.[2] The poem was first published in the collection *Miscellaneous Poems by Several Hands*, usually known as "Ralph's Miscellany," which appeared in April, 1729 *(C)*. This text was reprinted in the supplement of minor poems brought out in connection with the subscription edition of *The Seasons* in 1730.[3] The next significant text appeared in the third volume of Dodsley's *Collection of Poems*, January, 1748 *(D)*. Lastly, still further changes appeared in the version first printed posthumously in 1750 in Thomson's *Poems on Several Occasions* *(E)*, and reprinted in the *Works* of 1762, edited and published by Thomson's friends Patrick Murdoch and Andrew Millar. It is this version which has been regularly reprinted in later editions and anthologies, though its authenticity is open to question.

In general, Thomson texts published in the years immediately following his death may be suspect because of the possibility of tampering by Lyttleton.[4] Fortunately, as has been shown, the posthumous second edition of *The Castle of Indo-*

---

[1] See Hagstrum, *The Sister Arts*, p. 269; Alan D. McKillop, "Collins's Ode to Evening—Background and Structure," *Tennessee Studies in Literature*, V (1960), 73-83.

[2] *LD*, pp. 10-11; *MP*, XXV (1928), 447-48.

[3] See W. M. Sale, Jr., *Samuel Richardson: Master Printer* (Ithaca, 1950), pp. 209-10.

[4] See John Edwin Wells, "Thomson's *Seasons* 'Corrected and Amended,'" *JEGP*, XLII (1943), 104-14.

THE

SEASONS.

BY

Mr. THOMSON.

LONDON:

Printed in the YEAR M.DCC.XXX.

Title-page, *The Seasons*, subscription quarto, 1730

lence can be cleared of suspicion on this ground. But the revisions of "Solitude" that first appear in *(E)* raise some doubts. Their acceptance by Murdoch and Millar in 1762 is not conclusive, for, to cite only one other instance, this edition follows Lyttelton's arbitrary alterations in Canto II of *The Castle of Indolence*. The last revisions which we can confidently accept as from Thomson's hand are the slight changes which appear in *D*. It seems certain that Dodsley printed an authorized version of the poems by Thomson included in the first edition of his famous *Collection*. Lyttelton comes into the situation here also, for we are told that Dodsley submitted most of the pieces in his original three volumes to Lyttelton's judgment.[5] Lyttelton was personally close to Thomson, and his approval and Thomson's consent at this time would probably go together. It may be noted that Thomson's library included "Dodsley's Collection of Poems, vol. 2d and 3d. 1748" (Sale Catalogue, No. 60). Text *D* continued to appear in successive editions of Dodsley, though, as has been said, it has been otherwise superseded by *E*.

Under the circumstances, the changes of 1750 deserve close scrutiny, though the result can only be presumptive, not decisive. Among these changes, the alteration of "ever-pleasing Solitude" to "mildly pleasing Solitude" seems weak. The dropping of the line, "And Nature triumphs in your eye," revised in 1748 from the earlier "And nature dances in your eye," may mean that the reviser did not understand the subjectivity of this characteristically Thomsonian line. The expansion of the line on religion and the addition of a line on liberty seem commonplace:

> Religion's beams around thee shine,
> And chear thy glooms with light divine:
> About thee sports sweet Liberty.

The change of "soft-divided" to "calmed to friendship" in the compliment to the Countess of Hertford in line 19, though it gets rid of a difficult compound epithet, flattens the effect. The spelling *Harford* in line 20 has no parallel in Thomson's texts; elsewhere it is always *Hartford* or *Hertford*. The change of

---

[5] This statement is based on a passage in a letter from Dodsley to Shenstone, November 10, 1752 (British Museum, Addit. MS. 28, 959, f. 11ʳ). See W. P. Courtney, *Dodsley's Collection of Poetry: Its Contents and Contributors* (1910), p. 2.

"Philomela," originally an allusion to Mrs. Elizabeth Rowe and her friendship with Lady Hertford, to "Musidora" obscures such significance as there may be in the phrase "the rivalled nightingale," but Thomson by this time may have lost interest in his twenty-year old compliment. At one point, indeed, the 1750 text offers a clear improvement in the line,

> And rapt *Urania* sings to thee,

which is consistent with the shift from "you" to "thou" and "thee" made elsewhere in the revision of 1748, and corrects the common misspelling "wrapt." Most important is the rewritten conclusion, in which Thomson's reference to his friends Mallet and Murdoch is dropped, and a topographical reference to a country retreat at Norwood Hill is substituted. Norwood Hill, Wickham, Kent, was the residence of Gilbert West, a close friend of Lyttelton, and well known to Thomson also. Thomson and Lyttelton probably visited this spot more than once in the 1740's, and it is worth noting that another reference to Norwood Hill in Dodsley's *Collection* is from the pen of Lyttelton:

> Oft have I met her on the verdant side
> Of Norwood hill, and in the yellow meads
> Where Pan the dancing Graces leads,
> Array'd in all her flow'ry pride.[6]

The conclusion of *E*, moreover, seems to be authenticated by a parallel with Thomson's "Lines to Retirement," written at Lady Hertford's country place, St. Leonard's Hill, in 1735, and first printed by Miss Hughes from the Alnwick MSS. The concluding stanza of "Retirement" is as follows:

> And lo! where on Augusta's Shore,
> The Human Tempest roars amain;
> What wretches there their fate deplore!
> Oh cover me ye woods again![7]

Evidently the conclusion of *E* builds and improves upon this passage. It thus becomes impossible to reject the *E* readings entirely, though they probably include not only revisions agreed on by Thomson and Lyttelton but also unauthorized "improvements" introduced by Lyttelton after Thomson's death.

---

[6] "An Irregular Ode writ at Wickham in 1746," Dodsley's *Collection* (2d ed.; 1748), II, 67.

[7] *MP*, XXV (1928), 461.

In the "Hymn on Solitude" Thomson develops his Miltonic lyric by an opening and closing invocation, by imagining alternate forms or manifestations for his central persona, and by developing an attendant train of personifications. Dyer's "Grongar Hill," close in spirit and in time to "Solitude," moves in a somewhat different direction by absorbing the persona in a carefully located descriptive sequence.

HYMN ON SOLITUDE

Hail, mildly pleasing solitude,
Companion of the wise, and good;
But, from whose holy, piercing eye,
The herd of fools, and villains fly.

Oh, how I love with thee to walk,   5
And listen to thy whisper'd talk,
Which innocence, and truth imparts,
And melts the most obdurate hearts.
A thousand shapes you wear with ease,
And still in every shape you please.   10
Now wrapt in some mysterious dream,
A lone philosopher you seem;
Now quick from hill to vale you fly,
And now you sweep the vaulted sky.
A shepherd next, you haunt the plain,   15
And warble forth your oaten strain.
A lover now, with all the grace
Of that sweet passion in your face:
Then, calm'd to friendship you assume
The gentle-looking HARFORD's bloom,   20

1 mildly pleasing] ever-pleasing *A-D*
3 holy, piercing] awfull piercing *A*
5 with thee] with you *A*
6 thy whisper'd talk] your silent talk *A*
12 lone philosopher] sage Philosopher *A*
   Between ll. 12-13 A has:
   Now a religious port you bear
   And now a Hermit you appear
13 quick from hill to vale] o'er the meads and groves *A*] o'er the Hills and Vales *B*

Between ll. 14-15 A-D have:
   And nature dances in your eye.   dances] triumphs *C D*
   Then strait again you court the shade
   And pining hang the pensive head.
15 A shepherd next] A shepherd now *A B*
Between ll. 16-17 A has:
   Now a gay Huntress by the dawn
   You trip it o'er the dewy lawn
17-18 *These lines follow l. 24 in B*
After l. 18 A and B repeat ll. 9-10
19-24 *Added in B, following l. 16*
19 calm'd to friendship] soft-divided *B-D*
20 HARFORD's] *Hertford's B*] H---d's *C D*

125

As, with her MUSIDORA, she,
(Her MUSIDORA fond of thee)
Amid the long withdrawing vale,
Awakes the rival'd nightingale.
Thine is the balmy breath of morn,   25
Just as the dew-bent rose is born;
And while Meridian fervours beat,
Thine is the woodland dumb retreat;
But chief, when evening scenes decay,
And the faint landskip swims away,   30
Thine is the doubtful soft decline,
And that best hour of musing thine.
Descending angels bless thy train,
The Virtues of the sage, and swain;
Plain Innocence in white array'd,   35
Before thee lifts her fearless head:
Religion's beams around thee shine,
And chear thy glooms with light divine:
About thee sports sweet Liberty;
And rapt *Urania* sings to thee.   40
Oh, let me pierce thy secret cell!
And in thy deep recesses dwell;

21-22 MUSIDORA] PHILOMELA B-D
23 long withdrawing] long-withdrawing B

After l. 24 C and D repeat ll. 9-10.
For ll. 25-32 A has:
    Your's is the fragrant morning blush
    And your's the silent evening hush
    Your's the refulgent noonday gleam
    And your's ah then! the gelid stream
25 balmy breath] unbounded breath B-D
27 fervours] fervors B D] fevers C 1730
28 woodland B C E] woodland's D
31 soft decline] dear decline B-D

33 thy train] your train A
35 Plain Innocence] Soft innocence A
36 And Contemplation rears his head A-D   his head] the head C D
For ll. 37-40 A has:
    Religion with her awfull brow
    And all the muses wait on you
40 And wrapt Urania waits on you B C   wrapt] rapt C] wrap'd D

41 thy secret cell] your secret cell A] thy secret hill B
42 thy deep recesses] your deep recesses A

Perhaps from Norwood's oak-clad hill,
When meditation has her fill,
I just may cast my careless eyes   45
Where London's spiry turrets rise,
Think of its crimes, its cares, its pain,
Then shield me in the woods again.

After l. 42 A-D have as the conclusion of the poem:
 Forever from the world retir'd
 Forever with your raptures fir'd   your raptures *A*] thy raptures *B-D*
 Nor by a Mortal seen save he
 A Mallet or a Murdoch be.   A Lycidas, or Lycon be *B-D*
C and D interchange the first two lines of this passage

A Poem Sacred to the Memory of Sir Isaac Newton

INTRODUCTION

Sir Isaac Newton died on March 20, 1727, at the age of eighty-four, and was buried in Westminster Abbey on March 28. Thomson's poem to his memory was published on May 8 *(Daily Journal)*. Evidently the poet turned aside from his work on *Spring* to pay tribute to the great man whose fame had already spread far beyond the confines of the academic world and was fast becoming the property of the entire western republic of letters. Of course Newton's praise had long been sounded in terms comprehensible to the layman. The subtitle of Edmund Halley's Latin lines prefixed to the first edition of the *Principia* (1687) had referred to Newton and his work as "Saeculi Gentisque nostrae Decus egregium,"—"the illustrious ornament of our age and nation,"—and had praised him as the man who had single-handed disclosed the secrets of the universe. Moreover Halley set the model, eventually to be followed by Thomson and many others, of a specific enumeration in verse of Newton's discoveries.

The elevation of Newton to unique preëminence in the popular mind was the work of the next two generations. Addison's Oxford oration on the new philosophy (1693) praises Descartes at length as the great solitary genius who had brought the new truth; yet he seems to adapt Halley's epigraph for Newton when he remarks at the opening of his oration that it would be a shameful thing to transfer our praises to the ancients, "dum tam praeclarum aetatis hujusce specimen coram oculis praesens intuemur," translated by Rawlins, "when we survey the great ornament of the present age."[1] Sermon VII of Richard Bentley's Boyle Lectures (1692) shows the effective use of the *Principia* in physico-theology for the layman, with full acknowledgment to "that very excellent and divine Theorist Mr. *Isaac Newton*."[2] With continuing emphasis on such phrases as "decus egregium" and "divine Theorist," we have here a

---

[1] Addison, *Miscellaneous Works*, ed. A. C. Guthkelch (1914), II, 467-69. Cf. Marjorie Nicolson, *Mountain Gloom and Mountain Glory* (Ithaca, 1959), p. 302 and n.

[2] 5th ed., Cambridge, 1724, p. 253.

pattern in which a new philosophy instituted by one great man brings or promises to bring ultimate truth at a single revolutionary stroke. So it had been with Lucretius on Epicurus, with Cowley and Mulgrave on Hobbes. The claim is almost made by Glanvill for Descartes: "And yet had heaven afforded that miracle of men, the Illustrious *Des-Cartes* a longer day on earth, we might have expected the utmost of what ingenuity could perform herein: but his immature Fate hath unhappily disappointed us; and prevented the most desirable Complement of his not to be equall'd *Philosophy*."[3] But the major prophet for the new age must be clear of charges that his philosophy is mechanistic, heterodox, or merely speculative; no such charges were brought with any effect against Newton, and he speedily assumed the supreme position.

In the first generation of the eighteenth century, along with the advance of Newtonianism against the established Cartesian physics and in opposition to the rivalry of Leibniz, came an increasing demand for popular and polite expositions of the new philosophy.[4] On the popular level traditional material blended with the new operative ideas of Newtonian science both in the physico-theological manuals and the increasing number of descriptive-didactic poems that dealt with scientific subjects. This rich field has been widely and variously studied in recent years, and here we must limit ourselves to the fusion of panegyric and popular science that underlies Thomson's poem.[5] In the transition from the seventeenth to the eighteenth centuries one finds the original eulogistic phrase of Halley repeated, varied, and elaborated. In 1698 Dennis spoke of Newton and Locke as "Two of the living Glories of England." In 1720 he heightened his language: Newton, "whose Merit is above what the Muses themselves can Commend" has "oblig'd and astonish'd the Learned World by his Immortal and unparallel'd Treatises; those Treatises that have made him an Honour to his Country, an Advancer of the noblest Learning, and an Enlarger of the Empire of the Mind."[6]

---

[3] *The Vanity of Dogmatizing* (1661), p. 48.

[4] See E. W. Strong, "Newtonian Explications of Natural Philosophy," *JHI*, XVIII (1957), 49-83, especially 53 ff.

[5] For a convenient brief statement about the extensive but scattered literature on the subject, see W. Powell Jones, "Science in Biblical Paraphrase in Eighteenth-Century England," *PMLA*, LXXIV (1959), 41, n. 2.

[6] John Dennis, *Critical Works*, ed. E. N. Hooker (Baltimore, 1939-43), I, 161; II, 208.

The references in the *Spectator* will suffice to show the characteristic aspects of the popular tradition that was taking shape. In No. 543, November 22, 1712, Addison echoes his own earlier phrase and Halley's in a context which puts Newton at the center of modern science and physico-theology:

The more extended our Reason is, and the more able to grapple with immense Objects, the greater still are those Discoveries which it makes of Wisdom and Providence in the Work of the Creation. A Sir *Isaac Newton*, who stands up as the Miracle of the present Age, can look through a whole Planetary System; consider it in its Weight, Number, and Measure; and draw from it as many Demonstrations of infinite Power and Wisdom, as a more confined understanding is able to deduce from the System of an Human Body.

John Hughes, in *Spectator* No. 554, December 5, 1712, after naming Bacon and Boyle, mentions

a *Third,* who is yet living, and is likewise the Glory of our own Nation. The Improvements which others had made in Natural and Mathematical Knowledge have so vastly increased in his Hands, as to afford at once a wonderful Instance how great the Capacity is of an Human Soul, and how inexhaustible the Subject of its Enquiries; so true is that Remark in Holy Writ, that, tho' a wise Man seek to find out the Works of God from the beginning to the End, yet shall he not be able to do it.

Henry Grove in *Spectator* No. 635, December 20, 1714, combines the themes of the great soul illuminating the darkness of ignorance, the religious aspects of scientific discovery, and the extension of knowledge in the future life:

How doth such a Genius as Sir *Isaac Newton,* from amidst the Darkness that involves human Understanding, break forth, and appear like one of another Species! The vast Machine, we inhabit, lies open to him, he seems not unacquainted with the general Laws that govern it, and while with the Transport of a Philosopher he beholds and admires the glorious Work, he is capable of paying at once a more devout and more rational Homage to his Maker. But alas! how narrow is the Prospect even of such a Mind? and how obscure to the Compass that is taken in by the Ken of an Angel; or of a Soul but newly escaped from its Imprisonment in the Body! For my part, I freely indulge my Soul in the Confidence of its future Grandeur; it pleases me to think that I who know so small a portion of the Works of the Creator, and with slow and painful Steps creep up and down on the Surface of this Globe,

130

shall e'er long shoot away with the Swiftness of Imagination, trace out the hidden Springs of Nature's Operations, be able to keep pace with the heavenly Bodies in the Rapidity of their Career, be a Spectator of the long Chain of Events in the natural and moral Worlds, visit the several Apartments of the Creation, know how they are furnished and how inhabited, comprehend the Order and measure the Magnitudes, and Distances of those Orbs, which to us seem disposed without any regular Design, and set all in the same Circle, observe the Dependance of the Parts of each System, and (if our Minds are big enough to grasp the Theory) of the several Systems upon one another, from whence results the Harmony of the Universe.[7]

As Miss Nicolson has well shown, the new science took over the traditional cosmic voyage, which had long been associated in poetry with the flight of the religiously exalted free intelligence released from the body before or after death, and with a view of the heavens which might have scientific implications. In a well-known passage in the ode called "The Ecstacy" (modeled on Cowley's "Ecstasie"), written before 1717, John Hughes represents his soul as traveling with Newton's through the skies in endless acquisition of new knowledge, and Miss Nicolson has dwelt on the importance of this "little cosmic voyage" in setting the pattern for innumerable later tributes to Newton.[8]

In short, Thomson's lines stand out in the tradition which praises Newton as a unique culture-hero, describes his discoveries in some detail, represents them as a direct view of the cosmos comparable to the visions of the prophet and the insights of the poet, and anticipates the continuation and extension of this cosmic vision in the future life. We are dealing here with popular literature rather than with the history of science. Professor Guerlac has recently warned against an identification of popular Newtonianism with Newton's own discoveries and opinions or with the totality of eighteenth century scientific

---

[7] For further illustration, see *Background of Seasons*, pp. 22-25.

[8] See Marjorie Nicolson, *Voyages to the Moon* (1948), and, for the importance of Hughes' poem, *Newton Demands the Muse* (Princeton, 1946), pp. 10-11, and also Hoxie N. Fairchild, *Religious Trends in English Poetry*, I (1939), 251-52. The cosmic voyage is linked with elaborate scientific detail and extensive quotation from scientists, including Newton, in John Reynolds, *Death's Vision* (1709), repr. 1716 and 1719, and revised in 1725 as *A View of Death*. Similar ideas appear at this time in Henry Needler and William Hinchcliffe. See Maren-Sofie Røstvig, *The Happy Man*, II (Oslo, 1958), 31-32.

thought.[9] It is of course a legend that Newton reigned sole and supreme, and that in the first quarter of the eighteenth century he vanquished Descartes single-handed. Moreover, if we limit ourselves to popular literature in England, we can distinguish between the apotheosis of Newton and more broadly the spirit of the physico-theological poem which culminates in Thomson's *Seasons*. Here belong, for example, Blackmore's *Creation* (1712), Reynolds' *Death's Vision*, already mentioned, Richard Collins' *Nature Display'd* (1727, published a month after Thomson's Newton poem), Samuel Edwards' *The Copernican System* (1728), Robert Gambol's *Beauties of the Universe* (1732), and Henry Baker's *The Universe* (1734). J. T. Desaguliers' *The Newtonian System of the World, the Best Model of Government* (1728) is rather exceptional in being exclusively and technically Newtonian. Yet, after such qualifications have been made, it is still possible to say with Professor Guerlac, "There is little doubt that, as far as Britain and its American colonies were concerned, Newton was, in the words of Cotton Mather, 'the perpetual Dictator of the learned World.' "[10] Thomson's poem, linked in various ways, like all his work, with tendencies already clearly defined in the feeling and thought of his age, still conveys a fresh and authentic response to Newtonian science. Like the physico-theological pieces, it seeks some degree of precision, and in the tradition of philosophical panegyric it takes the highest ground. Among Thomson's shorter pieces it preëminently illustrates Miss Miles' excellent description of his mode as "an exceptionally panoramic and panegyric verse, emotional, pictorial, noble, universal, and tonal, rising to the height of heaven and of feeling in the style traditionally known as grand or sublime."[11] Or, using the terms of an earlier age, we may apply to this poem Dryden's description of his *Eleonora* (1692): "It was intended . . . not for an Elegie, but a Panegyrique. A kind of Apotheosis, indeed; if a Heathen Word may be applyed to a Christian use."

We need not claim for the young James Thomson any high proficiency in Newtonian physics. He might get a smattering

---

[9] Henry Guerlac, "Newton's Changing Reputation in the Eighteenth Century," in *Carl Becker's Heavenly City Revisited* (Ithaca, 1958), pp. 6 ff.

[10] *Ibid.*, p. 21 n.

[11] Josephine Miles, *Eras and Modes in English Poetry* (Berkeley, 1957), p. 57, quoted by Patricia Meyer Spacks, *The Varied God* (Berkeley, 1959), p. 184.

JAMES THOMSON
Portrait by William Aikman, 1725-26
Scottish National Portrait Gallery

JAMES THOMSON
Portrait by Stephen Slaughter, *c.* 1736
Leicester Museum

Newton's monument, *The Seasons*, 1730. See note on the opposite page.

of the new science from the curriculum at Edinburgh, and from popular lectures; possibly a closer view, as Grant suggests, from the curriculum of Watts' Academy, where he was a tutor for a few months in 1726.[12] Long afterwards Patrick Murdoch said that the poet was indebted for his account of Newton's discoveries "to the assistance he had of his friend Mr. *Gray, a* gentleman well versed in the *Newtonian Philosophy,* who, on that occasion, gave him a very exact, though general, abstract of its principles." But others among Thomson's friends thought Murdoch gave John Gray too much credit here.[13]

As a measure of Thomson's response to popular knowledge and sentiment, we may consider how closely much of what he says approximates the tribute to Newton in *Mist's Weekly Journal,* April 8, 1727.[14] After some general moralizing on the death of the great, this essay continues:

For we form a Notion of such People as common Benefactors to human Society, as sent amongst us by the more immediate Commission of the Deity, to enlighten the Understandings, correct the Errors, inform the Ignorance, and to be the publick Instructors of Mankind. While we dwell with Wonder and Admiration upon their illustrious Characters, we feel an unusual Ardour glowing within us, and conceive a Sort of Veneration for their sacred

---

[12] Cf. Herbert Drennon, "James Thomson's Contact with Newtonianism and his Interest in Natural Philosophy," *PMLA,* XLIX (1934), 72-74; *LD,* p. 2; Grant, pp. 56-58.

[13] Thomson, *Works* (1762), I, ix; *LD,* pp. 202-03, 214.

[14] Repr. *Political State of Great Britain,* XXXIII (March, 1727), 327-30.

The plate on the opposite page, drawn by William Kent and engraved by P. Fourdrinier, first appeared in the subscription quarto of 1730, facing p. 241. Kent was the designer of the monument, Rysbrack the sculptor. The plate does not correspond in all respects to the monument actually erected in Westminster Abbey; it is evidently based on preliminary sketches. The situation can best be understood by comparing this plate with the following illustrations in Mrs. M. I. Webb's *Michael Rysbrack: Sculptor* (1954): 19, facing p. 61, the monument in the Abbey; 32, facing p. 64, drawing by Kent in the Victoria and Albert Museum; 23, facing p. 64, drawing by Rysbrack in the British Museum. The plate of 1730 is on the whole closest to 23, which evidently represents the plan after Rysbrack had reworked it considerably. The following are the most striking differences between the plate and the monument: (a) in the plate, the pyramid rests on spheres which are on a level with the feet of the sarcophagus; in the monument, the pyramid rests squarely on a plinth; (b) in the plate, Newton's head is tangent to the sphere; in the monument, the head is considerably lower than the sphere; (c) in the plate, the volumes on which Newton's forearm rests are aligned vertically with the base; in the monument, the volumes project beyond the base. Limiting ourselves to these points, we may note that for (a) the sketch resembles Mrs. Webb's 22 (though in 22 the spheres are on a level with Newton's elbow); for (b) and (c) the plate resembles Webb's 23.

Memories. We take Fire, and are almost carried beyond our selves, upon a closer Review of those uncommon Excellencies, by which they have so happily distinguished themselves above the rest of the Creation. We are inspired into a generous, tho' distant, Emulation of those transcendent Virtues, which even on this Side the Grave, exalted the Possessors of them to a Degree beyond Mortality. When such great Examples as these are set before us, the Passions are necessarily quickened and excited, and the Soul with a becoming Pride dilates and extends it self, pleased as it were to behold the Dignity of human Nature.

I have been led into these common Reflections by the Death of the late Sir *Isaac Newton,* the greatest of Philosophers, and the Glory of the *British* Nation. Who by the Strength and Compass of his Genius, the vast Extent of his Capacities, and the Depth of his Judgment, together with the indefatigable Diligence and Application, has given greater Light to Philosophy, than all the Industry of former Ages. Who, by his subtil Speculations, and uncommon Penetration into the Principles of Things, has discovered to the World, and established upon the undeniable Evidence of Demonstration, what was once look'd upon as dark and inexplicable, and beyond the Limits of human Knowledge. Who by the most accurate Reasonings and Deductions has traced out the abstrusest Causes, solved the most difficult Phaenomena, and laid down such incomparable Rules and Propositions as may hereafter be the Foundation of new Improvements and Discoveries. Whose inestimable Writings are as far beyond the Reach of common Apprehensions, as they are useful and excellent; and seem to be delivered to the World like the sacred Oracles of old, which excluded the Profane and Vulgar, and admitted those only who had been solemnly initiated into the Mystery of the Deity.

How attentively did he survey the Operations of the supreme Wisdom, by what prescribed and stated Laws the whole Universe is governed; what a strict Concatenation and Subserviency ran thro' all Parts; how the same Laws exert themselves in all the Works of Nature, and are constantly observed with a wonderful Regularity? With what Art and Perspicuity did he explain the different Affections of Light, and the Origin of Colours? How ingeniously did he examine and compare his Quantities of Motion, the Powers of Gravity and Elasticity, the Actions and Properties of Fluids; and, from thence, by just and regular Conclusions, account for those Effects which were formerly ascribed to nothing but occult and unintelligible Causes, and the pompous Terms of Vanity and Ignorance? Behold him from this Earth extend his View yet farther into our System; and observe the Trajectories of Comets, the Orbits, Distances, Magnitudes of the Planets, their mutual Actions and Reactions upon one another, with what Equability and Constancy they perform their Revolutions, according to the Impression of the first great Mover. See him from hence enlarge the spacious Prospect, and, as far as the human Mind can expand it self, travel over the remotest Regions of the Universe; and from the Construction, Disposition, and Proportion of the Parts, and the Beautiful Order, Harmony, and Symmetry of the whole, draw Numberless Demonstrations of a divine intelligent Principle, an all-wise Creator. These were the Ends which this excellent Man proposed to himself in his Research after Truth: And this indeed is, or ought to be, the Scope of all Philosophy, namely, to lead Mankind from the Creature to the Creator, and to illustrate the Power and Magnificence of that eternal Wisdom, which has made all Things in Number, Weight, and Measure.

Though this passage repeats much that has been illustrated already, the gathering of all these themes into a single tribute in the early months of 1727 is worth our attention.

In his specific references to Newton's discoveries Thomson is probably following directly the precedent set by Halley's lines prefixed to the *Principia*. He depends on the physico-theological literature for such matters as "the mingling Power of *Gravitation* and *Projection*," and Miss Nicolson has rightly emphasized his important use of the *Opticks*.[15] But he placed on the title-page of the first edition Lucretius' lines in praise of Epicurus; and the solitary preëminence he gives to Newton is in the tradition of literary panegyric, the apotheosis of the seer, which has already been described. Newton is the central figure in a drama of revelation—almost a second creation, the theme epigrammatically expressed in Pope's "Epitaph intended for Sir Isaac Newton":

> Nature, and Nature's Laws lay hid in Night.
> God said, *Let Newton be!*—and All was Light.

Other poems close in time to Thomson's lines apply the formula of John Hughes' *The Ecstacy* to the theme of Newton's soul in the future life. Allan Ramsay's elegy, *An ode to the memory of Sir Isaac Newton,* published at Edinburgh (without date, but almost certainly 1727), shows how naturally the heavenly journey and the apotheosis could be combined in a memorial poem:

---

[15] *Background of Seasons*, pp. 32-33; *Newton Demands the Muse*, pp. 12 ff. See below, notes to ll. 46 ff., 96 ff.

The God-like *Man* now mounts the sky,
    Exploring all yon radiant Spheres;
And with one View can more descry,
    Than here below in eighty Years.

Tho' none, with greater Strength of Soul,
    Could rise to more divine a Height,
Or range the *Orbs* from *Pole* to *Pole*,
    And more improve the humane Sight.

Now with full Joy he can survey
    These Worlds, and ev'ry shining Blaze,
That countless in the *Milky Way*
    Only through glasses shew their Rays.

Thousands in thousand Arts excell'd,
    But often to one Part confin'd;
While ev'ry Science stood reveal'd
    And clear to his capacious Mind.

His Penetration, most profound,
    Launch'd far in that extended Sea,
Where humane Minds can reach no Bound,
    And never div'd so deep as he.[16]

Edward Young's *Cynthio* (June 1727), a poem on the death of the Marquis of Carnarvon, shows how naturally the Newtonian theme entered into contemporary elegy:

Tho' well the Sun may hide his Head,
And each Star mourn *their Newton* dead;
Who travell'd, with them, *Nature* round;
Who fathom'd all the *blue Profound;*
New Worlds of *Science* did explore
And *Light* upon the *Planets* pour;
Had not his Soul like these been blest,
Of every *tender Grace* possest,
To *learned Pride* this Truth I tell,
We less had lost, when *Newton* fell.

Andrew Motte's frontispiece to his translation of the *Principia* (1729) represents Newton as a prophet or apostle translated on a cloud, enveloped in celestial light, and further instructed or

---

[16] For a record of an apparently unique copy of the first edition, see *The Houghton Library: Report of Accessions for the Year 1958-59* (1959), p. 29.

inspired by the naked figure of Truth with a pair of compasses in her hand.[16a]

The slighting reference to Descartes appears in somewhat sharper form in the first edition of Thomson's poem than in the version of 1730. All who concerned themselves with Newtonian physics would of course, like Newton himself, have occasion to condemn Descartes' theory of vortices. Farther in the background was the old campaign against Descartes as a mechanist, tarred with the same brush as Hobbes, and as a speculative rather than an experimental scientist, whose method was opposed to the fruitful Baconian way. The popular literature was left with the idea that Descartes was a purveyor of "physical Romance," with the theory of vortices as the prime illustration. So in Swift: "*Cartesius* reckoned to see before he died, the Sentiments of all Philosophers, like so many lesser Stars in his *Romantick* System, rapt and drawn within his own *Vortex*."[17]

The one current theme which is strikingly absent from Thomson's poem is the emphasis on the limitations of human powers at their best. Great as Newton was, the argument might run, he had left much to do, and finally the most powerful genius will be brought to a stand in humility and ignorance. This was an almost inevitable development of the religious approach to the theme, as in Henry Grove's *Spectator* No. 635, already noted. And the tribute to Newton in *Mist's Journal*, April 8, 1727, had ended on this note.

We are not intimately acquainted even with the Objects that are within our Reach, they seem to mock our Enquiries, and flee from us as fast as we pursue: But when we would look into the Immensity of the Universe, the Mind starts back at the amazing Prospect, our Presumption is immediately check'd and baffled, and our Imagination loses it self in the boundless Reflection. I shall conclude in the Words of M. *Paschall: Tho' our Sight,* says he, *is limited, let our Thoughts at least pass beyond; yet even then we*

[16a] Reproduced and discussed by Martin K. Nurmi in *The Divine Vision,* ed. V. de Sola Pinto (1957), pp. 209 ff.

[17] *A Tale of a Tub,* etc., ed. A. C. Guthkelch and D. Nichol Smith (Oxford, 1920), p. 167; cf. also p. 245, *Gulliver's Travels,* III, viii, and Louis Landa's note in his edition of *Gulliver's Travels and Other Writings* (Boston, 1960), p. 526. John Hughes (d. 1720) wrote in his undated essay "Of the Pleasure in Being Deceived," "I do not question but Monsieur *Des Cartes* was as happy in contemplating his System of the *Vortices,* and some other of his Imaginary Notions, as if they had been true" (*Poems on Several Occasions* [1735], I, 260).

*may sooner exhaust the Power of conceiving, than Nature can want
a new Store to furnish out our Conceptions.*

In *Summer* Thomson had already said that the structure of the
universe is beyond the ken, not merely of the captious and
ignorant, but of the most sweeping vision; he had given Newton
a high and honorable place among British sages, but had not
assigned to him solitary eminence.[18]

It is *Summer,* however, which gives us Thomson's first specific treatment of Newtonian themes, and the relation of the
Newton poem to the poet's main line of development in *The
Seasons* may be briefly considered here. Gravitation and projection appear in the opening passages of *Summer:*

> With what a perfect, World-revolving Power
> Were first th' unweildy Planets launch'd along
> Th' illimitable Void!—
>
> ([1727]22-24)

and in the address to the sun:

> 'Tis by thy secret, strong, attractive Force,
> As with a Chain, indissoluble, bound,
> Thy System rolls entire; from the far Bourn
> Of slow-pac'd *Saturn,* to the scarce-seen Disk
> Of *Mercury,* lost in excessive Blaze.
>
> (89-93)

One senses the possibility of a catalogue of the planets, and
Thomson also moves toward his catalogue of the colors:

> The vegetable World is also thine,
> Parent of Seasons! from whose rich-stain'd Rays,
> Reflected various, various Colours rise.
>
> (102-04)

This leads a few lines farther on to the great catalogue of gems,
already brilliantly expounded by Miss Nicolson, but which we
may quote here in the original text as the pioneer and exem-
plary Newtonian color passage of the period:

---

[18] *Summer,* 318-33. From 1727 to 1738 the tribute to Newton read simply:
"Let comprehensive *Newton* speak thy Fame, / In all Philosophy." In the British
Museum manuscript revisions the expanded Newton passage, *Summer,* 1560-63,
is in Lyttelton's hand.

Th' unfruitful Rock, itself, impregn'd by Thee,
In dark Retirement, forms the *lucid Stone,*
Collected Light, compact!. . .
At Thee the *Ruby* lights his deepening Glow,
A bleeding Radiance! grateful to the View.
From Thee the *Saphire,* solid Aether! takes
His Hue cerulean; and, of evening Tinct,
The Purple-streaming *Amethyst* is thine.
With thy own Smile the Yellow *Topaz* burns.
Nor deeper Verdure dies the Robe of *Spring,*
When first she gives it to the Southern Gale,
Than the green *Emerald* shows. But, all combin'd,
Thick, thro' the whitening *Opal,* play thy Beams;
Or flying, several, from his Surface, form
A trembling Variance of revolving Hues,
As the Site changes in the Gazer's hand.[19]

The stage is further set for Newton at the end of *Summer,* after the long passage on the popular terror caused by the aurora borealis:

Not so the Man of *Philosophic* Eye,
And Inspect sage, *the waving Brightness,* He,
Curious surveys, inquisitive to know
The Causes, and Materials, yet unfix'd,
Of this Appearance beautiful, and new.
(1071-75)

Miss Nicolson has demonstrated the special influence on contemporary poets of Thomson's lines on the solar spectrum, beginning with Richard Glover's imitative but remarkable "Poem on Sir Isaac Newton" prefixed to Pemberton's *View of Sir Isaac Newton's Philosophy* (1728). Thomson indeed imitates himself in the description of the rainbow in *Spring* (1728):

Mean-time refracted from yon Eastern Cloud,
Bestriding Earth, the grand aetherial Bow
Shoots up immense! and every Hue unfolds,
In fair Proportion, running from the Red,
To where the Violet fades into the Sky.
Here, mighty *Newton,* the dissolving Clouds
Are, as they scatter round, thy numerous Prism,
Untwisting to the Philosophic Eye

---

[19] Ll. 127-29, 132-44. See *Newton Demands the Muse,* p. 28 and n.

The various Twine of Light, by Thee pursu'd
Thro' all the mingling Maze.[20]

One of the central questions in Thomson criticism is how far these scientific findings are merged or fused into a genuine imaginative view of the world. In the poet's best and most characteristic work the treatment of special effects and laws is drawn into a larger movement. The beauty of natural law appears in the gravity-passage in *Summer* and the spectrum-passage in *Newton*, but it is never a static beauty; there is the cosmic procession, the drama of revelation in which mind and spirit participate; and in connection with the emphasis on color there is always the special association of color with pervasive vitality and energy. Thomson's tribute to Newton is centered about his emphasis on the beauty and simplicity of the divine scheme as revealed by the master, who

> from MOTION's simple Laws,
> Could trace the boundless Hand of PROVIDENCE,
> Wide-working thro' this universal Frame.
>
> O unprofuse Magnificence divine!
> O WISDOM truly perfect! thus to call
> From a few Causes such a Scheme of Things,
> Effects so various, beautiful, and great,
> An Universe compleat![21]

The same principle appears in *The Seasons*:

> Unlavish *Wisdom* never works in vain.
>
> Mysterious round! what skill, what force divine,
> Deep-felt, in these appear! A simple train,
> Yet so harmonious mix'd, so fitly join'd,
> One following one in such inchanting sort,
> Shade, unperceiv'd, so softening into shade,
> And all so forming such a perfect whole,
> That, as they still succeed, they ravish still.[22]

The scheme connects the simple with the boundless, the unprofuse with the various. Unity and diversity appear together in Hutcheson's statement of the principle:

---

[20] Ll. 228-36. Cf. *Background of Seasons*, p. 59; *Newton Demands the Muse*, p. 31. In the first line quoted the first edition has the misprint "retracted" for "refracted."

[21] Ll. 14-16, 68-72. The discussion here follows in part my treatment of this point in *Background of Seasons*, pp. 30-31.

[22] *Spring* (1728), 681; *Hymn* (1730), 24-30.

140

There is another *Beauty* in Propositions, which cannot be omitted; which is this, When one *Theorem* shall contain a vast Multitude of Corollarys easily deducible from it. . . . In the search of *Nature* there is the like *Beauty* in the Knowledge of some great *Principles,* or universal *Forces,* from which innumerable Effects do flow. Such is *Gravitation,* in Sir Isaac Newton's Scheme; such also is the Knowledge of the Original of Rights, *perfect* and *imperfect,* and *external; alienable* and *unalienable,* with their manner of *Translations;* from whence the greatest Part of moral Dutys may be deduc'd in the various Relations of human Life.[23]

The conception of simplicity as applied to the arts moves in a somewhat different direction, emphasizing limitation and proportion, or design rather than color.[24] But in Thomson's practice the central simplicity or economy is easily connected with an infinite diversity of effect, and the endless pageant of nature is impelled by vital, not merely mechanical, forces.

ii

John Millan, who had previously published *Winter* and *Summer* for Thomson, brought out the Newton poem on May 8, 1727. James Roberts entered the piece for Millan in the Stationers' Register the same day. It was printed by Alexander Campbell of Westminster, who had also printed the first edition of Winter.[25]

This edition may be briefly described:
Title-page: Reproduced below, p. 149.
Collation: A-D².
Contents: Title-leaf, verso blank; Dedication, A²; text, [5]-15.
A "second edition" was advertised on May 13 *(London Journal),* a "fourth" on July 8 *(London Journal).* Later advertisements speak of a "fifth edition" *(Monthly Catalogue* I [March, 1728], 81), or vaguely of a "last edition" *(Craftsman,* May 17, 1729). All pre-1730 issues are really the same folio edition; along with the first, copies designated on the title-page as

---

[23] *An Inquiry into the Original of our Ideas of Beauty and Virtue* (1726), pp. 33-34.

[24] Raymond D. Havens, "Simplicity, a Changing Concept," *JHI,* XIV (1953), 3-32; Marjorie Nicolson, *Mountain Gloom and Mountain Glory,* p. 272.

[25] Campbell had had a shop in Union Street, near Palace Yard, in 1726, but by the following year had established himself "in King-street, near the Abbey." He did a good deal of printing for his fellow-Scot, John Millan, during these years.

"second," "third," "fourth," and "fifth" can easily be located, all with the date 1727 in the imprint. The only changes in text before 1730 are a few corrections introduced during the printing of the nominal "first edition," recorded in the textual notes. Richard Norris brought out the usual Dublin reprint or piracy before the end of 1727. The text was extensively revised for the subscription edition of 1730. The implications of the dedication to Walpole, and Walpole's reported present of fifty pounds to the poet, are discussed in connection with *Britannia* (see p. 160 below).

Thomson's contribution to Newtonian verse, though distinguished, merges with the general current; the lines echo and are echoed, and a study of influence is hardly in order. Richard Glover's "Poem on Sir Isaac Newton," prefixed to Pemberton's *View of Sir Isaac Newton's Philosophy* (1728), is rather wordy and imitative, though a remarkable performance for a boy of sixteen, and was no doubt written in full consciousness of Halley's lines, and Thomson's. Thomson may have passed on to later eulogists the idea of the sage surpassing the great names of antiquity; and in particular the striking line

> Untwisted all the shining robe of day

moved Glover to write in his apostrophe to light

> How Newton dar'd advent'rous to unbraid
> The yellow tresses of thy shining hair. . . .

Thomson's friend David Mallet promptly imitated the Newton lines in his *Excursion,* published in March 1728:

> This Spring of Motion, this hid Power infus'd
> Thro' universal Nature, first was known
> To Thee, great *Newton! Britain's* justest Pride,
> The Boast of human Race! whose towring *Thought,*
> In her amazing Progress unconfin'd,
> From Truth to Truth ascending, gain'd the Height
> Of Science, whither Mankind from afar
> Gaze up astonish'd. Now beyond that Height,
> By Death from frail Mortality set free,
> A *pure Intelligence,* He wings his Way
> Thro' wondrous Scenes, new-open'd in the World
> Invisible, amid the general Quire
> Of Saints and Angels, rapt with Joy divine,
> Which fills, o'erflows, and ravishes the Soul!

His Mind's clear Vision from all Darkness purg'd,
For God himself shines forth immediate there.
Thro' these Eternal Climes, the Frame of Things,
In its Ideal Harmony, to *Him*
Stands all reveal'd.—[26]

Though Mallet's version of the solitary preëminence of Newton and the identification of Newton's entry into the future life with the cosmic journey and with the translation of saint or prophet is undoubtedly Thomson's, these and related themes are so widespread in the multiplying eulogies of Newton that they cannot be recorded here.

For the situation a year after Newton's death we must reckon also with the reaction to Bernard Fontenelle's *Éloge*, which appeared in translation in *The Present State of the Republick of Letters,* I (January, 1728), 52-84, and also in three separate translations within the same month.[27] Fontenelle's attempt to put Descartes on an equal footing with Newton called forth adverse comment in England, and probably helped to bring anti-Cartesian sentiment to a focus again.[28] J. T. Desaguliers' piece, *The Newtonian System of the World, the Best Model of Government,* published in February 1728, and printed, incidentally, by the same Alexander Campbell who had printed Thomson's poem, is a clumsy but comprehensive performance by a practising scientist, who tries to combine the traditional exaltation of Newton and the extension of gravitation to the social and moral sphere, with much technical detail, fortified by illustrative plates. His reproaches against Descartes were repeated time and again, but it must have been evident to the most uncritical eye that verse could not carry this much technical science. Yet praise of Newton continued unabated, save for the somewhat obscure cautions incorporated in *The Dunciad.*

In the lines added to his poem in 1730 on the plans for a life of Newton to be written by his nephew John Conduitt, Thomson shows that he is in close touch with the developments that followed Fontenelle's *Éloge.* Conduitt had supplied Fon-

---

[26] *The Excursion* (1728), Book II, pp. 60-61.

[27] See Voltaire, *Lettres Philosophiques,* ed Lanson (Paris, 1909), II, 9, and British Museum Catalogue of Printed Books, under "Newton."

[28] *London Journal,* January 27, 1727-28.

tenelle with a manuscript memoir of Newton,[29] but was dissatisfied with Fontenelle's performance, and planned to write a full-length biography. In this project he asked the aid of the young Edinburgh mathematician Colin Maclaurin, the teacher of Thomson's friend Patrick Murdoch. Thomas Rundle, another friend of Thomson's, also favored the project, but it was never completed. Conduitt died in 1737, and Maclaurin's contribution, originally intended for Conduitt's use, was developed into his *Account of Sir Isaac Newton's Philosophy*, which Andrew Millar published by subscription in 1748. In 1730 John Conduitt had subscribed for ten copies of the quarto *Seasons* of 1730, where the lines complimenting him first appeared.[30]

We can also infer that Thomson followed with interest the plans for the monument to Newton, designed by William Kent the architect and executed by Michael Rysbrack, which was being erected in Westminster Abbey. John Conduitt and William Kent participated in the preliminary plans, which attracted wide attention. The monument was paid for by Conduitt. The plate representing the monument which appears in the subscription quarto in 1730 was drawn by Kent and engraved by Fourdrinier, but does not represent in all respects the monument as actually completed in April 1731; it is directly connected with one of the many preliminary sketches made for the project.[31]

Voltaire uses Fontenelle, the English comments on Fontenelle, and Pemberton's manual in his discussion of Newton in the *Lettres Philosophiques,* as Lanson has shown in detail, but only at one point, in the comparison of Newton with ancient conquerors, does it seem probable that he is directly echoing Thomson:

Il n'y a pas long-tems que l'on agitoit dans une compagnie célèbre cette question usée & frivole, quel étoit le plus grand homme de César, d'Alexandre, de Tamerlan, de Cromwel, &c.

Quelqu'un répondit que c'étoit sans contredit Isaac Newton; cet homme avoit raison, car si la vraie grandeur consiste à avoir reçu du Ciel un puissant génie, & à s'en être servi pour s'éclairer

---

[29] Printed long afterwards in Edmund Turnor's *Collections for the History of the Town and Soke of Grantham* (1806), pp. 158-67.

[30] Conduitt was also a member of the Jail Committee, praised by Thomson in a passage added to *Winter* in 1730. See Alan D. McKillop, "Thomson and the Jail Committee," *SP,* XLVII (1950), 66 n.

[31] See illustration opposite p. 133, and note.

soi-même & les autres, un homme comme Monsieur Newton, tel qu'il s'en trouve à en dix siècles, est véritablement le grand homme, & ces Politiques, & ces Conquerans dont aucun siècle n'a manqué, ne sont d'ordinaire que d'illustres méchans. C'est à celui qui domine sur les esprits par la force de la vérité, non à ceux qui font des esclaves par la violence, c'est à celui qui connoit l'Univers, non à ceux qui le défigurent, que nous devons nos respects.[32]

While Voltaire and Madame du Châtelet pursued their scientific studies a few years later, they were in communication with Francesco Algarotti, who visited them at Cirey. Algarotti's *Il Newtonianismo per le Dame, ovvero Dialoghi sopra la Luce e i Colori* (Naples, 1737) is clearly reminiscent of Thomson's poem, using at one point Thomson's line, "Untwisted all the shining robe of day."[33] The entire passage echoes Thomson at various points:

The Chaos of Chronology and History has from these Observations received its Light and Order. Sir *Isaac Newton,* that divine Philosopher who may be regarded as the Founder of human Knowledge, has from Observations drawn chiefly from the ordinary Course of Nature, ranged historical Facts in a certain Series, by joining Epochas, which the Ignorance or Pride of Mankind has set at a great Distance from each other, in the same Manner as a judicious Observation had united the Boundaries of the Earth in Geography.
    Conducted by this infallible Guide he, according to the Expression of one of his Countrymen,

>   Display'd the lucid Robe of Day,
>   [la lucida spiegò veste del giorno,]

and thence extracted the true Properties of Light and Colours (which had till that Time lain concealed and involved) without forming, like *Des Cartes* and his Followers, any imaginary System to explain the Nature of them.
    This is a World entirely new, enriched with the most shining Truths, and discover'd by *Newton* alone, for there are not the least Traces of any Philosopher who ever appear'd there before him.[34]

The following sentence in Algarotti shows the influence both of Voltaire and of Thomson: "What are the Triumphs of the *Caesars* and *Alexanders* (those miserable Conquerors who over-

---

[32] Lettre XII, ed. Lanson, I, 153.

[33] This is noted by Patrick Murdoch, in the memoir of 1762 (Thomson, *Works,* I, ix).

[34] *Sir Isaac Newton's Philosophy Explain'd for the Use of the Ladies,* trans. Elizabeth Carter (2 vols.; 1739), II, 17-18. The corresponding passage in the *Newtonianismo* is at p. 154.

turned two Particles [due particelle] of this Globe) when compared to the philosophical Triumph of him who first discovered the vast Extent of the Universe?"[35] Algarotti's continued interest in Thomson's piece is attested by some remarkably harsh expressions in a letter addressed to him by Lord Hervey, evidently written at the end of 1738: "As to Mr. Thomson's Poem on Sr. Isac Newton I beg you would not think of quoting any thing from him, for he is an Author so little esteem'd or rather so much decry'd, by all People of good Taste in this Country, that it will not do credit to any Body that cites him as an authority for any thing: he is an obscure, bombast, laborious *Diseur des riens.*"[36] It is probably due to reflex influence from Algarotti that Voltaire's lines to Madame du Châtelet, prefixed to his *Élémens de la Philosophie de Neuton* (1738) show the direct influence of Thomson's poem. Thus, speaking of the Cartesian vortices, he says:

> Déjà ces tourbillons, l'un par l'autre pressés,
> Se mouvant sans espace, & sans règle entassés,
> Ces fantômes savants à mes yeux disparaissent.
> Un jour plus pur me luit; les mouvements renaissent.

And the favorite theme of the "shining robe of day" reappears:

> Il déploie à mes yeux par une main savante,
> De l'astre des Saisons la robe étincelante,
> L'Émeraude, l'azur, le pourpre, le rubis,
> Sont l'immortel tissu dont brillent ses habits.
> Chacun de ses rayons dans sa substance pure,
> Porte en soi les couleurs dont se peint la Nature,
> Et confondus ensemble, ils éclairent nos yeux;
> Ils animent le monde, ils emplissent les cieux.[37]

In the wake of Voltaire's lines came the Abbé Yart's rather clumsy prose translation of Thomson's Newton poem in the fifth volume of his *Idée de la poésie angloise* (1754).

When Robert Shiels, an obscure but devoted admirer of Thomson, undertook to write an elegy on the poet, he followed the Newton lines in title and general plan—*Musidorus, A Poem Sacred to the Memory of Mr. James Thomson*—and exclaimed:

---

[35] *Ibid.,* II, 207; *Newtonianismo*, p. 274.

[36] From the original in the possession of Sir John Murray.

[37] This poem was translated by John Bancks, *Miscellaneous Works* (2 vols.; 1739), II, 241-50.

O could the Muse catch the poetic Flame
Which glows celestial in the sacred Page,
Where Newton's Glories to th' astonish'd Eye
Unbounded shine! then might she hope to raise
A Monument immortal as his Name.

THE TEXT OF *NEWTON*

A   First edition, 1727
1730 Second edition, in subscription edition of *The Seasons*
1750 *Works,* Vol. II, 1750
1762 *Works,* Vol. I, 1762

There was no significant revision after 1730. The copy-text followed is that of *Works,* Vol. I, 1744, substantially identical with 1730 and *Works,* Vol. I, 1738. The editions of 1727, 1730, and 1744 show an extensive use of small capitals for emphasis; 1738 uses only italics. Though the texts of 1750 and 1762 are untrustworthy, a few readings from these editions have been given, particularly when they seem to represent late manuscript corrections.

A POEM SACRED TO THE MEMORY OF
SIR ISAAC NEWTON

To
The Right Honourable
Sir ROBERT WALPOLE,
Knight of the
Most Noble Order of the Garter.

SIR,

Since I have ventur'd to write a Poem on a Gentleman who is universally acknowledg'd to be the Honour of our Country as a *Philosopher,* prompted by the same Ambition, I address it to her most illustrious *Patriot.*

Tho', by the wise Choice of the best of *Kings,* You are engag'd in the highest and most active Scenes of Life, balancing the Power of *Europe,* watching over our common Welfare, informing the whole Body of Society and Commerce, and even like Heaven dispensing Happiness to the Discontented and Ungrateful; tho' thus gloriously employ'd, yet are You not less attentive, in the Hour of Leisure, to the Variety, Beauty, and Magnificence of Nature, nor less delighted, and astonish'd at the Discoveries of the incomparable *Newton.* The same comprehensive Genius which Way soever it looks must have a steady, clear, and unbounded Prospect.

But not to encroach any further on Your important Moments all devoted to the Good of Mankind, I once more plead the Dignity of my Subject for my Excuse in this Approach, and beg Leave to subscribe my self, with the sincerest Veneration,
Sir,

> Your most faithful,
> humble Servant,
> JAMES THOMSON.

Shall the great Soul of NEWTON quit this Earth,
To mingle with his Stars; and every Muse,
Astonish'd into Silence, shun the Weight
Of Honours due to his illustrious Name?
But what can Man?—Even now the Sons of Light,   5
In Strains high-warbled to seraphic Lyre,

4 Name?] Name! *A*
6 In Strains such as delight the Ear of GOD *A*

A

P O E M

Sacred to the MEMORY of

SIR ISAAC NEWTON.

By J A M E S T H O M S O N.

His Tibi me Rebus quædam divina Voluptas
Percipit, atque Horror ; quòd fic Natura tuâ Vi
Tam manifefta patet ex omni Parte retecta.   LUCRETIUS.

L O N D O N:

Printed for J. MILLAN, at *Lock's Head* in *New-ftreet*, between
Marybone-ftreet and *Piccadilly* ; and Sold at his Shop near *Whitehall.*
MDCCXXVII.   (Price One Shilling.)

N. B. *Lately Publifh'd* ; By JAMES THOMSON. 1. WINTER, *a Poem. The 4th
Edition. Price* 1 s. 2. SUMMER, *a Poem. Price* 1 s. 6 d.

Title-page, *A Poem Sacred to the Memory of Sir Isaac Newton,* first edition

149

Hail his Arrival on the Coast of Bliss.
Yet am not I deterr'd, tho' high the Theme,
And sung to Harps of Angels, for with you,
Ethereal Flames! ambitious, I aspire   10
In Nature's general Symphony to join.

    And what new Wonders can ye show your Guest!
Who, while on this dim Spot, where Mortals toil
Clouded in Dust, from MOTION's simple Laws,
Could trace the secret Hand of PROVIDENCE,   15
Wide-working thro' this universal Frame.

    Have ye not listen'd while he bound the SUNS,
And PLANETS to their Spheres! th' unequal Task
Of Human-kind till then. Oft had they roll'd
O'er erring Man the Year, and oft disgrac'd   20
The Pride of Schools, before their Course was known
Full in its Causes and Effects to him,
All-piercing Sage! Who sat not down and dream'd
Romantic Schemes, defended by the Din
Of specious Words, and Tyranny of Names;   25
But, bidding his amazing Mind attend,
And with heroic Patience Years on Years
Deep-searching, saw at last the SYSTEM dawn,
And shine, of all his Race, on him alone.

    What were his Raptures then! how pure! how strong! 30
And what the Triumphs of old GREECE and ROME,
By his diminish'd, but the Pride of Boys
In some small Fray victorious! when instead
Of shatter'd Parcels of this Earth usurp'd
By Violence unmanly, and sore Deeds   35
Of Cruelty and Blood, Nature herself
Stood all subdu'd by him, and open laid
Her every latent Glory to his View.
    All intellectual Eye, our SOLAR ROUND
First gazing thro, he by the blended Power   40

7 Coast] Coasts *A*
15 secret] boundless *A*
36 Nature herself] *Nature herself A*
39-40 *A reads:*
    And first our *solar System* He survey'd
    With accurate Ken, and by the mingling Power

Of GRAVITATION and PROJECTION saw
The whole in silent Harmony revolve.
From unassisted Vision hid, the *Moons*
To chear remoter Planets numerous pour'd,
By him in all their mingled Tracts were seen.   45
He also fix'd the wandering QUEEN OF NIGHT,
Whether she wanes into a scanty Orb,
Or, waxing broad, with her pale shadowy Light,
In a soft Deluge overflows the Sky.
Her every Motion clear-discerning, He   50
Adjusted to the mutual MAIN, and taught
Why now the mighty Mass of Water swells
Resistless, heaving on the broken Rocks,
And the full River turning; till again
The Tide revertive, unattracted, leaves   55
A yellow Waste of idle Sands behind.

    Then breaking hence, he took his ardent Flight
Thro' the blue Infinite; and every STAR,
Which the clear Concave of a Winter's Night
Pours on the Eye, or astronomic Tube,   60
Far-stretching, snatches from the dark Abyss,
Or such as farther in successive Skies
To Fancy shine alone, at his Approach
Blaz'd into SUNS, the living Centre each
Of an harmonious System: all combin'd,   65
And rul'd unerring by that single Power,
Which draws the Stone projected to the Ground.

    O unprofuse Magnificence divine!
O WISDOM truly perfect! thus to call
From a few Causes such a Scheme of Things,   70
Effects so various, beautiful, and great,
An Universe compleat! And O belov'd

43-45 *A reads:*
    Drawn to his lengthen'd Eye th' attending *Moons*,
    Design'd to chear remoter Planets, were
    By Him in all their mix'd Proportions seen.
44 pour'd] form'd *1762*
46 the wandering] our wandering *MS Corrections 1762*
51 mutual MAIN] obsequious *Main A*
52 Water] Waters *A*
63 shine alone] only shine *A*
64 the living Centre] Th' enlivening Centre

Of Heaven! whose well-purg'd penetrative Eye,
The mystic Veil transpiercing, inly scan'd
The rising, moving, wide-establish'd Frame.   75

He, first of Men, with awful Wing pursu'd
The COMET thro' the long Elliptic Curve,
As round innumerous Worlds he wound his Way;
Till, to the Forehead of our evening Sky
Return'd, the blazing Wonder glares anew,   80
And o'er the trembling Nations shakes Dismay.

The Heavens are all his own; from the wild Rule
Of whirling VORTICES, and circling SPHERES,
To their first great Simplicity restor'd.
The Schools astonish'd stood; but found it vain   85
To keep at odds with Demonstration strong,
And, unawaken'd, dream beneath the Blaze
Of Truth. At once their pleasing Visions fled,
With the gay Shadows of the Morning mix'd,
When NEWTON rose, our philosophic Sun.   90

Th' aerial Flow of SOUND was known to him,
From whence it first in wavy Circles breaks,
Till the touch'd Organ takes the Meaning in.
Nor could the darting BEAM, of Speed immense,
Escape his swift Pursuit, and measuring Eye.   95

73-74 *A reads:*
        Of Heaven! into TH' ALMIGHTY's Councils thus
        To be admitted, and allow'd to scan
  76 He too, unbaffle'd in his Aim, pursu'd *A*
  79 our evening Sky] the Evening-Sky *A*
  80 Return'd] Reduc'd *A*
  81 *added in 1730*
82-85 *A reads:*
        The Heavens are all his own. Finish'd by Him
        The fair Discovery lies; and every Eye
        May lay the useless Telescope aside,
        Unless it be to hold the great Acquests
        By NEWTON made: Who from the wild Domain
        Of the *French Dreamer* rescu'd Heaven and Earth.   *Des Cartes*
        All *Europe* stood appall'd; but found it vain
  86 To keep at odds] to combat long *MS corrections 1750*] to combat still
    1762
  87 And lingering to resist the awakening Force   *A*
  93 Meaning] Message *A 1762*
  95 Eye] Glance *A*
  104 next] then *A*

Even LIGHT ITSELF, which every thing displays,
Shone undiscover'd, till his brighter Mind
Untwisted all the shining Robe of Day;
And, from the whitening undistinguish'd Blaze,
Collecting every Ray into his kind,   100
To the charm'd Eye educ'd the gorgeous Train
Of PARENT-COLOURS. First the flaming RED
Sprung vivid forth; the tawny ORANGE next;
And next delicious YELLOW; by whose side
Fell the kind Beams of all-refreshing GREEN.   105
Then the pure BLUE, that swells autumnal Skies,
Ethereal play'd; and then, of sadder Hue,
Emerg'd the deepen'd INDICO, as when
The heavy-skirted Evening droops with Frost.
While the last Gleamings of refracted Light   110
Dy'd in the fainting VIOLET away.
These, when the Clouds distil the rosy Shower,
Shine out distinct adown the watry Bow;
While o'er our Heads the dewy Vision bends
Delightful, melting on the Fields beneath.   115
Myriads of mingling Dyes from these result,
And Myriads still remain—Infinite Source
Of Beauty, ever-flushing, ever-new!

Did ever Poet image aught so fair,
Dreaming in whispering Groves, by the hoarse Brook!   120
Or Prophet, to whose Rapture Heaven descends!
Even now the setting Sun and shifting Clouds,
Seen, GREENWICH, from thy lovely Heights, declare
How just, how beauteous the REFRACTIVE LAW.

The noiseless TIDE OF TIME, all bearing down   125
To vast Eternity's unbounded Sea,
Where the green Islands of the Happy shine,
He stem'd alone; and to the Source (involv'd
Deep in primaeval Gloom) ascending, rais'd
His Lights at equal Distances, to guide   130
Historian, wilder'd on his darksome Way.

104 next] then *A*
110 Gleamings] Gleanings *A*
117 Infinite] th' exhaustless *A*
122 shifting] liveri'd *A*
128-129 *A reads:*
    He backward stem'd alone; and to it's Source
    Ascending, mark'd it's Periods, and hung out

153

But who can number up his Labours? who
His high Discoveries sing? when but a few
Of the deep-studying Race can stretch their Minds
To what he knew: in Fancy's lighter Thought,   135
How shall the Muse then grasp the mighty Theme?

What Wonder thence that his DEVOTION swell'd
Responsive to his Knowledge! For could he,
Whose piercing mental Eye diffusive saw
The finish'd University of Things,   140
In all its Order, Magnitude, and Parts,
Forbear incessant to adore that POWER
Who fills, sustains, and actuates the Whole?

Say, ye who best can tell, ye happy few,
Who saw him in the softest Lights of Life,   145
All unwithheld, indulging to his Friends
The vast unborrow'd Treasures of his Mind,
Oh speak the wondrous Man! how mild, how calm,
How greatly humble, how divinely good;
How firm establish'd on eternal Truth;   150
Fervent in doing well, with every Nerve
Still pressing on, forgetful of the past,
And panting for Perfection: far above
Those little Cares, and visionary Joys,
That so perplex the fond impassion'd Heart   155
Of ever-cheated, ever-trusting Man.
This, CONDUITT, from thy rural Hours we hope;
As thro' the pleasing Shade, where Nature pours
Her every Sweet, in studious Ease you walk;

135-136 *For these lines A has:*
        To image what He knew, as clear as They
        The Truths self-evident with which He link'd
        His farthest Views. For is there ought that's great,
        That's wonderful, and hard, deterring Search?
        That was his Prize! and worthy of his Toil
        Unfailing, Who the lonely *Monarch* reign'd
        Of *Science* thin-inhabited below.
137 thence] then *A*
140 University] *University*   Ms correction
148 Oh] O *A*
150 firm establish'd] firm, establish'd *A*
    Between ll. 150-51 A has:
        Pure as his Faith, and active as his Love,
156 perplex] befool *A*
158-62 *added in 1730; deleted in MS corrections; omitted in 1750, 1762*

The social Passions smiling at thy Heart,   160
That glows with all the recollected Sage.

And you, ye hopeless gloomy-minded Tribe,
You who, unconscious of those nobler Flights
That reach impatient at immortal Life,
Against the prime indearing Privilege   165
Of Being dare contend, say, can a Soul
Of such extensive, deep, tremendous Powers,
Enlarging still, be but a finer Breath
Of Spirits dancing thro' their Tubes awhile,
And then for ever lost in vacant Air?   170

But hark, methinks I hear a warning Voice,
Solemn as when some awful Change is come,
Sound thro' the World—" '*Tis done! The Measure's full;*
And I resign my Charge."—Ye mouldering Stones,
That build the towering Pyramid, the proud   175
Triumphal Arch, the Monument effac'd
By ruthless Ruin, and whate'er supports
The worship'd Name of hoar Antiquity,
Down to the Dust! what Grandeur can ye boast
While NEWTON lifts his Column to the Skies,   180
Beyond the Waste of Time.—Let no weak Drop
Be shed for him. The Virgin in her Bloom
Cut off, the joyous Youth, and darling Child,
These are the Tombs that claim the tender Tear,
And Elegiac Song. But NEWTON calls   185
For other Notes of Gratulation high,
That now he wanders thro' those endless Worlds
He here so well descried, and wondering talks,
And hymns their Author with his glad Compeers.

O Britain's Boast! whether with Angels thou   190
Sittest in dread Discourse, or fellow-blest,
Who joy to see the Honour of their Kind;
Or whether, mounted on cherubic Wing,

163 And you, ye hopeless] And say, ye downward, *A*
164 You] Ye *A*
174 *'Tis done!*] *He's dead. A*
179 hoar] grey *A*
183 Virgin] Beauty *A*

Thy swift Career is with the whirling Orbs,
Comparing Things with Things, in Rapture lost,   195
And grateful Adoration, for that Light
So plenteous ray'd into thy Mind below,
From LIGHT HIMSELF; Oh look with Pity down
On Human-kind, a frail erroneous Race!
Exalt the Spirit of a downward World!   200
O'er thy dejected Country chief preside,
And be her GENIUS call'd; her Studies raise,
Correct her Manners, and inspire her Youth.
For, tho' deprav'd and sunk, she brought thee forth,
And glories in thy Name; she points thee out   205
To all her Sons, and bids them eye thy Star:
While in Expectance of the second Life,
When Time shall be no more, thy sacred Dust
Sleeps with her Kings, and dignifies the Scene.

192 fellow-blest] Fellow-Saints *A*
195 Career] Careeer *A first issue*
    whirling Orbs] whirling Spheres *A*
197 grateful] lowly *A*
199 Oh] O *A*
201 Asswage the Madness of a frantic World! *A first issue*]
    jarring World! *A other issues*
202 But chiefly o'er thy Country's Cause preside *A*
203 her Studies raise] Her Councils steer *A*
205 tho' deprav'd and sunk] guilty as she is *A*
208 the second Life] th' arrousing Blast *A*

Britannia

INTRODUCTION

Britannia shows us the young poet moved to sharp political and patriotic utterance under circumstances which are not yet entirely clear. The lines on Newton, we have seen, had been dedicated to Walpole. *Britannia* expresses Opposition sentiment which perhaps had its origins in the year 1727, when Spain declared war on England and threatened Gibraltar. Admiral Hosier's death in that year, while in command of the British fleet in the West Indies, came in the minds of many to symbolize the Government's ineffective support of vigorous naval measures. Spain, so the general complaint went, continued to violate the freedom of the seas. Thomson's personal response can be inferred only from his verse; it has been suggested that since Bubb Dodington was one of his chief patrons after 1727, and since relations between Walpole and Dodington had been strained since the middle of that year, when Dodington paid court to the King's new favorite, Sir Spencer Compton, Thomson might now feel that he was free to follow his own inclination in criticizing Walpole.[1]

The publication of *Britannia* seems to have been timed to coincide exactly with the opening of Parliament on January 21, 1729 (*Daily Journal* of that date). The verses open with a reference to the arrival of Prince Frederick on English soil; after having been detained at Hanover by his father since 1727, he had landed at Harwich on December 3, 1728.[2] According to the court poets, his arrival was eagerly awaited:

> See! with impatience to the wide sea-shore
> They croud, and long to ken
> His *Navy*, whit'ning o'er the deep,
> And bounding o'er the surge to the expecting strand.[3]

Britannia was the only one of Thomson's works to be published anonymously, and the only one during his early period to appear without a dedication. The first edition may be briefly described:

---

[1] I owe this suggestion to one of my students, Tommy R. Burkett.

[2] See John Edwin Wells, "Thomson's *Britannia:* Issues, Attribution, Date, Variants," *MP,* XL (1942), 43-56, especially 52-53.

[3] James Ralph, *The Muses' Address to the King: An Ode* (1728), p. 28. Published September 7, 1728 (*London Journal*).

Title-page: Reproduced below, p. 167.
Collation: [ ]¹ B-D² E¹.
Contents: Title-leaf, verso blank; text, 3-16.

The bookseller whose name appears in the imprint, Thomas Warner, had not been hitherto concerned in bringing out Thomson's works. Thomson's regular booksellers, John Millan and Andrew Millar, immediately advertised *Britannia* along with *Newton* and the second edition of *Spring* (e.g., *London Journal,* February 15, 1729). On July 18, 1729, *Britannia* was included in the general assignment of Thomson's copyrights to Millan (*LD, p.* 64). Professor William M. Sale has discovered that the first edition was printed by Samuel Richardson.⁴

The details of publication show that Thomson and his booksellers or advisers wanted to put over some political ideas and at the same time to disguise or muffle political intentions and references. In the first edition praise of Frederick is associated with praise of the Throne and of "Royal Beauty," despite the fact that the Prince was on bad terms with his father. This passage was dropped in 1730, though earlier in the year Thomson had dedicated *Sophonisba* to the Queen and though the entire Royal Family had patronized the play. Thomson evidently adjusted the wording of his complimentary references to Royalty with great care. The exact political implications of such references may sometimes elude us; early in 1730 Thomson's primary purpose was evidently to solicit the favor of the Queen. Frederick dropped temporarily into the background. The dedication of *Sophonisba* shows again how the obligatory praise of Royalty blended with the theme of commerce and sea-power: "And to whom can this illustrious *Carthaginian* so properly fly for protection, as to a *Queen,* who commands the hearts of a *People,* more powerful at sea than *Carthage?* more flourishing in *commerce* than those *first Merchants?* more secure against conquest? and, under a *Monarchy,* more free than a *Commonwealth* itself?"⁵

The second edition of *Britannia* was published at almost exactly the same time as the subscription edition of *The Sea-*

---

⁴ *Samuel Richardson: Master Printer* (Ithaca, 1950), p. 209.

⁵ The original canceled dedication read simply "the *Queen* of a *People*"; the revision greatly heightens the praise. For a detailed account of this cancel, see D. F. Foxon, "Oh! *Sophonisba! Sophonisba!*-Oh!," *Studies in Bibliography,* XII (1959), 205-06. For later manipulation of details in references to the Royal Family, see *Background of Thomson's Liberty,* pp. 95-96.

sons, and is described in John Millan's advertisement of June 1, 1730, in the *Daily Journal* as "printed on a fine Royal Paper in Quarto, proper to be bound with the edition of Mr. Thomson's Four Seasons, &c." Though at first offered for separate sale, it was later regularly bound up and sold with the quarto *Seasons.* Similarly, the third edition of *Britannia,* brought out by Millan soon afterwards, was a separately titled and paged octavo which was regularly bound up with the octavo *Seasons.* This edition has the subtitle "Written in the Year, 1719," which would seem to be pure mystification. The changed subtitle "Written in the Year of 1727," which appears in the edition of 1738, may possibly point to the ultimate relation of the poem to political and military circumstances of 1727, if not, as Grant suggests, to composition in substantial part in that year.

Specific political intention and allusion were immediately detected in the piece. On January 28, 1729, the *Daily Journal,* a pro-Walpole paper, quoted the long passage in praise of peace (106-52), prefixing these comments:

The following Lines are so charming a Description of the Blessings of Peace, that I am persuaded your Readers will be exceedingly delighted with it, and find *Occasions* from it to extol and applaud the Pacific Measures that have hitherto been pursu'd by his Majesty and his Ministers, to preserve to us those invaluable Blessings; whatever Event their wise Endeavours may be attended with, from the Perverseness and Ambition of some of the Powers of Europe. I have borrow'd them from a Poem just publish'd, intitled *BRITANNIA,* which, tho' it seems to be written with *another* View, and even to rouze to *War* the British Nation, yet the happy Author, who has deprived us of the Pleasure of knowing his Name, has not been able to resist those charming Impulses which give so just a Preference to those *Divine Men,* as he aptly calls 'em, who study to cultivate the Arts of Peace.

The Tory *Fog's Weekly Journal* on February 1 countered this attempt to turn the poem to Walpole's advantage by bestowing high praise on the piece as a whole, and by printing another long extract, from the opening to the description of the defeat of the Armada (1-81): "The *Daily Journal* of last Tuesday having presented us with a Transcript in Praise of *Peace,* from an excellent Poem just publish'd intitled BRITANNIA; I hope you will oblige your Readers with the following Verses, from the same inimitable Piece; for tho' 'tis probable 'tis by this Time in the Hands of almost every Man of Taste or Judgment, yet I am confident, no one will think his Time ill-bestow'd to read a Part of it over again in your Paper."

In 1731 Eustace Budgell, conducting a campaign against the Walpole government in his *Letter to Cleomenes,* quoted the first fifteen lines of *Britannia,* and also later passages, 23-61 and 166-90, with the remark, "The Gentleman who wrote this Poem is still living; and if his future Works have but the same *Spirit,* with those he has already published, he will doubtless be placed by Posterity in one of the first Ranks of our *English* Poets."[6] In the same year *Britannia* was quoted in the advertisement and presumably on the title-page of a pamphlet called *A View of the Depredations and Ravages committed by the Spaniards on the British Trade and Navigation (London Evening-Post,* March 2-4, 1731).

Pro-Walpole journalists continued to look with disfavor on Thomson's apparent change of front from *Newton* to *Britannia.* In 1730, after the publication of the subscription edition of *The Seasons* and shortly before Thomson went abroad as traveling companion to young Charles Richard Talbot, his quest for favor was thus summed up by one of Walpole's journalists:

When Sir *Isaac Newton* died, a young Gentleman, fam'd for the Sublimity of his Genius, drew Bills on a certain *great Man,* by a courtly Dedication prefix'd to his incomparable Poem. *He also* [like Settle, referred to in the preceding paragraph] was rewarded with a Present of *fifty Pounds.* As he had shew'd his Parts on this Occasion, so he publish'd his Gratitude the following *Winter,* libell'd the Ministry in formidable Poetry; apply'd to them again in the *Spring,* and was ready to *travel* for the Good of the Publick with a Pension of *three hundreds* per Annum.

(*Free Briton,* August 13, 1730)

This statement may not be entirely accurate, and it almost certainly exaggerates the political significance of Thomson's association with the Talbots in 1730; but we can probably rely on the information that Walpole acknowledged the dedication of *Newton* with a gift of money (twenty guineas was the usual payment for a dedication), and we can infer that Thomson's attack in *Britannia* came as something of a shock to the Whig interest. Even now there was no open commitment against the Government; Thomson's support of the Jail Committee in

---

[6] *A Letter to Cleomenes* (1731), pp. 52-53.

1730 was consistent with the line taken by Talbot, and would also be approved by the more or less overt Opposition which was disposed to use any parliamentary investigation as a weapon against Walpole.[7] Whig journalists sometimes tried to claim Thomson as far as they could. Thus, in answer to an epigram in the *Grub-street Journal* about the Tory Harley's encouragement of writers, the *Daily Courant,* September 24, 1734, reports that before Swift, Harley had to be content with *"Trap, Yalden, Oldsworth,* and *Defoe,"* and continues:

> WALPOLE wants no such Bards.—His Worth is sung
> In Strains most sweet, and as sublime by Young,
> Justly extoll'd by *Thomson* him we find,
> And *Dodington* himself the Choir has join'd.

A note explains that the third line quoted refers to the Dedication of *Newton. Britannia* continued to be politically relevant for about ten years; indeed, in the agitations which preceded the declaration of war on Spain in 1739 it might seem to be more to the point than ever before. In March 1738 Andrew Millar, as part of the literary campaign of the Opposition, published a translation of Milton's *Manifesto of the Lord Protector,* "Wherein is shewn the Reasonableness of the Cause of this Republic against the Depredations of the Spaniards," with a quotation from *Britannia* on the title-page and the entire text of the poem appended. Lines from *Britannia* continued to crop up in political journalism; thus *Old Common Sense,* September 9, 1738, quotes the "pathetick, moving Strains" in which Thomson had described the frustrated return of Hosier's fleet (34-46). As late as October 27, 1744, the *Westminster Journal* reënforced a long essay on the importance of trade by a quotation from *Britannia* (173-81).

Britannia is a modification and to some extent a reversal of the praise of Britain in *Summer* (1727):

> HAPPY BRITANNIA! where the Queen of Arts,
> Inspiring Vigour, LIBERTY, abroad,
> Walks thro' the Land of Heroes, unconfin'd,
> And scatters Plenty with unsparing Hand.
> (498-501)
> Bold, firm, and graceful, are thy generous Youth,
> By Hardship sinew'd, and by Danger fir'd,

---

[7] For further detail see Alan D. McKillop, "Thomson and the Jail Committee," *SP,* XLVII (1950), 64-67.

Scattering the Nations where They go; and first,
Or on the listed Plain, or wintry Seas.
Mild are thy Glories too, as o'er the Arts
Of thriving Peace thy thoughtful Sires preside;
In Genius, and substantial Learning high;
For every Vertue, every Worth renown'd.
Sincere, plain-hearted, hospitable, kind,
Yet like the mustering Thunder when provok'd;
The Scourge of Tyrants, and the sole Resource
Of such as under grim Oppression groan.

(523-34)

Island of Bliss! amid the Subject Seas,
That thunder round thy rocky Coasts, set up,
At once the Wonder, Terror, and Delight
Of distant Nations; whose remotest Shore
Can soon be shaken by thy naval Arm.
Not to be shook Thy self, but all Assaults
Baffling, like thy hoar Cliffs the loud Sea-Wave.

(585-91)

In the optimistic exuberance of *Spring* (1728), Britain's over-seas commerce is blended with the general theme of Nature's fecundity.

Ye generous *Britons* cultivate the Plow!
And o'er your Hills, and long with-drawing Vales,
Let *Autumn* spread his Treasures to the Sun,
Luxuriant, and unbounded. As the Sea,
Far thro' his azure, turbulent Extent,
Your Empire owns, and from a thousand Shores
Wafts all the Pomp of Life into your Ports,
So with superior Boon may your rich Soil,
Exuberant, Nature's better Blessings pour
O'er every Land; the naked Nations cloath,
And be th' exhaustless Granary of the World.

(65-75)

But in 1729 Thomson reaches the point at which one line of "Whig panegyric," to use a convenient though possibly over-worked term, diverges into "dissident Whig panegyric," and thus points forward ominously to the editorial vein which reaches its height in *Liberty*. Mrs. Spacks has recently described this tendency with considerable precision as a shift from interest in "man in nature" to "man in society."[8] On the positive

---

[8] Patricia Meyer Spacks, *The Varied God: A Critical Study of Thomson's The Seasons* (Berkeley and Los Angeles, 1959).

side, this patriotic poetry exalts the peaceful spread of British power through commerce, as Cecil A. Moore long ago demonstrated in a classic essay.[9] Current benevolism, fusing then as now in a strange way with Anglo-Saxon politics, delighted to dwell on peace as an international blessing conferred by a righteous nation. Ideally the panegyrist would lay equal stress on peace, prosperity, and power. But power is always accompanied by "mustering Thunder." This theme appears at the end of the description of the port of London in *Autumn* (1730), after a glowing account of warehouse, river, and shipping—

> While deep the various voice of fervent toil
> From bank to bank increas'd; whence ribb'd with oak,
> To bear the BRITISH thunder, black, and bold,
> The roaring vessel rush'd into the main.
>
> (130-34)

Yet an indefatigable panegyrist like Edward Young was eager to see the war clouds roll away and to celebrate peaceful imperialism, as in his *Imperium Pelagi,* inspired by the Treaty of Seville at the end of 1729:

> Trade springs from Peace, and Wealth from Trade,
> And Power from Wealth.
> . . . . . .
> Then perish War!—Detested War!

But *Britannia* strikes a different note. Though the poem still formulates the ideal of peaceful imperialism, it reverts to the contrast between the unique and glorious situation and mission of Britain and the present state of things—the pattern that had been set in the dying speech of John of Gaunt in *Richard II.* The goddess in *Britannia,* no longer the triumphant sea-born figure of earlier iconography,[10] contemplates "her degenerate Sons" on a melancholy coast, and is not at all certain that she rules the waves. Britain is the last resort of Liberty, "the World almost in slavish Sloth dissolv'd." The poem *Liberty* elaborates the same framework: in each poem the goddess appears and speaks movingly and at length of the visualized

---

[9] C. A. Moore, "Whig Panegyric Verse, 1700-1760: a Phase of Sentimentalism," *PMLA,* XLI (1926), 362-461, reprinted in *Backgrounds of English Literature,* pp. 104-44.

[10] For some examples, see Hans Marcus, "Die Entstehung von 'Rule Britannia,'" *Beiblatt zur Anglia,* XXXVI (1925), 30 ff., 78 ff.

situation while the Muse records her words, then vanishes, leaving the poet in the desolate scene presented at the beginning—the wild coast in *Britannia,* the ruins of Rome in *Liberty.* In both poems, past glories are contrasted with the present shameful decline; the opposition between luxury and liberty is emphasized; tendentious political utterances merge with universally acceptable political, moral, and social generalizations. Except in the passage on the Armada, and perhaps the lines on the sources of the Nile, reflecting the geographical reading which underlies part of *The Seasons,* Thomson is far from being at his best here. Yet his remarkable feeling for public opinion and public sentiment should not go unnoticed; his sensitiveness to the winds that were blowing is as evident here as in the *Newton,* though it appears in a less engaging form. In *Britannia* he set a model for dissident Whig panegyric; some instances of his influence here have been briefly noted above, and Moore has recorded further echoes in this kind.[11] The note is caught up clearly in patriotic song and ballad; in Richard Glover's *Admiral Hosier's Ghost,* to take a notable example, present triumph and past disaster are balanced somewhat as present disaster and past triumph in *Britannia.* A somewhat similar balance is struck in Kipling's *Recessional.* Though we immediately connect "Rule, Britannia" with this vein in Thomson's verse, his famous "Ode in Honour of Great Britain" differs somewhat from *Britannia* and *Liberty* in its massive and unqualified panegyric.

THE TEXT OF *BRITANNIA*

A   First edition, 1729
1730 Second edition, 1730
1738 *Works,* Vol. I, 1738
1744 *Works,* Vol. 1, 1744
1750 *Works,* Vol. II, 1750
1762 *Works,* Vol. I, 1762

There was no significant revision of *Britannia* after 1730. The copy-text followed is 1738, with the adoption of a few corrections made in 1744. Readings of 1738 are to be preferred in ll. 39, 46, 175 (?), 222, 265, 269, 279. The 1744 text seems to bypass 1738 and go back directly to 1730, including the reproduction of a mistake

---

[11] *Backgrounds of English Literature,* pp. 143-44.

in numbering (l. 19 misnumbered 20 and so to the end); 1744 also follows 1730 in using italics for all proper names, with no small capitals. Though the texts of 1750 and 1762 are untrustworthy, a few readings from these editions have been given, particularly when they seem to represent late manuscript corrections.

The type-facsimile of *A* published by the Oxford University Press in 1925 varies from the original only on these points: it supplies a period in the imprint after "DCC," drops the punctuation mark at the end of 1.155, and reads "slacken'd" in 1. 214.

BRITANNIA

As on the Sea-beat Shore *Britannia* sat,
Of her degenerate Sons the faded Fame,
Deep in her anxious Heart, revolving sad:
Bare was her throbbing Bosom to the Gale,
That hoarse, and hollow, from the bleak Surge blew;   5
Loose flow'd her Tresses; rent her azure Robe.
Hung o'er the Deep, from her majestic Brow
She tore the Laurel, and she tore the Bay.
Nor ceas'd the copious Grief to bathe her Cheek;
Nor ceas'd her Sobs to murmur to the Main.   10
Peace discontented nigh, departing, stretch'd
Her Dove-like Wings. And War, tho' greatly rous'd,
Yet mourn'd his fetter'd Hands. While thus the Queen
Of Nations spoke; and what she said the Muse
Recorded, faithful, in unbidden Verse.   15

Even not yon Sail, that, from the Sky-mixt Wave,
Dawns on the Sight, and wafts the Royal Youth,
A Freight of future Glory to my Shore;
Even not the flattering View of golden Days,
And rising Periods yet of bright Renown,   20
Beneath the Parents, and their endless Line
Thro' late revolving Time, can sooth my Rage;
While, unchastis'd, the insulting *Spaniard* dares
Infest the trading Flood, full of vain War
Despise my Navies, and my Merchants seize;   25
As, trusting to false Peace, they fearless roam
The World of Waters wild, made, by the Toil,
And liberal Blood of glorious Ages, mine:
Nor bursts my sleeping Thunder on their Head.
Whence this unwonted Patience? this weak Doubt?   30
This tame beseeching of rejected Peace?
This meek Forbearance? this unnative Fear,
To generous *Britons* never known before?
And sail'd my Fleets for this; on *Indian* Tides
To float, unactive, with the veering Winds?   35

6 Robe.] Robe *A Corrected in errata published in Daily Journal, January 24,*
1729
7 Deep,] Deep: *A*] Deep *1730 1738 1744 Corrected in errata of January 24,*
1729

B R I T A N N I A.

A

P O E M.

——— *Et tantas audetis tollere Moles ?*
Quos Ego — *fed motos præftat componere Fluctus.*
Poft mihi non fimili Pœna commiffa luetis.
Maturate Fugam, Regique hæc dicite veftro :
Non illi Imperium Pelagi, Sævumque Tridentem,
Sed mihi forte datum. ———

V I R G.

L O N D O N :
Printed for T. WARNER, at the *Black-Boy*, in *Pater-Nofter-Row.* M.DCC XXIX.

Title-page, *Britannia,* first edition

167

The Mockery of War! while hot Disease,
And Sloth distemper'd, swept off burning Crouds,
For Action ardent; and amid the Deep,
Inglorious, sunk them in a watry Grave.
There now they lie beneath the rolling Flood,   40
Far from their Friends, and Country unaveng'd;
And back the drooping War-Ship comes again,
Dispirited, and thin; her Sons asham'd
Thus idly to review their native Shore;
With not one Glory sparkling in their Eye,   45
One Triumph on their Tongue. A Passenger,
The violated Merchant comes along;
That far-sought Wealth, for which the noxious Gale
He drew, and sweat beneath Equator Suns,
By lawless Force detain'd; a Force that soon   50
Would melt away, and every Spoil resign,
Were once the *British* Lion heard to roar.
Whence is it that the proud *Iberian* thus,
In their own well-asserted Element,
Dares rouze to Wrath the Masters of the Main?   55
Who told him, that the big incumbent War
Would not, ere this, have roll'd his trembling Ports
In smoky Ruin? and his guilty Stores,
Won by the Ravage of a butcher'd World,
Yet unaton'd, sunk in the swallowing Deep,   60
Or led the glittering Prize into the *Thames?*

    There was a time (Oh let my languid Sons
Resume their Spirit at the rouzing Thought!)
When all the Pride of *Spain*, in one dread Fleet,
Swell'd o'er the lab'ring Surge; like a whole Heaven   65
Of Clouds, wide-roll'd before the boundless Breeze.
Gaily the splendid Armament along
Exultant plough'd, reflecting a red Gleam,
As sunk the Sun, o'er all the flaming Vast;
Tall, gorgeous, and elate; drunk with the Dream   70
Of easy Conquest; while their bloated War,

36 hot Disease] foul Disease *A*
39 a watry Grave] the watry Grave *1744*
42 drooping *Correction in Thomson's hand in British Museum copy, 1750 1762*]
    weeping *1729-1744*
46 on their Tongue] in their Tongue *1744*
57 ere] e'er *1738 Corrected to* ere *in Thomson's hand in British Museum copy*

Stretch'd out from Sky to Sky, the gather'd Force
Of Ages held in its capacious Womb.
But soon, regardless of the cumbrous Pomp,
My dauntless *Britons* came, a gloomy few,   75
With Tempest black, the goodly Scene deform'd,
And laid their Glory waste. The Bolts of Fate
Resistless thunder'd thro' their yielding Sides;
Fierce o'er their Beauty blaz'd the lurid Flame;
And seiz'd in horrid Grasp, or shatter'd wide,   80
Amid the mighty Waters, deep they sunk.
Then too from every Promontory chill,
Rank Fen, and Cavern where the wild Wave works,
I swept confederate Winds, and swell'd a Storm.
Round the glad Isle, snatch'd by the vengeful Blast,   85
The scatter'd Remnants drove; on the blind Shelve,
And pointed Rock, that marks th' indented Shore,
Relentless dash'd, where loud the Northern Main
Howls thro' the fractur'd *Caledonian* Isles.

Such were the Dawnings of my liquid Reign;   90
But since how vast it grew, how absolute,
Even in those troubled Times, when dreadful BLAKE
Aw'd angry Nations with the *British* Name,
Let every humbled State, let *Europe* say,
Sustain'd, and ballanc'd, by my naval Arm.   95
Ah what must these immortal Spirits think
Of your poor Shifts? These, for their Country's Good,
Who fac'd the blackest Danger, knew no Fear,
No mean Submission, but commanded Peace.
Ah how with Indignation must they burn?   100
(If aught, but Joy, can touch etherial Breasts)
With Shame? with Grief? to see their feeble Sons
Shrink from that Empire o'er the conquer'd Seas,
For which their Wisdom plan'd, their Councils glow'd,
And their Veins bled thro' many a toiling Age.   105

Oh first of human Blessings; and supreme!
Fair *Peace!* how lovely, how delightful Thou!
By whose wide Tie, the kindred Sons of Men,
Like Brothers live, in Amity combin'd,
And unsuspicious Faith; while honest Toil   110
Gives every Joy, and to those Joys a Right,

169

Which idle, barbarous Rapine but usurps.
Pure is thy Reign; when, unaccurs'd by Blood,
Nought, save the Sweetness of indulgent Showers,
Trickling distils into the vernant Glebe;   115
Instead of mangled Carcasses, sad-seen,
When the blythe Sheaves lie scatter'd o'er the Field;
When only shining Shares, the crooked Knife,
And Hooks imprint the vegetable Wound;
When the Land blushes with the Rose alone,   120
The falling Fruitage, and the bleeding Vine.
Oh, *Peace!* thou Source, and Soul of social Life;
Beneath whose calm, inspiring Influence,
Science his Views enlarges, Art refines,
And swelling Commerce opens all her Ports;   125
Blest be the Man divine, who gives us Thee!
Who bids the Trumpet hush his horrid Clang,
Nor blow the giddy Nations into Rage;
Who sheaths the murderous Blade; the deadly Gun
Into the well-pil'd Armoury returns;   130
And, every Vigour from the Work of Death,
To grateful Industry converting, makes
The Country flourish, and the City smile.
Unviolated, him the Virgin sings;
And him the smiling Mother to her Train.   135
Of him the Shepherd, in the peaceful Dale,
Chaunts; and, the Treasures of his Labour sure,
The Husbandman of him, as at the Plough,
Or Team, he toils. With him the Sailor sooths,
Beneath the trembling Moon, the midnight Wave;   140
And the full City, warm, from Street to Street,
And Shop to Shop, responsive, rings of him.
Nor joys one Land alone; his Praise extends
Far as the Sun rolls the diffusive Day;
Far as the Breeze can bear the Gifts of Peace,   145
Till all the happy Nations catch the Song.

    What would not, *Peace!* the Patriot bear for thee?
What painful Patience? What incessant Care?
What mixt Anxiety? What sleepless Toil?
Even from the rash protected what Reproach?   150

133 The City flourish, and the Country smile *A "It does not seem certain that this change was deliberate."—Editor of Oxford Facsimile*

For he thy Value knows; thy Friendship he
To human Nature: but the better thou,
The richer of Delight, sometimes the more
Inevitable *War*; when Ruffian Force
Awakes the Fury of an injur'd State.   155
Then the good easy Man, whom Reason rules;
Who, while unhurt, knew nor Offence, nor Harm,
Rouz'd by bold Insult, and injurious Rage,
With sharp, and sudden Check, th'astonish'd Sons
Of Violence confounds; firm as his Cause,   160
His bolder Heart; in awful Justice clad;
His Eyes effulging a peculiar Fire:
And, as he charges thro' the prostrate War,
His keen Arm teaches faithless Men, no more
To dare the sacred Vengeance of the Just.   165

    And what, my thoughtless Sons, should fire you more,
Than when your well-earn'd Empire of the Deep
The least beginning Injury receives?
What better Cause can call your Lightning forth?
Your Thunder wake? Your dearest Life demand?   170
What better Cause, then when your Country sees
The sly Destruction at her Vitals aim'd?
For oh it much imports you, 'tis your All,
To keep your Trade intire, intire the Force,
And Honour of your Fleets; o'er These to watch   175
Even with a Hand severe, and jealous Eye.
In Intercourse be gentle, generous, just,
By Wisdom polish'd, and of Manners fair;
But on the Sea be terrible, untam'd,
Unconquerable still: let none escape,   180
Who shall but aim to touch your Glory there.
Is there the Man, into the Lion's Den
Who dares intrude, to snatch his Young away?
And is a *Briton* seiz'd? and seiz'd beneath
The slumbring Terrors of a *British* Fleet?   185
Then ardent rise! Oh great in Vengeance rise!
O'erturn the Proud, teach Rapine to *restore*:
And as you ride sublimely round the World,
Make every Vessel stoop, make every State

175 o'er These *1738*] o'er that *A 1730 1744*
180 Unconquerable] Inconquerable *A*

At once their Welfare and their Duty know.   190
This is your Glory; this your Wisdom; this
The native Power for which you were design'd
By Fate, when Fate design'd the firmest State,
That e'er was seated on the subject Sea;
A State, alone, where *Liberty* should live,   195
In these late Times, this Evening of Mankind,
When *Athens, Rome,* and *Carthage* are no more,
The World almost in slavish Sloth dissolv'd.
For this, these Rocks around your Coast were thrown;
For this, your Oaks, peculiar harden'd, shoot   200
Strong into sturdy Growth; for this, your Hearts
Swell with a sullen Courage, growing still
As Danger grows; and Strength, and Toil for this
Are liberal pour'd o'er all the fervent Land.
Then cherish this, this unexpensive Power,   205
Undangerous to the Public, ever prompt,
By lavish Nature thrust into your Hand:
And, unencumber'd with the Bulk immense
Of Conquest, whence huge Empires rose and fell,
Self-crush'd, extend your Reign from Shore to Shore,   210
Where'er the Wind your high Behests can blow,
And fix it deep on this eternal Base.
For should the sliding Fabrick once give way,
Soon slacken'd quite, and past Recovery broke,
It gathers Ruin as it rolls along,   215
Steep-rushing down to that devouring Gulph,
Where many a mighty Empire buried lies.
And should the big redundant Flood of Trade,
In which ten thousand thousand Labours join
Their several Currents, till the boundless Tide   220
Rolls in a radiant Deluge o'er the Land,

197 *Athens, Rome,* and *Carthage*] *Carthage, Rome,* and *Athens A*
212 this eternal Base] his eternal Base *1738*
213 *After this line A has:*
And on the Brink of Fate begin to nod,
214 slacken'd] blacken'd *A Corrected in errata published in Daily Journal January 24, 1729*
221 Deluge] Torrent *A*
After this line A has:
Fruitful of Wealth, Magnificence, and Joy,
Of every glittering Harvest, richer far
Than what *Hesperian* Gardens bore of old;

Should this bright Stream, the least inflected, point
Its Course another way, o'er other Lands
The various Treasure would resistless pour,
Ne'er to be won again; its antient Tract   225
Left a vile Channel, desolate, and dead,
With all around a miserable Waste.
Not *Egypt,* were her better Heaven, the *Nile*
Turn'd in the Pride of Flow; when o'er his Rocks,
And roaring Cataracts, beyond the Reach   230
Of dizzy Vision pil'd, in one wide Flash
An *Ethiopian* Deluge foams amain;
(Whence wondr'ing Fable trac'd him from the Sky)
Even not that Prime of Earth, where Harvests croud
On untill'd Harvests, all the teeming Year,   235
If of the fat o'erflowing Culture robb'd,
Were then a more uncomfortable Wild,
Steril, and void; than of her Trade depriv'd,
Britons, your boasted Isle: her Princes sunk;
Her high-built Honour moulder'd to the Dust;   240
Unnerv'd her Force! her Spirit vanish'd quite;
With rapid Wing her Riches fled away;
Her unfrequented Ports alone the Sign
Of what she was; her Merchants scatter'd wide;
Her hollow Shops shut up; and in her Streets,   245
Her Fields, Woods, Markets, Villages, and Roads,
The cheerful Voice of Labour heard no more.

    Oh let not then waste Luxury impair
That manly Soul of Toil, which strings your Nerves,
And your own proper Happiness creates!   250
Oh let not the soft, penetrating Plague
Creep on the free-born Mind! and working there,
With the sharp Tooth of many a new-form'd Want,
Endless, and idle all, eat out the Heart
Of *Liberty*; the high Conception blast;   255
The noble Sentiment, th' impatient Scorn
Of base Subjection, and the swelling Wish
For general Good, erazing from the Mind:
While nought save narrow Selfishness succeeds,

222 inflected] infected *1730 1744*
238 than] then *1738*

And low Design, the sneaking Passions all   260
Let loose, and reigning in the rankled Breast.
Induc'd at last, by scarce-perceiv'd Degrees,
Sapping the very Frame of Government,
And Life, a total Dissolution comes;
Sloth, Ignorance, Dejection, Flattery, Fear,   265
Oppression raging o'er the Waste he makes;
The human Being almost quite extinct;
And the whole State in broad Corruption sinks.
Oh shun that Gulph: that gaping Ruin shun!
And countless Ages roll it far away   270
From you, ye Heaven-beloved! may *Liberty*,
The Light of Life! the Sun of Human Kind!
Whence Heroes, Bards, and Patriots borrow Flame,
Even where the keen depressive North descends,
Still spread, exalt, and actuate your Powers!   275
While slavish Southern Climates beam in vain.
And may a public Spirit from the *Throne*,
Where every Virtue sits, go copious forth
Wide o'er the Land! the finer Arts inspire;
Make thoughtful Science raise his pensive Head,   280
Blow the fresh Bay, bid Industry rejoice,
And the rough Sons of lowest Labour smile.
As when, profuse of Spring, the loosen'd West
Lifts up the pining Year, and balmy breathes
Youth, Life, and Love, and Beauty o'er the World.   285

But haste we from these melancholy Shores,
Nor to deaf Winds, and Waves, our fruitless Plaint
Pour weak; the Country claims our active Aid;
That let us roam; and where we find a Spark

260 sneaking] gloomy *A*
265 Fear,] Fear. *1744*
269 that gaping Ruin] and gaping Ruin *1744*
279 Wide *A 1730 continuously paged octavo 1738*] Live *1730 1744*
284 balmy] luscious *A*
288 Pour weak] Pour out *A*
289 roam] rome *A Corrected in errata published in Daily Journal January 24, 1729*

Of public Virtue, blow it into Flame.   290
And now my Sons, the Sons of Freedom! meet
In awful Senate; thither let us fly;
Burn in the Patriot's Thought, flow from his Tongue
In fearless Truth; myself, transform'd, preside,
And shed the Spirit of *Britannia* round.   295

  This said; her fleeting Form, and airy Train,
Sunk in the Gale; and nought but ragged Rocks
Rush'd on the broken Eye; and nought was heard
But the rough Cadence of the dashing Wave.

290 *After this line A has:*
  The THRONE be chief our Care, th' aetherial Streams
  Of Wisdom, Justice, and Benevolence,
  That issue thence, refreshing all the Land,
  Joyous to swell: and o'er the lovely Round
  Of ROYAL BEAUTY, which about it glows,
  To hover fond, prophetick of those Days
  That, FREDERICK! dawn delightful in thy Eye.

Rule, Britannia

INTRODUCTION

From the complex political background of *Britannia* and *Liberty* emerged "Rule, Britannia," Thomson's most famous poem. The place of "Rule, Britannia" in the history of popular song and patriotic music cannot be fully considered here, but some points connected with its early history may be noted. It was originally sung near the conclusion of *Alfred,* a masque written by Thomson and Mallet and produced at Cliveden House before the Prince and Princess of Wales on August 1 and 2, 1740, to celebrate the birthday of their daughter, the Princess Augusta. The piece had been rehearsed at Drury Lane on July 28 (*Gentleman's Magazine,* X [1740], 356). The extended description of the entertainment at Cliveden given by the *London Daily Post and General Advertiser* for August 2 and August 5 has often been quoted, most recently by Grant, pp. 192-94. This report, however, does not mention "Rule, Britannia" or the composer of the music, Thomas Arne. The *Daily Advertiser* for August 6 gives a good deal of information about the allocation of the songs among the cast and ends its account by adding, "after which, a new Ode, in Honour of Great Britain, was sung by Mr. Salway." This gives what we may call the original title. Salway, who was cast as the shepherd Corin, evidently doubled as the Bard on this occasion, and thus had the honour of singing the "new Ode" in public for the first time.[1]

The program at Cliveden also included Congreve's *Judgment of Paris* with Arne's music. Plans for immediate production of *Alfred* on the public stage fell through, though license seems to have been given in 1741.[2] *The Judgment of Paris* was produced at Drury Lane on March 19, 1742, and both *The Judgment of Paris* and *Alfred,* with special mention of the "celebrated Ode," during Arne's 1744 season in Dublin.[3] At

---

[1] W. H. Cummings, *Dr. Arne and 'Rule Britannia'* (1912), p. 120, says Thomas Lowe took the part of the Bard, but this statement seems to go back to a conjecture made by W. H. Husk in *N&Q,* 2 S.V (1858), 320.

[2] For details, see Alan D. McKillop, "Thomson and the Licensers of the Stage," *PQ,* XXXVII (1958), 453.

[3] Allardyce Nicoll, *A History of English Drama 1660-1900,* II (Cambridge, 1955), 315; Cummings, pp. 124-25.

some time after the former production the following score was published:

The Music in / The Judgment of Paris. Consisting of All the Songs, Duettos and Trio with / The Overture, in Score. / As perform'd by / Mr. Beard, Mr. Lowe, Mrs. Arne, / Mrs. Clive, Miss Edwards, and others. / At the Theatre Royal in Drury Lane. / To which (By particular Desire of Several Encouragers of this Work) are added / The celebrated Ode in Honour of Great-Britain / call'd / Rule Britannia. / And Sawney & Jenney, a favourite Dialogue in yᵉ Scotch Stile. / The whole Compos'd by / Thomas Augustine Arne. / Opera sesta. / London: / Printed for Henry Waylett, at the Black Lyon in Exeter Change in yᵉ Strand, / and Sold by him, and at all the Music Shops in London and Westminster. / Where may be had five other Volumes of yᵉ Authors Works.[4]

This title-page is also to be connected with the prominent use of "Rule, Britannia" in Arne's musical adaptation of *Alfred,* produced at Drury Lane in March and April 1745; the libretto was immediately published by Andrew Millar as *Alfred. An Opera.* Arne's advertising says explicitly of this piece: "Part of the Musick was composed by Command of his Royal Highness Frederick Prince of Wales, and never perform'd in England, but at his Royal Highness's Palace at Cliefdon. The rest is new compos'd. The Poem was written by Mr. Thomson and Mr. Mallet. . . . The Musick by Mr. Arne. To conclude with a celebrated Ode in Honour of Great Britain, in Imitation of those formerly sung at the Banquets of Kings and Heroes."[5] As to the exact dating of the published score of *The Judgment of Paris* and "Rule, Britannia," W. H. Husk pointed out that the piece called "Sawney and Jenney" denounces Pope and Pretender in a way that points to 1745, and that Miss Edwards, named in the cast, became Mrs. Mozeen in 1746.[6] The date 1745-46 seems certain for this score. Arne continued to assert his special claim to the music. When Mallet's altered version of *Alfred* was produced in 1751, Arne was at pains to announce

---

[4] From the copy in the Wells Collection, Swarthmore College Library. Cummings, p. 122, transcribes this title-page. There was also a performance of *The Judgment of Paris* with Arne's music at Drury Lane, April 20, 1748 (Dougald MacMillan, *Drury Lane Calendar 1747-1776* [Oxford, 1938], p. 266), but the cast as listed does not correspond with that given on the title-page above, which clearly refers to the earlier performance.

[5] *Daily Advertiser,* March 15, 1745. For further detail, see Grant, p. 239.

[6] *N&Q,* 2 S.V (1858), 320.

in the *General Advertiser,* February 26, 1751, that the music was not his except for the two songs "O Peace thou fairest child of Heav'n" and "Rule, Britannia."[7] We can deal with the complicated record of the versions of *Alfred* only as it touches on the fortunes of "Rule, Britannia." The song did not originally conclude the masque, but in 1745 it assumed the position of a grand finale, with alternate stanzas sung by Alfred and Eltruda. The 1740 text of the song presented in this way was kept in Arne's various productions, and appears entire in the first published score, but was reduced to four stanzas in Arne's "Oratorio" or "Drama for Music" published in 1753 and 1754, and also in undated editions.

The connection in diction and thought with other works of Thomson makes it unnecessary to argue at length for his authorship as against any claims for Mallet, though the question has been much discussed.[8] It has long been known that the song had already appeared over Thomson's initials in the miscellany called *The Charmer* (Edinburgh, 1749). In the Advertisement to his 1751 version of *Alfred* Mallet says that of Thomson's part in the original masque he has kept only "three or four speeches, and a part of one song." But the song kept in part may be "Rule, Britannia," and Mallet makes no explicit claim here.

The Huntington Library has the manuscript copy of the 1751 *Alfred* submitted by Garrick and Lacy for licensing on February 14. The piece was elaborately staged at Drury Lane for nine nights from February 23. The manuscript shows some uncertainty about the way in which "Rule, Britannia" is to be used. At first the Bard is introduced about as in 1740:

> But see, my lord,
> Aged and blind, our venerable bard.
> Yet ere you go, in our lov'd country's praise,
> That noblest theme, hear what his rapture breathes.

Then follows the direction, "After a prelude on the British harp, the Bard sings." Both the speech and the direction are then deleted, and instead the Hermit calls Alfred's attention to an elaborate scenic effect: "Scene opening discovers the ocean, and ships sailing along. Two boats land their crews. One

---

[7] Quoted by V. Schoelcher, *N&Q*, 2 S.V. (1858), 91.

[8] The best survey of the case is still that of J. Churton Collins, *Ephemera Critica* (1902), pp. 321-28.

sailor sings the following Ode: after which, the rest join in a lively dance." After the Ode, the manuscript has the following deleted direction: "The scene opens behind and shows a dock-yard, with the hull of a large ship on the stocks. Towards each side of its stem are caulkers at work on a scaffold. Enter a crew of ship-carpenters and sailors, who to the tune of the caulker's hammers join in a gay lively dance." It was perhaps Aaron Hill, in his comments on the *Alfred* of 1740, who gave Mallet the suggestion that the revised masque should end with Alfred's resolution "to *build* and *man* a fleet, and fix the safety of his too oft insulted kingdom, on the future guard and sovereignty of the ocean."[9] Hill of course took his cue from the original "Rule, Britannia," but his suggestion and Mallet's proceedings here strikingly confirm Langley's comment: "It is dignity that pre-dominates in 'Rule, Britannia!' and it is dignity more than any other quality that has been lost in the process of popularising which followed immediately on the first overwhelming suc-cess. Had 'Rule, Britannia!' been the jolly Jack Tar sort of song that it has since become, it is doubtful whether it would ever have been heard outside the garden wall of Cliveden."[10]

The 1751 manuscript also shows Mallet, probably in col-laboration with Bolingbroke, tampering with the Ode itself. The first two stanzas are identical with the text of 1740. The third stanza is a weak addition:

> Should War, should faction shake thy Isle,
> And sink to poverty and shame;
> Heaven still shall on BRITANNIA smile,
> Restore her wealth, and raise her name.

The fourth stanza of 1751 inverts and weakens the third stanza of 1740:

> As the loud blast that tears thy skies,
> Serves but to root thy native oak;
> Still more majestic shalt thou rise,
> From foreign, from domestic stroke.

The last three stanzas of 1740 are replaced by two weak stanzas over which Mallet (and/or Bolingbroke?) labored consider-ably. We have in the body of the manuscript:

---

[9] Aaron Hill, *Works* (1753), II, 165-66.
[10] Hubert Langley, *Doctor Arne* (Cambridge, 1938), p. 31.

How blest the prince, whose patriot reign
Shall bid thy towns with commerce shine!
Awe with thy fleet the farthest main,
And make, at home, true freedom thine.

And lo! these blessings long desir'd,
This monarch's day, the muses see:
And all proclaim, by heaven inspir'd,
Their Alfred shall this monarch be.

This goes down badly, and two alternative stanzas (eventually printed) are inserted on a slip, apparently in Mallet's hand:

Happy the prince reserv'd by fate,	Happy the prince]
In adverse days to mount the throne;	How blest the prince
Renew thy once triumphant state,	*printed*
And on thy grandeur found his own.	found] build *printed*

His race shall long, in times to come,
So heaven ordains, the sceptre wield,
Rever'd abroad, belov'd at home,
And be, at once, thy sword and shield.

The last two stanzas, and the one beginning "Should War, should faction shake thy Isle," are later said to have been "written by the late Lord Bolingbroke, in 1751."[11] The Ode in this form had some currency; thus it was this 1751 text that was sung in the Norwich production of 1764 by "Mr. Kear in the Character of a British Tar."[12] In Garrick's production of Mallet's masque in 1773, the garbled version of the Ode is given in the libretto, but the 1740 text is added on a separate leaf with the cryptic note, "The following Song was altered by the author, and is now printed as it is sung." It should also be noted that Mallet himself, apparently revising the 1751 text of the masque for inclusion in the 1759 edition of his works, though he used the garbled Ode, took it away from the British Tar and gave it back to the Bard with his harp, much as in 1740 and the first draft of 1751.

---

[11] Mallet, *Works* (1759), III, 69; Thomas Davies, *Life of Garrick* (3rd ed.; 1781), II, 41-42.
[12] *The Songs, in the Masque of Alfred* (Norwich, 1764), Air XIV. Copy in Huntington Library.

AN ODE

[RULE, BRITANNIA]

1.

When *Britain* first, at heaven's command,
  Arose from out the azure main;
This was the charter of the land,
  And guardian angels sung *this* strain:
    "Rule, *Britannia*, rule the waves;   5
    Britons never will be slaves."

2.

The nations, not so blest as thee,
  Must, in their turns, to tyrants fall:
While thou shalt flourish great and free,
  The dread and envy of them all.   10
    "Rule, *&c.*

3.

Still more majestic shalt thou rise,
  More dreadful, from each foreign stroke:
As the loud blast that tears the skies,
  Serves but to root thy native oak.   15
    "Rule, *&c.*

4.

Thee haughty tyrants ne'er shall tame:
  All their attempts to bend thee down,
Will but arrouse thy generous flame;
  But work their woe, and thy renown.   20
    "Rule, *&c.*

5.

To thee belongs the rural reign;
  Thy cities shall with commerce shine:
All thine shall be the subject main,
  And every shore it circles thine.   25
    "Rule, *&c.*

6.

The Muses, still with freedom found,
   Shall to thy happy coast repair:
Blest isle! with matchless beauty crown'd,
   And manly hearts to guard the fair.   30
      "Rule, *Britannia,* rule the waves;
      Britons never will be slaves."

List of References

This list includes only works referred to several times, often by the author's or editor's name, or by short title or abbreviation. Unless otherwise indicated, the place of publication is London or New York.

Aldine edition. *The Poetical Works of James Thomson.* Memoir by Sir Harris Nicolas, revised by Peter Cunningham. 2 vols. 1860, repr. 1862, 1866, etc.

Arthos, John, *The Language of Natural Description in Eighteenth-Century Poetry.* Ann Arbor, 1949. University of Michigan Publications: Language and Literature, XXIV.

ELH. ELH: A Journal of English Literary History.

FQ. The Faerie Queene. See Spenser.

Grant, Douglas. *James Thomson, Poet of 'The Seasons.'* 1951.

Hagstrum, Jean. *The Sister Arts: The Tradition of Literary Pictorialism and English Poetry from Dryden to Gray.* Chicago, 1958.

JEGP. Journal of English and Germanic Philology.

JHI. Journal of the History of Ideas.

LD. James Thomson (1700-1748): Letters and Documents, ed. Alan D. McKillop. Lawrence, Kansas, 1958.

McKillop, Alan D. *The Background of Thomson's Liberty.* Rice Institute Pamphlet, XXXVII (1951), No. 2.

———— *The Background of Thomson's Seasons.* Minneapolis, 1942.

MLN. Modern Language Notes.

MP. Modern Philology.

Moore, Cecil A. *Backgrounds of English Literature 1700-1760.* Minneapolis, 1953.

Morel, Léon. *James Thomson: sa vie et ses œuvres.* Paris, 1895.

Nicolson, Marjorie. *Newton Demands the Muse: Newton's 'Opticks' and the Eighteenth Century Poets.* Princeton, 1946.

Oxford edition. *The Complete Poetical Works of James Thomson,* ed. J. Logie Robertson. Oxford, 1908.

OED. Oxford English Dictionary.

PL. John Milton, *Paradise Lost,* ed. Merritt Y. Hughes, 1935.

PMLA. Publications of the Modern Language Association of America.

PQ. Philological Quarterly.

PR. John Milton, *Paradise Regained,* ed. Merritt Y. Hughes. 1937.

RES. Review of English Studies.

Ritter, Otto. *Quellenstudien zu Robert Burns 1773-1701.* Berlin, 1901. Palaestra, XX.

Robertson. James Thomson, *The Seasons and The Castle of Indolence,* ed. J. Logie Robertson. Oxford, 1891. Clarendon Press edition.

Sale Catalogue. *A Catalogue of all the Genuine Household Furniture, Plate, China, Prints & Drawings, &c. of Mr. James Thomson. . . together with*

REFERENCES

His compleat Library of Books. [May 15, 1749.] [Copy in Mitchell Library, Glasgow.]

SC. The Shepherd's Calendar. See Spenser.

Spenser. *The Works of Mr. Edmund Spenser,* ed. John Hughes. 6 vols. 1715. References are to this edition, as the one used by Thomson. Sale Catalogue, No. 83.

SP. Studies in Philology.

Thomson. *Liberty.* Quotations follow the first edition, 1735-36, but for convenience in reference the line numbering of the Oxford edition is followed.

———— *The Seasons.* Unless some other edition is indicated, quotations follow the edition of 1746, but for convenience in reference the line numbering of the Oxford edition is followed whenever possible.

Explanatory Notes

THE CASTLE OF INDOLENCE

In the following notes, though some attention has been given to Thomson's diction, the principal purpose has been to supplement the account of his literary background given in the Introduction. Numerous cross references to the Introduction and to Thomson's other works have been supplied. In addition to the abbreviated references sufficiently covered by the foregoing general list, a few special abbreviations are used here. The Glossary in Hughes' edition of Spenser (1715) is referred to by the symbol H, Thomson's "Explanation of the obsolete Words" (pp. 68-69) by the symbol T. A word glossed in a substantially identical way by both is marked HT; entries are quoted from H only when there is no equivalent in T. As in the Introduction, the text of Spenser used is that of Hughes.

Argument   1   *hight:* T.
           2   *false Luxury.* Cf. *Summer,* 68: "Falsely luxurious, will not Man awake. . .?"

  i   3   *moil:* T.
      3-4   Genesis iii:19: "In the sweat of thy face shalt thou eat bread."
      5   *certes:* HT.
      8   *Bale:* HT.

  ii   Introduction, pp. 15-16.
      5   *ween:* HT.
      6   *atween:* HT.
      8   *Sooth:* HT.
      9   *ne:* HT.

  iii-v   Introduction, pp. 16-19. For the sequence and correspondence of details with Thomson's description of Hagley Park, cf. iii.6 to v.2 with the following:

> "There along the Dale,
> With Woods o'er-hung, and shag'd with mossy Rocks,
> Whence on each hand the gushing Waters play,
> And down the rough Cascade white-dashing fall,
> Or gleam in lengthen'd Vista thro' the Trees,
> You silent steal; or sit beneath the Shade
> Of solemn Oaks, that tuft the swelling Mounts
> Thrown graceful round by Nature's careless Hand,
> And pensive listen to the various Voice
> Of rural Peace: the Herds, the Flocks, the Birds,
> The hollow-whispering Breeze, the Plaint of Rills,
> That, purling down amid the twisted Roots
> Which creep around, their dewy Murmurs shake
> On the sooth'd Ear." (*Spring,* 909-922)

  iii   3   *kest:* HT. Only once in Spenser as past tense of *cast, FQ* VI.xii.15.7.

6-7 Cf. *Summer,* 448-50: "The very Streams . . . impatient, seem / To hurl into the Covert of the Grove."

7 *sheen:* HT.

iv 3 Cf. *Spring,* 200: "the distant Bleatings of the Hills."

4 *vacant:* carefree.

8 *Coil . . . keep: OED, coil, sb.²,* sense 4a.

9 *yblent:* HT.

v Introduction, pp. 18-19.

4 *Idless:* HT.

6 *ay.* Spenser has *ay* or *aye* in the sense of "always"; Thomson regularly uses *ay.*

6-7 Robertson quotes Genesis xv:12: "A deep sleep fell upon Abram; and, lo, an horror of great darkness fell upon him." He also quotes Thomson's "Soporifick Doctor": "Through every joint a gentle horror creeps, / And round you the consenting audience sleeps."

vi 1 *Drowsy-hed:* H. Only once in Spenser, *FQ* I.ii.7.5: "The royall Virgin shook off drowsy-hed."

8 *Noyance:* HT. Only twice in Spenser. Cf. *FQ* I.i.23.7: "That from their noyance he no where can rest." For the relation of this stanza in Spenser to I.xxx below, see Introduction, p. 35.

vii 1 *Landskip:* the regular eighteenth century form for *landscape.*

7 *wicked Wight.* Used by Spenser of the spider Aragnoll in *Muiopotmos,* 243. Spenser's description of the spider lying in wait to entrap the butterfly influenced Thomson's account of the Wizard. See II.xl.9 below.

viii 3 *breathe:* to stop to catch breath. Cf., e.g., *FQ* IV.ii.18.7.

6-7 Introduction, p. 22. Cf. also Thomson to Elizabeth Young, May 14, 1743; *LD,* p. 155: ". . . when seduced by that most fatal Syren Indolence and false Pleasure."

7 *Ymolten:* T. H has *ymolt.*

ix-xi Introduction, pp. 5-6, 22-23.

ix 4 *wintry Tomb.* Cf. *Liberty,* V.11-12: "And let the little Insect-Artist form, / On higher Life intent, it's silken Tomb." Cf. also Introduction, p. 8.

x 5 *emove: emmove* or *enmove* in Spenser. Cf. II.lxvi.7 below.

7 *nodding Sheaves.* G. C. Macaulay, *James Thomson* (1908), p. 200, quoting this stanza, gives and defends the reading "nodden sheaves," which I do not find in any early edition.

xi 1 *Outcast of Nature, Man!* Cf. *Autumn,* 47-48: "Raiser of Human Kind! by Nature cast, / Naked, and helpless, out amid the Woods."

2 *sweltry:* HT. *OED,* sense 1b.

3 Cf. *L'Allegro,* 135: "eating Cares."

7 *the Plain:* the earth.

9 *soft milky Streams.* Cf. *Spring* (1728), 311-12: "The Rivers foam'd with Nectar; or diffuse, / Silent, and soft, the milky Maze devolv'd." This is part of a description of the Golden Age; the rivers flowing with nectar and milk are from Ovid, *Metamorphoses,* I.111.

xii Introduction, p. 23.

1-5 The punishment of Sisyphus as described in the *Odyssey,* XI. 593-601. Thomson improves on Pope's excessively onomatopoetic translation:

"With many a weary step, and many a groan,
Up the high hill he heaves a huge round stone;
The huge round stone, resulting with a bound,
Thunders impetuous down, and smoaks along the ground.
Again the restless orb his toil renews,
Dust mounts in clouds, and sweat descends in dews."

xiii 2 *Stounds:* H: "Hour, Time, Season; sometimes it signifies Misfortune, as ill Stound, like the Fr. *Malheur.*" Cf. *FQ* I.viii.25.5: "That she could not endure that doleful Stound." *OED*, sense 2a: "a hard time, a time of trial or pain."

      3 *louting:* HT.

xiv   Introduction, p. 43. Cf. also the description of the Cave of Sleep in Ovid, *Metamorphoses,* XI.592 ff. Thomson's stanza is later echoed by Cowper in his description of the lodge called "the peasant's nest," *The Task,* I.228-23:

"far remote
From such unpleasing sounds as haunt the ear
In village or in town, the bay of curs
Incessant, clinking hammers, grinding wheels,
And infants clam'rous whether pleas'd or pain'd,
Oft have I wish'd the peaceful covert mine."

xiv 5 *sear:* HT. A variant of the adjective *sere,* "dry, withered," but also connected in meaning with the verb *sear,* "to burn."

      6 *Tradesman:* "In Scotland one who works with his hands at a trade. In England a shopkeeper."—[James Beattie], *Scoticisms* (1787). The first meaning may fit here, but another possible meaning is "hawker," one who cries his wares in the street.

xv   1 *Candour: OED,* sense 4: "Freedom from malice, favourable disposition, kindliness."

      2 Quoted by Wordsworth, *Prelude,* VI.182.

      3 Cf. Goldsmith, *The Traveller,* 242, of France: "Pleas'd with thyself, whom all the world can please."

xvi   Introduction, p. 23.

xvii 8-9 Scipio Africanus Major retired early to Liternum, near Cumae and Naples, on the coast of Campania. Cf. *Winter,* 517-20; *Liberty,* V.419-21. Milton compares his withdrawal from active life, and that of Fairfax, to the retirement of Scipio at Liternum (*Pro Se Defensio* and *Defensio Secunda,* Columbia edition, IX, 4-7; VIII, 216-17). In Congreve's *Old Bachelor,* II.i, Captain Bluffe says: "I am content to retire—live a private person—Scipio and others have done it." Cf. also Pope, *Windsor Forest,* 257.

xviii 5-7 Cf. the long angling passage, *Spring,* 379-442, added in 1744.

      5 *Gear:* HT.

      7 *amus'd:* in a state of musing or reverie, a favorite word of Thomson's.

      8 *the hoarse Stream.* Cf. *Newton,* 120.

xix   The entire stanza paraphrases Ecclesiastes ii:18-23, with specific echoes of viii:15 in line 2, and of i:2 in line 8. Cf. also Psalms xxxix:6.

      3 Cf. *Lycidas,* 75: "Comes the blind Fury with th' abhorred shears."

      6 *Pluto's Reign. FQ* II.vii.21.4: "*Pluto's* griesly Reign."

xx   Introduction, p. 34.

      1 *trembling Ears.* Cf. *Lycidas,* 77.

187

xxi 4 *han:* HT.

7 *perdie:* HT. Cf. I.lvi.5.

xxii 2 *strait.* Thomson's regular spelling in the sense *straightway.*

9 Cf. Burns, "Caledonia": "Whoe'er shall provoke thee, th' encounter shall rue."—Ritter.

xxiii 7 *Losel's:* HT.

xxiv-xxvi Introduction, p. 40.

xxiv 7 Cf. Pope, "Elegy to the Memory of an Unfortunate Lady," 17 ff.: "Most souls, 'tis true, but peep out once an age," etc.

xxv 2 *to weet:* HT.

xxvi *Undress:* the informal costume worn by men at home. The "gown," often called "nightgown," was much like the modern dressing gown; there was also the "Banjan" or "Indian night-gown," a loose coat extending about to the knees. These were usually worn with nightcap and slippers. See C. Willett and Phillis Cunnington, *Handbook of English Costume in the Eighteenth Century* (1957), pp. 73-75. Such costumes often appear in eighteenth century portraits (see the portraits of Thomson above), and were often worn when receiving or paying informal visits, and in coffeehouses and other public places.

xxvii 6 *Nepenthe.* Homer describes the power of the magic drug Nepenthes to produce forgetfulness of trouble and insensibility even to the death of one's parents or children (*Odyssey,* IV.220 ff.); Spenser describes Nepenthe as a sovereign drink reserved by the gods for the sober and wise, with power to obliterate the memory of past cares and bestow eternal happiness (*FQ* IV.iii.43-45). The "cordial Julep" in *Comus,* 672-78, is said to surpass Homer's Nepenthes in "power to stir up joy." In spite of the reference to Homer, Thomson's lines are closest to Spenser. Spenserian also is the fountain in the court (*FQ* II.xii.60 ff.). But the association of Homer's Nepenthes with the magic draught offered by Circe, and so with the spells of Spenser's Acrasia, Thomson probably got from *Comus.* He may also have remembered the cup extended by the Wizard in *The Dunciad,* IV.517 ff.

7 *Dan* HOMER. H: "Dan, an old Title signifying Master, like the Spanish Don." Since Spenser and Shakespeare used in poetic diction especially of gods ("Dan Cupid") or poets ("Dan Chaucer," "Dan Prior"), often in a playful or humourour way. Cf. I.xxxvii.3, lviii.3 below.

xxviii Introduction, p. 40.

1 *inly.* Frequent in Spenser with reference to a state of mind, but probably not felt to be a Spenserianism in the eighteenth century.

xxix Introduction, p. 35.

2 Besides *Il Penseroso,* 7-8, cf. Chaucer, Wife of Bath's Tale, 868: "As thikke as motes in the sonne-beem."

3 *eftsoons.* With T cf. H: "quickly."

9 *you . . . was.* Common as the second person singular form in the eighteenth century.

xxx Introduction, p. 35. From among the innumerable comments on this stanza Joseph Warton's may be cited (*Essay on the Genius and Writings of Pope* [5th ed., 1806], I,349): "I cannot at present recollect any solitude so romantic." Cf. William Lisle Bowles, *The Spirit of Discovery; or, The Conquest of Ocean* (Bath, 1804), p. 14:

"As in the skiey mirage, when the seer
From lonely Kilda's western summit sees
A wondrous scene in shadowy vision rise."

Cf. also Wordsworth, *Prelude*, III.510-16:

"Hitherto I had stood
In my own mind remote from social life,
(At least from what we commonly so name,)
Like a lone shepherd on a promontory
Who lacking occupation looks far forth
Into the boundless sea, and rather makes
Than finds what he beholds."

	1	*Hebrid-Isles.* "Those Islands on the western Coast of *Scotland* called the *Hebrides.*"—Thomson's note.
xxxi		Introduction, p. 36.
	5	Cf. *Comus*, 44: "What never yet was heard in Tale or Song."
xxxii		Introduction, pp. 37-38.
	2	*Imp:* HT.
	8-9	Cf. Burns, "The Vision," II.iv: "Some rouse the patriot up to bare / Corruption's heart."—Ritter.
xxxiii		Introduction, p. 43. See also note to I.liii below.
	3	*Self-open'd into Halls.* Cf. *PL* V.254: "The gate self-opend wide."
xxxiv		Introduction, pp. 44-46.
	9	*thick the Glasses play'd:* "The light gleamed on innumerable glasses."—Robertson. *OED, play,* sense 3b: "to exhibit a play of light or colour."
xxxv	3	*saintly Spleen:* Puritan censoriousness.
	4	*pall:* weaken. *FQ* V.iv.5.9: ". . . forestal / Their furious Encounter, and their Fierceness pall." Dryden, *Palamon and Arcite,* III.686: "A miracle . . . / Their joy with unexpected sorrow pall'd."
	5-7	Introduction, p. 40.
	9	*carol:* HT.
xxxvi-xxxviii		Introduction, pp. 25-29.
xxxvii		Cf. *Liberty,* II.3-6:

"First, in the dawn of Time, with eastern Swains,
In Woods, and Tents, and Cottages, I liv'd;
While on from Plain to Plain they led their Flocks,
In search of clearer Spring, and fresher Field."

	2	*Depeinten:* H: "Depeinten, painted." *SC,* April 69: "In either Cheek depeinten lively chear."
xxxviii		This famous stanza describes imaginary and generalized landscapes presenting the changes of the seasons, the contrast between storm and sunshine, and picturesque views of mountain, waterfall, and ocean. To illustrate this range of effect Thomson names Claude Lorrain, Salvator Rosa, and Nicolas Poussin, adding Titian in stanza xliv. These references became so widely known as to affect the course of later Thomson criticism; thus James More quotes one critic as saying that "the pieces of *Poussin* are not more uncommon, exotic, and classical, the sketches of *Lorenese* more daring and sublime, or the descriptions of *Titian* more happy, natural, graceful, varied and charming" than Thomson's; another critic, according to More, says that "the scenes of

189

Thomson are frequently as wild and romantic as those of
Salvator Rosa" (*Strictures, Critical and Sentimental, on
Thomson's Seasons* [1777], p. 182). The subject has received
much attention, and too sweeping claims have been made
for the influence of these painters on English poetry
by Elizabeth Wheeler Manwaring (*Italian Landscape in
Eighteenth Century England* [1925]), and Christopher Hussey
(*The Picturesque* [1927]). The whole question of Thomson's
relation to Italian painting has been effectively explored and
clarified by Jean Hagstrum (*The Sister Arts* [1958]). At the
same time, the dominant influence of Italian masters like
Domenichino, the Carracci, Maratti, and Reni need not ex-
clude a special interest in Italianate landscape which comes
to the fore in *The Castle of Indolence*. In the present passage Thomson is not undertaking a comprehensive account
of painting—he resists the temptation to extend his iconic
passages—but is simply pointing up variety and contrast in
picturesque landscape by familiar examples.

That these examples lay ready to hand can be illustrated
from George Turnbull's *Treatise on Ancient Painting* (1740).
Thomson and several of his friends subscribed for this work,
it praises Thomson's *Liberty,* and a copy remained in the
poet's library (Sale Catalogue, No. 251). Turnbull uses the
painters named by Thomson to illustrate the interaction or
interchangeability of the picturesque in nature and in art,
the real theme of Thomson's stanza: "Nor is another Pleasure
to be passed by unmentioned, that the Eye formed by right
Instruction in good Pictures, to the accurate and careful
Observance of Nature's Beauties, will have, in recalling to
mind, upon seeing certain Appearances in Nature, the Landscapes of great Masters he has seen, and their particular
Genius's and Tastes. He will ever be discerning something
suited to the particular Turn of one or other of them; something that a *Titian,* a *Pousin,* a *Salvator Rosa,* or a *Claud
Lorrain,* hath already represented, or would not have let go
without imitating, and making a good Use of in Landscape.
Nature would send such a one to Pictures, and Pictures
would send him to Nature: And thus the satisfaction he
would receive from the one or the other would be always
double" (p. 146). For Salvator Rosa we have in Turnbull:
"Who does not see in *Salvator Rosa's* Pictures, the Savageness
of his Imagination? His Genius led him most strongly to
paint Battles. He painted likewise *Paisages* and Sea-ports;
but always in a whimsical, wild, and savage Taste" (p. 164).
And again: "*Salvator Rosa* should have painted for me
several Battles, and a great Variety of wild savage Prospects"
(p. 169). These passages, to be sure, are based on André
Félibien's *Entretiens sur les vies et les ouvrages des plus
excellens peintres* (1685-88), a work which was also in
Thomson's library (Sale Catalogue, No. 194), but the fixed
epithet "savage" may come to Thomson from Turnbull.
For "learned Poussin" Turnbull had adopted the comment
in Du Bos, *Réflexions critiques* (1719): "Nicolas Poussin,
says the ingenious Author of the Reflections on Poetry and
Painting, was justly called by his Contemporaries *Le Peintre
des gens d'esprit;* or, a Painter for those who look for Enter-

190

tainment to their Understanding, by Truth, Science, Learning, Correctness, and good Disposition in Pictures, or for Exercise to their Passions by just Force of Expression" (p. 165). Here Thomson may have been helped to the epithet "learned," although he had already written in *Liberty*, V.500-02,

"From *Rome*, awhile, how PAINTING, courted long,
With POUSSIN, came; *Ancient Design*, that lifts
A fairer Front, and looks another Soul."

The contrast between Lorrain and Rosa was evidently current. "So *Claud de Lorain* in his Landskips, Figures, &c. his great Inclination to Retirement, Quietness, and Stilness, his Perspicuity, as well as Capacity, Judgment, and good Choice of Nature, may all plainly enough be observed in his Paintings; whereas *Salvator Rose*, on the contrary, shows a more particularly chagrin, savage, satyrical, smart Genius, by his vast Spirit and Fire, with his constant Imitation and Choice of wild and gloomy Nature in all his Works" (*A Letter on the Nature and State of Curiosity* [1736], pp. 22-23).

For what is probably an elaboration of Thomson's brief view of the picturesque painters, cf. Byron, *Don Juan*, XIII. lxxi-lxxii.

xxxix 1 *Languishment: OED*, sense 2b: "expression of sentimental emotion."

xl-xli   See Appendix A.

xli 2 *Diapasan:* diapason.

    4 With reference to this line, quoted as "And let it down again into the soul," and erroneously said to be the concluding line of the stanza, Henry Mackenzie writes in *Anecdotes and Egotisms 1745-1831*, ed. H. W. Thompson (1927), pp. 39-40: "The beautiful stanza in his *Castle of Indolence* describing the tones of the instrument then recently invented, the Eolian Harp, he had left on his table unfinished, the concluding line being wanting, for which, not having pleased himself, he had left a blank; it was filled up by a young man of very limited talents and not a spark of poetical genius, who was the pupil of his intimate friend Murdoch, described in that poem as the 'little oily man of God,' young Forbes of Culloden, son of the illustrious President Duncan Forbes, who happened to come into the room in the absence of Thomson and filled up the blank with a most happy line."

    9 Cf. *L'Allegro*, 134; *PL* V.297.

xlii   A reminiscence of the Arabian Nights. Cf. also I.xlv.8 below.

    4 *of Ladies store.* Cf. *FQ* V.iii.2.8; *L'Allegro*, 121.

    6 "The *Arabian Caliphs* had Poets among the Officers of their Court, whose Office it was to do what is here mentioned."— Thomson's note.

    8 *Composing:* soothing.

xliii   Introduction, p. 32. Cf. John Armstrong, *The Art of Preserving Health* (1744), I.288-95:

"O! when the growling winds contend, and all
The sounding forest fluctuates in the storm,
To sink in warm repose, and hear the din
Howl o'er the steady battlements, delights
Above the luxury of vulgar sleep.
The murmuring rivulet, and the hoarser strain

Of waters rushing o'er the slippery rocks,
Will nightly lull you to ambrosial rest."
It is possible that Armstrong had seen the manuscript of
Thomson's Canto I, in whole or in part, and that he is
following Thomson here.

xliv	6	*Titian.* See note on I.xxxviii above.
xlv-xlviii		Introduction, pp. 32-33.
xlvi	1	*Sooth:* HT.
xlvii	5	*Rome.* The rime with such words as "bloom" and "gloom" occurs occasionally through the eighteenth century, indicating a survival of the old pronunciation.
xlviii	7-8	*warbling Maze / Of the wild Brooks.* Cf. *PL* III.30-31: "the flow'ry Brooks beneath / That . . . warbling flow."
xlix	1	Introduction, p. 46.
xlix	5	*Idly-busy.* Cf. Goldsmith, *The Traveller,* 256, of the French people: "Thus idly busy rolls their world away."
l	2	*Muckworm.* Cf. Pope, "To Mr. John Moore," 23: "Misers are Muckworms." In Matthew Draper's comedy *The Spend-Thrift* (1731) a character named Muckworm is described as a citizen "of a covetous, griping Disposition, not scrupling to grow rich at any Rate." I owe this reference to Mr. J. Stuart Wilson.
	5	*Gallow-Tree.* Cf. *FQ* V.iv.Argument.
	7	Sir Andrew Freeport's favorite maxim, *Spectator,* No. 2.
li	1-4	For the insect metaphor, cf. *Winter,* 644-45: "While, a gay Insect in *his* Summer-shine, / The Fop, light-fluttering, spreads his mealy Wings." Cf. also Pope, "To Mr. John Moore," 17-18: "The Fops are painted Butterflies, / That fllutter for a Day."
	6-7	Perhaps suggested by the first two plates of Hogarth's *Rake's Progress.*
	8	*Ghost from Limbo-Lake.* Cf. *FQ* I.ii.32.5: "What Voice of damned Ghost from *Limbo* Lake."
lii	4	*Thespian Rage.* A frenzy of inspiration such as might seize a writer of tragedy.
liii	5	Introduction, p. 43. For the thundering knock of the servants of the great, cf. Jean Marishall, *History of Alicia Montague* (1767), I, 342, when the heroine is selling laces from door to door: "She should have given a single knock," but instead "gave a rat-tat as loud as would have been given by the footman of a lady of quality." Cf. also *Tatler,* No. 105; *Tom Jones,* XIII,4; Cowper, *The Task,* IV.145-47.
liv	5	The meaning seems to be that the eyes of the political busy-body are half closed in intense speculation, somewhat as in *The Rape of the Lock,* III.117-18: "Coffee, which makes the Politician wise, / And see thro' all things with his half-shut Eyes."
liv	6	*Lucifer.* "The Morning-star."—Thomson's note.
lvi		Introduction, p. 46.
lvii-lix		Introduction, p. 47. Thomson's letter of April 1748, quoted in the Introduction, p. 6, makes it virtually certain that these lines refer to William Paterson, a fellow-student of Thomson at Edinburgh, later a friend and literary associate of the poet in London. Paterson is said to have been Thomson's amanuensis for a time. His opposition play *Arminius* was prohibited by the Lord Chamberlain in 1740 as Thom-

son's *Edward and Eleonora* had been in 1739. He became
Thomson's deputy or joint patentee as Surveyor General of
the Leeward Islands. For additional details see *LD*, pp. 198-99,
Grant, under Paterson, and also Lewis M. Wiggin, *The
Faction of Cousins* (New Haven, 1958), p. 135. In spite of the
evidence for Paterson, scholars have been tempted to take
these fine stanzas as a portrait of the poet William Collins,
also a friend of Thomson's in the middle 1740's and for a
time a resident of Richmond. The suggestion goes back at
least as far as Moy Thomas' Memoir in the Aldine edition
of Collins (1858), pp. xxiii-xxiv, and Professor Garrod has
been disposed to entertain it (*Collins* [Oxford, 1928], p. 106).
This is an attractive but groundless theory. Though we know
little of Paterson's personality, he inspired the finest letter
of Thomson's that has come down to us; and we may conclude that Thomson here gives a playfully idealized portrait
of his friend. It may be added that W. J. Courthope, in a
purely speculative way, has taken this passage as an idealized
portrait of Thomson himself (*History of English Poetry*
[1911], V, 310-11).

lvii 2 *special grave Remark. OED* cites this line under *remark*,
sense 2b: "air of observation, look," but the meaning also
involves sense 1, "the fact or quality of being worthy of
notice or comment." The phrase may be expanded thus:
"specially worthy of notice because of his grave and penetrating air."

5 *soot:* H: "Soote, sweet, or sweetly." See textual note.

7 *ybury'd stark.* Here *stark* combines the adverbial meaning,
"utterly, absolutely," with the meaning "stiff in death."

9 *boon Nature.* Cf. *PL* IV.241-43:
"Flow'rs worthy of Paradise which not nice Art
In Beds and curious Knots, but Nature boon
Pour'd forth profuse on Hill and Dale and Plain."
John Philips, *Cyder* (1708), II.442-43: "Boon Nature, that
thus annually supplies / Their vaults." *Liberty*, II.98: "All
that boon Nature could luxuriant pour." Collins, "The
Manners," 71: "O Nature boon." Cf. also II.xii.5 below.

lviii 1 *incontinent:* precipitately, with an eagerness that admitted
no delay. Probably after Spenser.

3 *Dan Sol.* Cf. I.xxvii.7 above.
to slope his Wheels. Cf. *Lycidas*, 30-31: "Oft till the Star that
rose at Ev'ning bright / Toward Heav'n's descent had slop'd
his westering wheel."

7 *Welkin's Bound.* H: "Welkin, Sky." Cf. *PL* II.236: "Heav'n's
Bound."

lix 9 *Tract.* See textual note. This line is verbally close to *Timon
of Athens,* I.i.49-50: "But flies an eagle flight, bold and forth
on / Leaving no tract behind." Cf. *Newton*, 45; *Britannia*,
225; *Autumn* (1730-38), 394: "For Sport alone takes up the
cruel Tract."

lx This stanza describes Dr. John Armstrong, author of *The
Art of Preserving Health*, who provided the conclusion of
this canto, and whose "spleen" was almost proverbial among
his associates. Cf. Thomson to Paterson, April 1748; *LD*, p.
198: "Tho the Doctor increases in his Business, he does not
decrease in Spleen; but there is a certain Kind of Spleen

that is both humane and agreeable, like Jacque's in the Play." The central part of this stanza is evidently colored by Shakespeare's account of the misanthropic woodland musings of Jaques. See further Lewis M. Knapp, "John Armstrong, Littérateur," *PMLA*, LIX (1944), 1019-58; *LD*, p. 173.

lxi   No original for the slovenly recluse here described has been found among Thomson's friends. The Aldine edition refers to the account of Henry Welby given in Granger's *Biographical History of England* (5th ed.; 1842), III, 103. Welby, after his brother had made an attempt on his life, shut himself up in his rooms. "In these he kept himself so closely retired, that for forty-four years he was never seen by any human creature, except an old maid that attended him, who had only been permitted to see him in some cases of great necessity." Details of his spare diet follow, with an account of his solitary studies and devotions. He died in 1636. The description of Welby's retirement is a close enough parallel to be striking, but it is hard to see how this eccentric solitary of a century before got into Thomson's Castle.

3 *loathly Toad.* Cf. *FQ* I.i.20.7; II.xi.12.5.

5 *practis'd:* devised, placed by special arrangement.

lxii-lxiv   The *joyous Youth* was John Forbes, son of Duncan Forbes of Culloden. He took the grand tour with his tutor Patrick Murdoch, served in the army, and was evidently a great favorite with Thomson and his circle. See *LD*, 108-09, and note to xli.4 above.

lxii 2 *took:* charmed.

lxiv 1 *a burnish'd Fly.* In William Robertson's reminiscences of Thomson, reported by Thomas Park and printed in William Goodhugh, *The English Gentleman's Library Manual* (1827), p. 280, is the following remark about the young poet James Hammond: "Hammond was a gentleman and a very pleasant man. Yet Thomson, I remember one day called him a burnished butterfly." For the insect figure, cf. li.1-4 above.

9 *mazy Round.* Cf. *Essay on Man*, II.25: "Or tread the mazy round his follow'rs trod."

lxv-lxvi   George Lord Lyttelton, Thomson's friend and chief patron during the 1740's. As secretary to the Prince of Wales, Lyttelton secured political patronage for the poet; in and after 1743 Thomson paid summer visits to Lyttelton's estate, Hagley Park, Worcestershire (cf. lxvi.9). For further details see Rose Mary Davis, *The Good Lord Lyttelton* (Bethlehem, Pa., 1939), *LD*, Grant. Despite this personal intimacy, it will be noticed that Thomson is respectful and eulogistic in these stanzas, without the touch of facetiousness that we find in the stanzas on Forbes and Murdoch. For the theme of Lyttelton's retirement at Hagley, cf. Shenstone's *Judgment of Hercules* (1741):

"While blooming spring descends from genial skies,
By whose mild influence instant wonders rise;
From whose soft breath Elysian beauties flow;
The sweets of HAGLEY, or the pride of STOWE;
Will LYTTELTON the rural landskip range,
Leave noisy fame, and not regret the change?"

lxvi 5 *ill apaid:* ill repaid. Always with the sense *displeased* in Spenser.

194

lxvii 1 *the* ESOPUS *of the Age.* Thomson refers to James Quin, using the name of Claudius Aesopus, the principal Roman tragic actor of the first century B.C. For the friendship of Thomson and Quin see *LD*, pp. 200-01. Smollett echoes this line ironically in the passages attacking Quin in *Peregrine Pickle* (H. S. Buck, *A Study in Smollett* [New Haven, 1925], pp. 105-06).

2-4 Cf. Thomson to Paterson, April 1748, *LD*, pp. 196-97: "Coriolanus has not yet appeared upon the Stage, from the little dirty Jealousy of Tullus—I mean of him who was desired to act Tullus, towards him who alone can act Coriolanus. Indeed, the First has intirely jockyed the Last off the Stage for this Season; but, I believe, he will return on him next Season, like a Gyant in his Wrath." "The First" is Garrick; "the Last" is Quin. What Thomson means by "jockyed off the Stage" seems to be simply that Garrick has prevented Quin from playing Coriolanus, not that he has kept Quin off the stage altogether during the season 1747-48. In the month when Thomson wrote this letter Quin was playing Cato and Falstaff at Covent Garden (*General Advertiser*, April 14, April 18). Thomson applies to the transactions concerning *Coriolanus* the lines he has written for *The Castle of Indolence.* But the lines themselves have a somewhat different reference; they seem to say that after a period of retirement Quin has returned to the stage with redoubled energy. Quin did not act at all during the seasons 1743-44 and 1745-46 (cf. Aline Mackenzie Taylor, "The Patrimony of James Quin," *Tulane Studies in English*, VIII [1958], 104). The present lines probably refer to his return to the stage after one or both of these periods.

lxviii Reprinted in *Gentleman's Magazine*, XVIII (September, 1748), 423, with the caption, "Character of Mr. THOMPSON."

2-9 "The following Lines of this Stanza were writ by a Friend of the Author."—Thomson's note. The implication is that Thomson himself wrote the first line. Elton attributes this line to Armstrong, apparently without authority (*Survey of English Literature 1730-1780* [1928], I, 364). Lyttelton was the friend who wrote lines 2-9, according to a note in Fawkes and Woty, *Poetical Calendar*, XII (1763), 106. These lines were erroneously attributed to Murdoch by the *DNB*, under "Murdoch," and to Armstrong by Courthope (*History of English Poetry* [1911], V, 311).

Thomson's death on August 27, 1748, was so close in time to the publication of *The Castle of Indolence* that an obituary notice, written no doubt by a friend, perhaps Lyttelton or Andrew Mitchell, may be quoted as a companion-piece to this stanza:

"Saturday morning at Four o'Clock died of a violent Fever at his House in Kew-Lane, the celebrated Mr. James Thomson, Author of the Seasons, &c. an honest Man, who has not left one Enemy behind him. His Abilities as a Writer, his Works sufficiently witness to all the World; but the Goodness of his Heart, which overflowed with Benevolence, Humanity, universal Charity, and every amiable Virtue, was best known to those who had the Happiness of his Acquaintance, by every one of whom he was most tenderly beloved, and now most sincerely and most deservedly lamented."

(*General Advertiser*, Monday, August 29,
1748. Reprinted in *Jacobite's Journal*,
September 3, from *Whitehall Evening-Post*.)

4   *his unpremeditated Strain.* Cf. *PL* IX.24: "my unpremeditated Verse."

lxix   Patrick Murdoch, a friend of Thomson since their student days at Edinburgh, tutor to the "joyous Youth" John Forbes (cf. lxii-lxiv above), from 1738 vicar of Stradishall, Suffolk, and later Thomson's biographer. In a letter to George Ross, January 12, 1738, *LD*, p. 117, Thomson gives what is virtually a preliminary sketch of this stanza: "Pe[t]ie came here two three Days ago. I have not yet seen the round Man of God, to be. He is to be Parsonifyed, a few Days hence. How a Gown and Cassock will become him! And with what a bold Leer he will edify the devout Females! There is no Doubt of his having a Call; for he is immediately to enter upon a tolerable Living—God grant him more, and as fat as himself." Thomson's lines "To the Incomparable Soporifick Doctor" are usually taken to refer to Murdoch. This piece (Ralph's Miscellany, 1729) satirizes in the manner of *The Dunciad* a dull and corpulent preacher. But Murdoch, as appears above, was not in the pulpit until 1738, when Thomson addressed to him some lines praising tranquillity and philosophic ease, first published in *Poems on Several Occasions* (1750), dated 1738 in *Works* (1762).

3   This line, which perpetuates a nickname for Murdoch, became almost proverbial. See *LD*, p. 118. Cf. also Thomas Love Peacock, *Maid Marian,* chap. 1: "a little round oily friar." The line echoed more remotely in Burns' memory when he wrote ("Sketch," Oxford edition [1910], p. 276): "A little upright, pert, tart, tripping wight." Burns remembered at the same time II.xxxiii.1 below.

lxx   4   Cf. *PL* I.601-03: "care / Sat on his faded cheek, but under Brows / Of dauntless Courage."

6   *Hall of Smoak.* The italics probably indicate a specific reference to a gathering place in Richmond.

7   *the sage Berry:* the coffee bean. Cf. *Rape of the Lock*, III.106: "The Berries crackle, and the Mill turns round."

8   *inward Eye.* Cf. I.liv.5 above, and note. The phrase appears in a very different context in the lines contributed by Mrs. Wordsworth to "I Wandered Lonely as a Cloud": "They flash upon that inward eye / Which is the bliss of solitude."
smoak-enroll'd. Cf. *FQ* I.xi.44.4: "Enroll'd in duskish Smoak."

lxxi-lxxii   Introduction, p. 48. With this passage is to be associated a stanza said by Sir Harris Nicolas to have appeared in an edition with the impossible date "1746" and supposed to describe Lady Lyttelton (here reprinted from Aldine edition, 1866):

> "One nymph there was, methought, in bloom of May,
> On whom the idle fiend glanced many a look,
> In hopes to lead her down the slippery way
> To taste of pleasure's deep deceitful brook:
> No virtues yet her gentle mind forsook;
> No idle whims, no vapours filled her brain,

But prudence for her youthful guide she took,
And goodness, which no earthly vice could stain,
Dwelt in her mind; she was ne proud I ween or vain."
It is possible that this stanza is genuine, and was intended
as a companion-piece to the compliment to Lyttelton. Lady
Lyttelton's death in January 1747 may have prevented pub-
lication.

Inserted in a copy of the second edition in the Wells
Collection, Swarthmore College Library, is "An additional
Stanza to the Castle of Indolence after Stanz. 72, Cant.
1" dated 1758 and signed with an illegible monogram:
"Here too a gentle Lass was sometimes seen,
Fair as the Hawthorn-Flow'r in bloom of May;
Who, tho' sage *Pallas* was her rightful Queen,
Yet oft at *Idless'* shrine would homage pay,
And loit'ring wast the livelong Hour away.
Her books & pen the while were thrown aside,
And rich Instruction all suspended lay.
Nathless, so meek and patient was her guide,
In vain he strove to frown & c.ᵈ as little chide."

lxxii   5   *with tottering Step and slow. PL* XII.648: "with wand'ring
steps and slow."

7   *Strait.* Cf. I.xxii.2 above.

9   *the vapoury God:* the god of vapours or spleen. See I.lxxv-
lxxvii below, and note.

lxxiii   Introduction, p. 48.

2   *eftsoons.* Cf. xxix.3 above.

9   *Fierce Fiends, and Hags of Hell.* Cf. *FQ* II.ix.50.8.

lxxiv-lxxvii   These stanzas were contributed by Dr. John Armstrong (see
lx above). Armstrong's stanzas, presumably in the form in
which he submitted them to Thomson, are printed in his
Miscellanies (2 vols.; 1770), I, 164, with the title, "An Imitation of Spencer. Written at Mr. Thomson's desire, to be
inserted into the Castle of Indolence." See textual notes. The
immediate model for the passage was the catalogue of
diseases in the vision shown by Michael to Adam, *PL* XI.477
ff. William Thompson's *Sickness* (1745), I. 359 ff. also has a
catalogue imitated, as he says, from
                 "the execrable crew
Which Michael, in vision strange, disclos'd
To Adam, in the *Lazar-house of woe*;
A colony from hell."
Armstrong connects with Thomson's account of Indolence
the diseases associated with an inactive life, particularly the
complex of diseases described, in Dr. George Cheyne's words,
as "the Spleen, Vapours, Lowness of Spirits, Hysterical, or
Hypochondriacal Disorders" (*The English Malady: or, A
Treatise of Nervous Diseases of All Kinds* [fifth ed., 1735], pp.
192 ff.). As Swift remarks, spleen "only seizeth on the *lazy,*
the *luxurious,* and the *rich*" (*Gulliver's Travels,* IV.vii).
There was much medical literature on the subject. (For a
survey, see Lawrence Babb, "The Cave of Spleen," *RES*, XII
[1936], 165-76; C. A. Moore, "The English Malady," in *Backgrounds of English Literature,* pp. 179-235.)

The "moping Mystery" of Armstrong's lines, clad in
variegated robes, called by some the "hypochondriack fit,"

and running in imagination the gamut of all the diseases, represents the infinite variety of symptoms covered by such terms as "the spleen" and "the vapours." This "Lady proud," called Hypochondria in the final text, with a "listless Maiden by her side," also presents the idea, familiar from *The Rape of the Lock,* that the disease is particularly incident to women. The "Robes of various Dye" suggest the figure of Fancy in Addison's *Spectator* No. 558, who "was cloathed in a loose flowing Robe, embroidered with several Figures of Fiends and Spectres, that discovered themselves in a thousand chimerical Shapes, as her Garment hovered in the Wind. There was something wild and distracted in her Looks." Among the human ills cast down before Addison's Fancy is a packet called "the Spleen," which "was a Complication of all the Diseases incident to Human Nature, and was in the Hand of a great many fine People." The idea was greatly elaborated by medical writers such as Cheyne: "In general, when the Symptoms are *many, various, changeable,* shifting from one Place to another, and imitating the *Symptoms* of almost every other Distemper described, if they are attended with no other apparent, real, determined original Distemper, . . . then they may be properly call'd *Vapours*" (pp. 195-96). Reserving this term for the first stage, Cheyne goes on to describe the second stage of the disease as marked by acute emotional disturbances, "sometimes unaccountable Fits of *Laughing,* apparent *Joy, Leaping* and *Dancing*; at other times, of *Crying, Grief,* and *Anguish*; and these generally terminate in *Hypochondriacal* or *Hysterical Fits*" (p. 199). The third stage, if no cure is effected, "is generally some *mortal* and incurable Distemper, such as *Dropsy, Black Jaundice, Consumption, Palsy, Epilepsy,* or *Apoplexy,* &c." (p. 200). Since Armstrong names hydropsy and apoplexy, along with the tertian fever and gout, some such prognosis as this may have helped him to his catalogue.

Boswell, in No. 5 of the series of essays which he contributed to the *London Magazine* under the pseudonym of "The Hypochondriack," quotes the last four lines of lxxv and the whole of lxxvi (*Boswell's Column,* ed. Margery Bailey [1951], pp. 45-46). Unaware of Armstrong's authorship, he compares this passage with the lines on melancholy in Armstrong's *Art of Preserving Health,* IV.

lxxiv   4   *Lubbard:* Variant form of *lubber.* The association of this word with "Lethargy" and a catalogue of diseases suggests that Armstrong may have in mind here and throughout these stanzas Allan Ramsay's poem entitled "Health," especially his description of "Lethargus," which ends:

"Thus does the sluggard health and vigour waste,
With heavy indolence, till at the last,
Sciatic, jaundice, dropsy, or the stone,
Alternate makes the lazy lubbard groan."
(*Poems* [1800], I,96)

lxxv   7   *in Robes of various Dye.* Cf. Collins' description of Humour, "The Manners," 48: "in Robe of wild contending Hues."

lxxvi   7-9   Lady Winchilsea dwells on the varying moods of the victims of this disease in "The Spleen," 44-52:

"In ev'ry One thou dost possess,
New are thy Motions, and thy Dress:
Now in some Grove a list'ning Friend
Thy false Suggestions must attend,
Thy whisper'd Griefs, thy fancy'd Sorrows hear,
Breath'd in a Sigh, and witness'd by a Tear;
  Whilst in the light, and vulgar Croud,
  Thy Slaves, more clamorous and loud,
By Laughters unprovok'd, thy Influence too confess."
Cf. Beattie, *The Minstrel*, I.141-42: "And now his look was
most demurely sad, / And now he laugh'd aloud, yet none
knew why."

lxxvii 7-9 Cf. *FQ* VI.xii.30.7-8.

CANTO II

i   Introduction, pp. 48-49.

ii   2   *Parnassus' barren Soil*. Locke, *Some Thoughts Concerning
Education* (1693), p. 207, says of Parnassus: " 'Tis a pleasant
Air, but a barren Soil." Cf. also *LD*, p. 95.

   4   *swink:* HT. The phrase *swink and moil* is modeled on
Spenser's *swinke and sweate*. Cf. *SC,* November, 154; *FQ*
II.vii.8.7.

iii   Introduction, p. 49. Cf. Burns, "Epistle to Davie":
"What tho' like commoners of air,
We wander out, we know not where,
  But either house or hal',
Yet nature's charms, the hills and woods,
The sweeping vales, and foaming floods,
  Are free alike to all."

—Ritter.

   6   *living Stream*. Cf. *PL* V.651-52: "their Camp extend / By
living Streams."

   8   *great Children*. Perhaps italicized as an adaptation of Dryden's line, *All for Love:* "Men are but children of a larger
Growth." Cf. Thomson to Mrs. Robertson, November 27,
1742, *LD*, p. 139: "What a round of silly amusements, what
a giddy circle of *nothing* do these children of a larger size
run every day!"

iv   2   *lig:* T.

   3   For the effect of the repeated *l*'s, cf. *Essay on Criticism*, 357.

   6   *Imp of Fame*. Cf. I.xxxii.2 above.

v-vii   Introduction, p. 50.

v   4-5   Cf. I.x.6-7 above, and note.

   9   Cf. *FQ* VII.vii.29.8: "Had hunted late the Libbard or the
Boar."

vi   2   *Prick'd:* HT.
      Lawn: OED: "an open space between woods; a glade."

   5   *Fray:* assault, attack.

   7   *Needments:* HT. *FQ* I.i.6.4; I.vi.35.9; *Colin Clout*, 195.

   9   *compress'd*. For this sense, cf. Dryden, *Hind and Panther*,
352; *Aeneid*, XII.214.

vii   3   *Lustyhed:* H: "Lustiness, Vigour."

   9   *Winter breme:* H: "Breem or breme, fierce, fiercely."
SC, February, 43; December, 148.

viii   1   *youthly*. Several times in Spenser in such phrases as "prime
of youthly Years," *FQ* I.ii.35.1.

7   *Wonne:* HT.

4-9   Thomson has in mind the games of the classical epic, with a general reminiscence of *PL* II.528 ff. The entire passage is close to John Dyer's account of Roman sports on the Campus Martius (*The Ruins of Rome* [1740], p. 15):

> "There to their daily Sports the noble Youth
> Rush'd emulous; to fling the pointed Lance;
> To vault the Steed; or with the kindling Wheel
> In dusty whirlwinds sweep the trembling Goal;
> Or wrestling, cope with adverse swelling Breasts,
> Strong grappling Arms, clos'd Heads, and distant Feet."

7-8   The reference is to Roman chariot-racing. The driver tries to round the goal *(meta)* without slackening speed. Cf. Horace, *Odes,* I.i.3-5; *FQ* III.vii.41; *PL* II.531-32; Dyer, *The Ruins of Rome,* as quoted in the preceding note.

9   *Compeer.* Cf. *Newton,* 189.

xi   2   *th' Etherial Round:* the vault of heaven, and also the region of the air. See note to 4,5-7 below.

4   *Reigns.* The traditional division of nature into the animal, vegetable, and mineral kingdoms. Cf. *Winter,* 1026-27: "How dead the Vegetable Kingdom lies! / How dumb the tuneful!" See following note.

5-7   *Domains* is used (line 5) for the political divisions of the earth, and also (line 7) with reference to the traditional division of nature into the four elements, earth, fire, air, and water. See Arthos, under *Empire, Kingdom, Region, Reign.*

9   *moral Seeds.* An extension of the ancient conception of elements or atoms as seeds. See Arthos, under *Seed.* Cf. *Autumn,* 50-54, on the state of primitive man:

> "With various Seeds of Art deep in the Mind
> Implanted, and profusely pour'd around
> Materials infinite: but idle all.
> Still unexerted, in th' unconscious Breast,
> Slept the lethargic Powers."

Cf. also *Liberty,* III.539-40, on the northern peoples who overran the Roman Empire: "Long in the barbarous Heart the bury'd Seeds / Of *Freedom* lay, for many a wintry Age"; *Tancred and Sigismunda,*I,i: "In Love included all the finer Seeds / Of Honour, Virtue, Friendship, purest Bliss."

xii   1-2   Cf. Pope, *Epistle to Arbuthnot,* 340-41.

5   *boon Earth.* Cf. I.lvii.9 above, and note.

7   *Draught.* The rime with *taught,* etc., was regular, according to the "Dictionary of Rhymes" in Bysshe's *Art of English Poetry.*

xiii   3-4   Introduction, p. 30.

5   *Pygmalion's Wife.* Pygmalion the sculptor fell in love with his own creation, the statue of a woman. Brought to life by Aphrodite, the woman became his wife. Ovid, *Metamorphoses,* X.243 ff.

xiv   1   *issu'd.* Here, as in xxxv.1 below, accented on the second syllable.

2   *bold Emprize.* H: "Emprise, Enterprise, Undertaking, (Fr.)." *FQ* II.iii.35.4; IV.iv.36.1; VII.vi.22.9. Cf. *Comus,* 610: "I love thy courage yet, and bold Emprise."

xv   8   *rascal Rout. Rascal* is almost a fixed epithet in Spenser with such words as *rout, flock, crew, rabblement,* etc. Cf. xli.2 below.

xvi-xvii   Introduction, p. 50.

xvi   1-3   For the westward progress of culture, associated with the course of the sun, cf. *Liberty,* II.41-42: "West with the living Day to GREECE I came: / Earth smil'd beneath my Beam"; *Liberty,* III.4: "To what new Region stream'd the *Human Day?*"

xvii   6   *bouncing:* bounding.

      9   Thomson derived from the historian Rapin de Thoyras the idea that the Britons were never actually conquered by Rome. Cf. *Liberty,* IV.640-41: "Witness, *Rome,* / Who saw'st thy *Cesar,* from the naked Land, / Whose only Fort was *British Hearts,* repell'd."

xix   Introduction, p. 50.

xxi   With the familiar theme of the fall of Constantinople in 1453 as the beginning of the Revival of Learning, Thomson combines the progress of liberty and the arts from Greece to Britain. Cf. *Liberty* throughout, and "Rule, Britannia": "The Muses, still with freedom found, / Shall to thy happy coast repair."

      2   "Constantinople."—Thomson's note.

      5   *another Castalie.* Another kingdom of the Muses, so named from the Castalian spring on the slopes of Parnassus at Delphi. Cf. Spenser, *Tears of the Muses,* 57: "And thou our sire, that reignst in *Castalie.*"

    7-9   Cf. *Lycidas,* especially 24, 103, 189.

xxiv   9   *vacant.* Cf. I.iv.4 above.

xxv   1   *Deva's Vale:* the valley of the river Dee. Except for the reference in *Lycidas,* 55, there seems to be no special reason for the use of this name here.

      6   *sided: OED side,* sense lc: "to walk or stand by the side of."

xxvi   9   *vild:* HT.

xxvii   Introduction, p. 51.

      2   *amusing.* Cf. I.xviii.7 above.

xxviii   Introduction, p. 30.

    1-4   For Thomson's view of gardening as "dressing" or "improving" Nature, see his conversation with Shenstone, *LD,* pp. 185-86.

      5   *immingled.* Cf. *Summer,* 551: "Where Purity and Peace immingle Charms." Johnson's *Dictionary* quotes only Thomson for this word.

      6   *Pales:* the Roman goddess of sheepfolds and pastures.

      7   *fand:* provided, offered.

xxix   8   *overlaid.* Cf. *SC,* July, 151: "And with leud Lust was overlaid."

xxx   5-6   "Vice leads the van, bearing the standard; Corruption commands the rear."—Robertson. *Arrier-ban* originally meant "summons to military service," but Thomson probably took it to be equivalent to "arrear-band," or "rear band."

xxxi   8   *Eld:* H: "Old Age, (Sax.)."

xxxii   2   *Archimage. Archimago* or *Archimage* is the name of the enchanter in *FQ,* but Thomson's gloss leaves it uncertain whether he takes it to be a proper name or not. Among the

Spenserian imitators before Thomson—Croxall, West, Cambridge, and Upton—it had come to be used as a common noun. See *OED*. The word is not printed in italics or small capitals in Thomson's text, as it would almost certainly be if used as a proper name.

4 *Benempt:* called, bearing the name. Spenser has *nempt* in this sense once, *FQ* III.x.29.5; he uses *benempt* in the sense of "mentioned by name" in *SC,* July, 214; November, 46.

6 Thomson connects the net with the weaving of the Fates in Greek mythology.

8 *Replevy:* H: "To redeem a pledge." More accurately here, "bail given for a person." Cf. *FQ* IV.xii.31.8: "It to replevy, and my Son reprieve."

xxxiii   Joseph Warton, *Essay on the Genius and Writings of Pope* (5th ed., 1806), II, 325-26, says this stanza refers to Pope.

1 *Druid-Wight.* For the poet as druid, see J. M. S. Tompkins, "In Yonder Grave a Druid lies," *RES,* XXII (1946), 1-16, especially 10-11. Cf. *"British* Harp," xlvi.3 below.

3 *bedight:* H: "dress'd, adorn'd."

xxxiv   4 PHILOMELUS: "Lover of Music." Thought of as a masculine form of Philomela, the nightingale. Cf. "his Sister of the Copses green,'" xxxiii.4 above.

xxxv   1 *Issuing.* Cf. II.xiv.1 above.

3-4 *the generous Breed,* etc. Probably a reference to the Aurora of Guido Reni. Cf. Hagstrum, *The Sister Arts,* p. 260.

6 *milk-white Palfrey. FQ* III.i.15.2.

9 *yfere they yode:* HT. Apparently Spenser does not use these archaisms together.

xxxvi   4 *refel:* refute. Common in this sense in the eighteenth century.

xxxvii   Introduction, p. 18.

3 *Palmers:* originally "pilgrims who had been to the Holy Land," but often, as here, "travelers."

5 *Wonne.* Cf. II.viii.7 above.

8 *tufted Groves.* Cf. *Comus,* 225: "And casts a Gleam over this tufted Grove."

xxxix   Introduction, p. 52.

1 *sicker:* T.

3 Cf. *Measure for Measure,* III.i: "But how out of this can she avail?"

6 *Glaive:* T.

xl   2 *cursed Carle:* H: "Carl, a Clown. (Sax.)." *FQ* IV.vii.18.4: "this accursed Carle."

9 *wily Fox.* Spenser's spider Aragnoll in *Muiopotmos,* 401, is compared to a "wily Fox." Cf. I.vii.7 above, and note.

xli   2 *Rabble-Rout.* Cf. II.xv.8 above, and note.

7 *magic Dust.* Cf. *Comus,* 164-65: "When once her eye / Hath met the virtue of this Magic dust." *Tancred and Sigismunda,* I.iv, quoted in Introduction, p. 24.

xlii   3 *transmew'd to Stone.* Cf. *FQ* I.vii.35.6: "Men into Stones there-with he could transmew."

9 *back'ning.* The first example under *backen* given in *OED.* Cf. Aaron Hill, "The Happy Man" (*Works* [1753], III, 163): "High, o'er the winding of a cliffy shore, / From whose *worn* steep, the *back'ning* surges roar."

xliii   2   *Retiarius:* "A Gladiator, who made use of a Net, which he threw over his Adversary."—Thomson's note.

         7   *flounced:* floundered, struggled. Cf. Thomson, "A Paraphrase of Psalm civ," 93: "Monsters that flounce upon the boiling tide"; *Winter,* 285, of the traveler caught in a snowstorm: "Impatient flouncing thro' the drifted Heaps."

         9   *felly:* in a malignant way. With the whole line, cf. *FQ* IV.viii.23.8: "Gnawing her Nails for Felness, and for Ire." With the rejected stanza given in the textual note, cf. John Gay, *The Beggar's Opera,* II, ix, Air xxvii:

> "Thus when a good huswife sees a Rat
> In her trap in the morning taken,
> With pleasure her heart goes pit a pat,
> In revenge for her loss of bacon.
> Then she throws him
> To the Dog or Cat,
> To be worried, crush'd and shaken."

xliv   3   *deform'd.* Cf. *Spring,* 19-21: "Winter . . . bids his driving Sleets / Deform the Day delightless"; *Britannia,* 76.

xlv   3   *Rabblement.* Cf. II.xli.2 above, and note.

      5   *Shoal.* Cf. *SC,* May, 20: "a Shole of Shepherds."

xlvi   2   *in seemly Sort.* Cf. Spenser, *Mother Hubberd's Tale,* 662; *Tears of the Muses,* 198; *FQ* IV.xii.18.7.

      3   *British Harp.* Cf. II.xxxiii.1 above, and note.

      4   *deffly:* H: "finely or nimbly." Cf. *SC,* April, 111. Erroneously changed to *deftly* by many later editors.

      9   *ten Thousands.* Cf. *FQ* II.xii.25.1: "All these, and thousand thousands many more."

xlvii-xlviii   Introduction, p. 52.

xlviii   8   *fondly:* foolishly.

xlix   3   *active Ether:* a vital force pervading the atmosphere. Cf. *vital Sky,* I.lxiv.3 above. See Maynard Mack's note on Pope, *Essay on Man,* III.115-18, Twickenham edition.

l   A brief restatement of themes treated in *Liberty,* II-III.

      4   *keen.* Rare as a verb. Cf. *Summer,* 1259: "when cold Winter keens the brightening Flood."

      7   *her conquering Dart.* Cf. *PL* XI.491-92: "And over them triumphant Death his Dart / Shook."

lii   4   *Mincian Reeds.* Cf. *Lycidas,* 86. The Mincius is a river near the birthplace of Virgil, in the vicinity of Mantua. Pastoral poetry traditionally associates a poet with a river near his birthplace or residence. Cf. Thomson's references to the Tweed and the Jed in *Autumn,* 889-91, and line 9 below.

      9   *Mulla's Plains. Mulla* is Spenser's poetical name for the Awbeg, a river near his home at Kilcolman, Ireland. Cf. Shenstone, *The School-Mistress,* 165: "the bard by *Mulla's* silver stream."

liii   3-4   Cf. *Winter* (1730-38), 595-97: "that Ray / Of purest Heaven, which lights the glorious Flame / Of Patriots, and of Heroes."

liv   7   *absorpt: absorptus,* past participle of *absorbeo.*

lv   4   *houghs:* hoes.

lvi   9   *Losel.* Cf. I.xxiii.7 above.

lvii   6   *slugs.* Cf. *FQ* II.i.23.3: "to slug in Sloth"; III.vii.12.8: "But all the Day before the sunny Rays / He us'd to slug, or sleep in slothful Shade."

lviii	6	*Younglings:* young animals, as in *SC.*
	9	*Plesaunce.* Cf. I.xxvii.7 above.
lxii	3-4	Proverbs xxii: 13; xxvi:13.
lxiii		Introduction, p. 52.
lxv	5	*agen.* Not a Spenserian form, but a common poetic spelling of *again.*
lxvi	6	*Sabbath of our Time.* Cf. Pope, *First Epistle of the First Book of Horace,* 3: "the Sabbath of my days."
	7	*emove.* Cf. I.x.5 above.
lxvii-lxviii		Introduction, p. 54.
lxix		Introduction, p. 55.
	3	*Depeinten.* Cf. I.xxxvii.2 above.
lxx	6	*eternal Chains.* Cf. *PL* I.48.
lxxii	8	Cf. *Lycidas,* 181, and the biblical sources of this line, Isaiah xxv:8; Revelation vii:17, xxi:4.
lxxiii	3	*sears.* Cf. I.xiv.5 above, lxxviii.5 below.
lxxiv		Introduction, p. 55.
lxxv		*dispreds.* Frequent in Spenser.
lxxvi	4	*mossy Cell.* Cf. *Il Penseroso,* 169.
	7	*Delves:* H: "Dell or Delve, Pit, or Hole in the Ground." Cf. *Alfred,* II.i: "O'er many a delve."
lxxvii-lxxix		Introduction, pp. 55-56.
lxxviii	4	*Auster:* the south wind, often associated with cold rain and storms in Virgil, e.g., *Georgics,* I.462: "umidus Auster."
	5	*Caurus.* The cold northwest wind. Cf. *Georgics,* III.356: "semper spirantes frigora Cauri"; *Winter,* 836: "frosty Caurus."
		sear'd. Usually used of the effect of heat, but here with reference to cold. Cf. I.xiv.5, II.lxxiii.3 above.
	9	*moe:* T.
lxxix	4	*hollow Eyne. FQ* I.ix.35.6-7: "his hollow Eyne / Look'd deadly dull."
lxxx	2	*Hell . . . in baleful Bower.* Cf. *SC,* October, 29: "*Pluto's* baleful Bower"; *Gnat,* 313: "the darksome Bowre of *Herebus*"; *FQ* IV.x.58.5: "the *Stygian* Prince's Bow'r."
	3	*keen'd.* Cf. II.l.4 above.
lxxxi		Introduction, p. 56. In this stanza Thomson also has in mind the "Boar and Sow" passage in *The Rehearsal,* I, especially the concluding couplet:
		"Pensive in mind they wallow all alone,
		And snort, and gruntle to each others moan."
		Cf. *LD,* pp. 50, 52.
lxxxi	1	*Brentford Town.* Thomson refers to Brentford under the influence of Pope's catalogue of Thames-side towns in "The Alley," and also because of the reputation of Brentford as an unattractive place. This may well have been a local joke in neighboring towns like Richmond and Kew, but seems to have been fairly widespread. Many years later, when Adam Smith was praising Glasgow, Dr. Johnson asked him abruptly, "Pray, Sir, have you ever seen Brentford?" In annotating this passage Powell cites, besides this stanza in *The Castle of Indolence,* Gay's *Epistle to Lord Burlington*: "Three dusty miles reach Brentford's tedious town; / For dirty streets, and white-legged chickens known"—and Gray to West, April 21, 1741, describing a fair at Reggio: "Does not this sound magnificent? Yet is the city of Reggio but one step above

Old Brentford" (Boswell, ed. Hill-Powell, IV, 186, 513). Thomson may have in mind the appearance of Brentford High Street on a market day. Cf. Fred Turner, *History and Antiquities of Brentford* (Brentford, n.d.), p. 59: "In the time of Charles II, a very extensive trade in cattle, sheep, and pigs, was established in connection with the market."

9 *Fone:* H. Spenser uses this form only in the riming position.

Appendix

The Harp of Aeolus

To I.xl.9 Thomson adds a note: "This is not an Imagination of the Author; there being in fact such an Instrument, called *Aeolus's Harp,* which, when placed against a little Rushing or Current of Air, produces the Effect here described." The post also adds the note "Aeolus's harp" to the following lines in his "Ode to the Winter Solstice" (printed by Ralph M. Williams, *MLN*,LXX[1955], 256-57), no doubt written about 1748:

> Why, gentle Aura, dost thou thus complain,
> And touch my trembling harp with such soft woe.

The note to Thomson's "Ode on Aeolus's Harp," first published in Dodsley's *Collection* (1748,III[second edition],211), is also probably from the poet's hand: "Aeolus's Harp, is a musical Instrument, which plays with the wind, invented by Mr. Oswald; its properties are fully described in the Castle of Indolence." With a footnote likewise referring to the passage in *The Castle,* William Collins in his *Ode on the Death of Mr. Thomson* (June 1749) identifies the harp with Thomson's poetic genius and adapts the passage to the uses of pastoral elegy:

> In yon deep bed of whisp'ring reeds
> His airy harp shall now be laid,
> That he whose heart in sorrow bleeds
> May love thro' life the soothing shade.
>
> Then maids and youths shall linger here;
> And while its sounds at distance swell,
> Shall sadly seem in Pity's ear
> To hear the Woodland Pilgrim's knell.

The note appended to William Mason's "Ode to an Aeolus's Harp," Dodsley's *Collection* (1755),IV,274, gives another brief statement about the history of the instrument: "This instrument appears to have been invented by KIRCHER: who has given a very accurate description of it in his MUSURGIA. After having been neglected above an hundred years, it was again accidentally discovered by Mr. OSWALD." The Jesuit Athanasius Kircher is generally said to have invented the wind-harp about 1650;

the supposed rediscovery by the Scottish musician James Oswald must have come in the late 1740's, not long before Thomson's references to the subject. The only full account of what we may call the Anglo-Scottish rediscovery has been given by Geoffrey Grigson (*The Harp of Aeolus*[1948],pp.24-29). Thomson, a friend of Oswald's, was evidently greatly interested. An advertisement in the *General Advertiser,* October 29, 1751, reads: "By Authority This Day is Published Aeolus's Harp—A new-invented musical instrument, which is played by the wind, as described by Mr. Thomson, in his *Castle of Indolence.* Sold only by the Inventor, J. Oswald, at his music-shop in St. Martin's church-yard" (quoted by Lewis M. Knapp, *Tobias Smollett: Doctor of Men and Manners* [Princeton, 1949], p. 60 n.). The name was apparently not Oswald's invention, though the continuous history of the term dates from this time; Grigson points out that J. J. Hofmann's seventeenth-century *Lexicon Universale* calls the harp "Aeolium instrumentum."

A detailed account of Oswald's supposed discovery was afterwards given by William Jones:

When Mr. Pope was translating Homer, he had frequent occasion to consult the Greek commentary of Eustathius; where he met with a passage, in which it was suggested, that the blowing of the wind against musical strings would produce harmonious sounds. This was communicated to Mr. Oswald, a master of the violoncello from North Britain, and an ingenious composer in the Scotch style, who himself gave me the following account many years ago, when I was under him as a practitioner in music. When he had received the hint of Mr. Pope's discovery in Eustathius, he determined to try whether he could reduce it to practice. Accordingly he took an old lute, and having put strings upon it, he exposed it to the wind in every manner he could think of; but all without effect. When he was about to give the matter up as a mystery or a fable, he received some encouragement to a farther trial from an accident which happened to an harper on the Thames; who having his instrument with him in a house-boat, perceived that a favourable stroke of the wind brought some momentary sounds from the strings, as if they had been suddenly touched after that manner, which, from the genius of the instrument, is called *arpeggio*. The man was charmed with the accident, and made many trials to procure a repetition of the same sounds from a like turn of the wind, but could never succeed: the music was vanished like an apparition. Upon this ground, however, Mr. Oswald persevered; and it came at last into his mind, that perhaps the strings ought to be exposed to a more confined current of air. With this view he drew up the sash of his chamber-window, so as to let in a shallow stream of air, and exposed his lute to it. In the middle of the night the wind rose and the instrument sounded; which being heard by the artist, he sprang out of bed to examine all the circumstances of its situation, and noted down everything with the most scrupulous precision; after which, as the principle was now ascertained, he never failed of the effect.[1]

Mrs. A. M. Bernhard-Smith communicates to me a tradition which has come down in her family that Thomson himself made an Aeolian harp and presented it to a friend.

Another friend of Oswald and Thomson, Tobias Smollett, wrote on this subject a few years later in a strain which may have been influenced by Thomson's verses. Ferdinand Count Fathom uses the instrument in an attempt to seduce the maiden Celinda.

Some years ago, a twelve-stringed instrument was contrived by a very ingenious musician, by whom it was aptly intitled the harp of Aeolus, because, being properly applied to a stream of air, it produced a wild, irregular variety of harmonious sounds, that seem to be the effect of inchantment, and wonderfully dispose the mind for the most romantic situations. Fathom, who was really a virtuoso in musick, had brought one of these new-fashioned guittarres into the country, and as the effect of it was still unknown in the family, he that night converted it to the purposes of his amour, by fixing it in the casement of a window belonging to the gallery, exposed to the west-wind, which then blew in a gentle breeze. The strings no sooner felt the impression of the balmy zephyr, than they began to pour forth a stream of melody more ravishingly delightful than the song of Philomel, the warbling brook, and all the concert of the wood. The soft and tender notes of peace and love were swelled up with the most delicate and insensible transition, into a loud hymn of triumph and exultation, joined by the deep-toned organ, and a full choir of voices, which gradually decayed upon the ear, until it died away, in distant sound, as if a flight of angels had raised the song in their ascent to Heaven. Yet the chords hardly ceased to vibrate after the expiration of this overture, which ushered in a composition in the same pathetic stile; and this again was succeeded by a third, almost without pause or intermission, as if

---

[1] William Jones, *Physiological Disquisitions* (1781), pp. 339-40. I owe this reference to Robert Bloomfield's collection of references to this subject, published as *Nature's Music* (1808) and reprinted in *The Remains of Robert Bloomfield* (3 vols.; 1824), I, 93-143.

the artist's hand had been indefatigable, and the theme never
be exhausted. His heart must be quite callous, and his ear lost
all distinction, who could hear such harmony without emotion.[2]

A passing reference in *Rasselas* may be noted. Among th
"engines of recreation" provided in the Happy Valley are "i1
struments of soft musick, . . . of which some played by the im
pulse of the wind, and some by the power of the stream" (chap
vi).

The comprehensive survey of Georges Kastner, *La Harpe
d'Éole et la musique cosmique* (Paris, 1856), gives a chain of
references from ancient times down to French and German
romanticism. Of the earlier literary references, Thomson would
certainly remember in this connection Spenser's line in *The
Ruines of Time* describing the "stellification" of Orpheus' lyre:

> At length out of the River it was rear'd,
> And borne above the Clouds to be devin'd,
> Whilst all the way most heav'nly Noise was heard
> Of the Strings, stirred with the warbling Wind.
>
> (610-13)

---

[2] *The Adventures of Ferdinand Count Fathom* (2 vols.; 1753), chap. xxxiv,
I, 256-58.

HYMN ON SOLITUDE

After 14, A-D. And nature dances in your eye. The line associates a vision of nature with the movement of perception and imagination. A somewhat similar association of ideas appears in the opening lines of the early version of Dyer's "Grongar Hill," published in Savage's *Miscellany:*

> *"Fancy!* Nymph that loves to lye
> On the lonely Eminence;
> Darting Notice thro' the Eye,
> Forming Thought and feasting Sense:
> Thou! that must lend Imagination Wings,
> And stamp Distinction, on all worldly Things!"

21-22 *B-D Philomela.* The pen-name of Mrs. Elizabeth (Singer) Rowe, regularly used in her literary correspondence with Lady Hertford. See Helen Sard Hughes, *The Gentle Hertford* (1940), and her article, "Elizabeth Rowe and the Countess of Hertford," *PMLA,* LIX (1944), 726-46. "Philomela" addressed verses to Thomson "on the Countess of Hertford's praising his poems" (*The Gentle Hertford*, p. 23). Mrs. Rowe died in 1737, and this fact may help to account for the change from "Philomela" to "Musidora," but it is not certain that this change is from Thomson's own hand.

40 *rapt:* often confused in spelling and in meaning with *wrapt. Urania.* Milton's "heav'nly Muse," *PL* I.6, VII.1.

41 *secret cell.* Cf. *Comus,* 387: "The pensive secrecy of desert cell."

43 *Norwood's oak-clad hill.* See Introduction, p. 123. In the last line, *B-D,* Thomson substituted the pastoral names *Lycidas* and *Lycon* for *Mallet* and *Murdoch* in *A.* For Lycidas as Mallet, cf. *Winter* (1726), 296-300:

> *"Silence!* thou lonely *Power!* the Door be thine:
> See, on the hallow'd Hour, that none intrude,
> Save *Lycidas,* the Friend, with Sense refin'd,
> Learning digested well, exalted Faith,
> Unstudy'd Wit, and Humour ever gay."

This passage may refer to Thomson's period of residence with Mallet at the country house of the Duke of Montrose near Winchester (see *LD,* pp. 20-21), and would then be close in time to the *B* version of "Solitude," at the end of 1725 or the beginning of 1726. The origin of the familiar name "Lycidas" needs no explanation. As to "Lycon," a common name in pastoral verse, perhaps Thomson picked it up from the *Idylls* of Theocritus, II, 76, and paired it with "Lycidas" for the sake of the alliteration.

NEWTON

10 *Ethereal Flames.* About equivalent to Milton's "fiery Seraphim," *PL* II.512.

13 *this dim Spot.* Cf. *Comus,* 5.

14 See Introduction, p. 140.

15-16 Cf. *Spring* (1728), 802-06:
"He ceaseless works alone, and yet alone
Seems not to work, so exquisitely fram'd
Is this complex, amazing Scene of Things.
But tho' conceal'd, to every purer Eye
Th' informing Author in his Works appears."

16 *Frame.* See Arthos, under *Frame.*

18 *Spheres:* orbits. See Arthos, under *Orb* and *Sphere,* for this sense.

36-38 These lines echo the motto from Lucretius, *De Rerum Natura,* III.28-30, on the title-page of the first edition. See reproduction above, p. 149. The motto was dropped in 1730. Thomson, at least at a later date, owned a copy of the second edition (1717) of Creech's Latin text (Sale Catalogue, No. 40). Though this is not necessarily the edition he used in 1727, it is cited in the present notes.

41 See Introduction, p. 135.

42 *silent Harmony.* The Pythagorean and Platonic idea of the music of the spheres, associated with the ancient theory of the heavens (cf. "the full consenting Choir," *Liberty,* III.44), had become part of the heritage of modern poetry. A familiar theory was that the music was not heard because of the grossness of the body and the brutalizing effects of sin (cf., e.g., *Merchant of Venice,* V.i.60-65; Milton "Second Prolusion," "At a Solemn Music," 17-21; "Arcades," 72-73). Sir Thomas Browne explains that the harmony is rational, "for those well-ordered motions, and regular paces though they give no sound unto the eare yet to the understanding they strike a note most full of harmony" (*Religio Medici,* II, 9). Addison, in the age of Newton, gives us the best-known restatement of this idea (*Spectator,* No. 465):
"What though, in solemn Silence, all
Move round the dark terrestrial Ball?
What tho' nor real Voice nor Sound
Amidst their radiant Orbs be found?
In Reason's Ear they all rejoice. . . ."
Cf. *Spring* (1728), 810-12: "The glittering Stars, / By the deep Ear of Meditation heard, / Still in their Midnight Watches sing of Him." Cf. also the related ideas of "silent-working *Heaven*" (846) and of divine power as "a Language rather felt than heard" (796). Edward Young characteristically develops the theme of the silent eloquence of the skies:
"There dwells a noble *Pathos* in the Skies,
Which warms our Passions, proselytes our Hearts:
How eloquently shines the glowing Pole?
With what Authority it gives its Charge,
Remonstrating great Truths in Style sublime,
Tho' silent, Loud! heard Earth around; above
The Planets heard; and not unheard in Hell."
(*Night Thoughts,* IX.1636-40)

45 *Tracts:* orbits. Cf. *Castle of Indolence,* I.lix.9 and note.

55 *revertive.* The only example of this word given in *OED.*

68 ff. See Introduction, pp. 140-41.

76-81 Comets served as a classic example of the discovery of exact mathematical law in a spectacular view of the heavens, and at the same time as a signal instance of popular superstition dispelled by scientific enlightenment. See, e.g., *Guardian,* No. 103. In the first edition of *Summer* Thomson gave a long description of the northern lights, with comments on popular superstition. In the final version

211

this passage was replaced by an elaborate description of a comet, including Newton's speculations as to the possible uses of comets. With the present passage in *Newton,* especially 79-81, cf. *Summer,* 1720-22:

> "While, from his far Excursion thro' the Wilds
> Of barren Ether, faithful to his Time,
> They see the blazing Wonder rise anew."

Thomson's elaboration of the theme of the comet may have been partly suggested by Mallet's *Excursion (Background of Seasons,* p. 68).

79 Cf. *Lycidas,* 171: "Flames in the forehead of the morning sky."

83 *whirling Vortices.* The Cartesian theory, familiar not only to the scientists of the period but to laymen. Its appearance in the poems of John Norris of Bemerton, whose works were well known to Thomson, is worth noting. In the cosmic journey of "The Elevation" the soul is said to be "drawn by the Bent of the Ethereal tide," explained as an allusion "to the *Cartesian* Hypothesis of Vortices or Whirl-pools of subtile Matter"; and in "A Divine Hymn on the Creation" we have the line: "With lucid *whirl-pools* the vast Arch does shine" (*Collection of Miscellanies* [5th ed., 1710], pp. 44, 47, 68).

A 84 *Acquests.* For the passage from Lucretius quoted below, note on 132-36, Creech's prose paraphrase has "acquisita" in the last clause, and this may possibly be connected with Thomson's use of the rare word *Acquests* here.

A 87 *All Europe stood appall'd.* Cf. *Liberty,* III.10: "All LATIUM stood arrous'd."

88-90 Cf. Lucretius, III.1056-57, of Epicurus: "Qui genus humanum ingenio superavit, & omneis / Praestinxit, stellas exortus uti aetherius Sol."

96 ff. See Introduction, pp. 142, 145.

119 Cf. *Tancred and Sigismunda,* II. viii: "Did ever Tyrant image aught so cruel!"

120 *the hoarse Brook.* Cf. *Castle of Indolence,* I. xviii.8.

123 *Greenwich.* The hill in Greenwich Park commands a fine view, and is mentioned here also because of its associations with science, as the site of the Royal Observatory.

125 ff. Though Newton's own writings in chronology had not been fully published in English at the time Thomson's poem appeared, his contributions had become known through the publication of an unauthorized French translation of his manuscript abridgment (Paris, 1725) and through the controversy that ensued during the last two years of his life. Toward the end of 1727 the abridgment was published as *Sir Isaac Newton's Chronology Abridg'd by Himself,* dated 1728 on the title-page, and, also late in 1727 dated 1728, the full-length *The Chronology of Ancient Kingdoms Amended.* The latter appeared under the sponsorship of John Conduitt. Newton's method in chronology was to correlate and harmonize the evidence yielded by the Bible, classical history, and astronomical data in such a way as to produce what he considered a consistent scheme.

132-36 Cf. Lucretius, V.1-5:

> "Quis potis est dignum pollenti pectore carmen
> Condere, pro rerum majestate, hisque repertis?
> Quisve valet verbis tantum, qui fundere laudes
> Pro meritis Ejus possit, qui talia nobis
> Pectore parta suo, quaesitaque praemia liquit?"

212

138   *Responsive:* responding readily to some influence. First example given for this sense in *OED* 1762.

140   *University of things.* OED gives no example of *university* in the sense of *universe* after the seventeenth century. But Thomson may have taken the phrase directly from the Latin. Cf. Addison's oration of 1693, speaking of Descartes: "totam tam dilucide depinxit rerum universitatem ut nulla iam Qualitas relicta sit occulta" (*Miscellaneous Works,* ed. A. C. Guthkelch [1914], II, 467).

143   Cf. Introduction to *Castle of Indolence,* p. 52 n.

158   *Conduitt.* John Conduitt married Newton's favorite niece, Catharine Barton, and served as Newton's deputy as Warden of the Mint. For his plans for a life of Newton, see Introduction, p. 143. Since he died in 1737 without having written the projected life, it was probably Thomson's intention to delete ll. 158-62 for the edition of 1744. See textual notes.

158   *thy rural Hours.* Here, and in the following lines, Thomson presumably refers to Conduitt's country seat at Cranbury Park, near Winchester.

163 ff.   An attack on those who deny the immortality of the soul.

169-71   The traditional physiology, handed down from the ancients, taught that the brain received "vital spirits" in the form of blood and generated "animal spirits," a subtle fluid which the nerves, thought of as hollow tubes, then conveyed to the various parts of the body.

BRITANNIA

Motto on title-page, reproduced above, p. 167, from *Aeneid,* I.134-39.

1 ff.   For the general parallel of the opening passage with *Liberty,* see Introduction, p. 163. A political satire of 1741, *The Year Forty-One: Carmen Seculare,* imitative of both *Liberty* and *Britannia,* has a similar vision on Dover Cliff:

> "Methought, on the bleak Beach *Britannia* sate,
> Waiting, with *Neptune,* her disastrous Fate.
>
> . . . .
>
> Sunk in Despair she, sick'ning, *droop'd* her Head,
> The Laurel Wreath, that grac'd her Temples, dead."

Further imitations appear in two later patriotic musical entertainments inspired in part by Thomson and Mallet's *Alfred* (1740). Richard Rolt's *Eliza* (Haymarket, 1754) opens with "a mountainous Country, with a prospect of the Sea; and Britannia discovered under the Rock, in a melancholy Posture." Mallet's own *Britannia* (Drury Lane, 1755) begins: "On one hand a rocky coast; woods and fields on the other: the whole terminated by a view of the ocean. BRITANNIA is seen reclining against a cliff, in a pensive posture: her helmet, shield and spear strewed negligently on the ground."

6-8   Cf. the allegorical figure in *Liberty,* I.29-34, with "her bright Temples bound with *British* Oak," and her "sea-green Robe." Cf. also *Liberty,* V.311-13:

> "Should they BRITANNIA's well-fought Laurels yield
> To *slily-conquering Gaul*; even from her Brow
> Let *her own Naval Oak* be basely torn."

16-18   "*Frederic* Prince of *Wales,* then lately arrived."—Note 1762. See Introduction, p. 157.

27   *World of Waters.* Cf. *PL* III.11.

29   *on their Head.* Cf. *Winter* (1744), 169, 924: "The wintry *Baltick* thundering o'er their Head"; "The long long Night, incumbent o'er their Head." For both we have the correction "Heads" in the errata of 1744, but the first line quoted has "Head" in 1730 and 1738. Such an expression as "their Head" was probably idiomatic for Thomson. Cf. 45-46 below: *their Eye . . . their Tongue.*

34 ff.   The passage seems to fit Admiral Hosier's West Indian expedition of 1727.

44   *review:* to see or behold again.

57   *roll'd:* enveloped. Cf. *Castle of Indolence,* I.lxx.8.

62 ff.   Thomson may have in mind the picture of the defeat of the Spanish Armada in the House of Lords, alluded to in Edward Young's *Imperium Pelagi:*

> "What naval scene adorns the seat
> Of awful Britain's high debate,
> Inspires her counsels, and records her power?"

For comment on the pictorial quality of Thomson's description here, see Hagstrum, *The Sister Arts,* p. 258.

64   Cf. *Liberty,* IV.938: "And dash'd the *Pride of Spain* around *their Isle.*"

69   *the flaming Vast.* Cf. *PL* VI.203: "the vast of Heav'n"; James Ralph, *Clarinda* (1729): "a Vast of Wonder"; *Liberty,* IV.383: "the watry Vast."

71   *War.* See *OED,* sense 6b.

76   *deform'd.* Cf. *Castle of Indolence,* II.xliv.3.

82-84   *Promontory . . . Winds.* Cf. *Lycidas,* 91-94.

83   *where the wild Wave works.* Cf. *Winter* (1730), 760-61: "And into various shapes (as fancy leans) / Work'd by the wave, the crystal pillars heave."

85   *the glad Isle.* Cf. "Rule, Britannia," 29, and note.

86   *Shelve:* sandbank.

88-89   Cf. *Autumn,* 862-65:

> "Or where the *Northern* Ocean, in vast Whirls
> Boils round the naked melancholy Isles
> Of farthest *Thule,* and th' *Atlantic* Surge
> Pours in among the stormy *Hebrides.*"

Both passages are inspired by *Lycidas,* 154-58, as is *Liberty,* III.227-29. Cf. also *Castle of Indolence,* I. xxx.

89   *fractur'd Caledonian Isles.* Cf. *Winter,* 69: "fractur'd Mountains wild."

91 ff.   Even in the troubled times of the Civil War and the Commonwealth, Blake maintained and advanced British naval power. Thomson has particularly in mind Blake's last great victory, the destruction of the Spanish West Indian fleet in 1657.

106 ff.   See Introduction, p. 159.

115   *vernant.* Cf. *PL* X.679; *Spring,* 82.

118-21   Cf. Isaiah ii:4, and especially Micah iv:3-4: "They shall beat their swords into plowshares, and their spears into pruning hooks; . . . they shall sit every man under his vine and under his fig tree."

118   *shining Shares.* Cf. *Spring,* 41.

127   *the Trumpet . . . horrid Clang.* Cf. Milton, "Nativity Ode," 156-57.

146 ff.   See Introduction, p. 159.

162   *effulging.* The earliest example for this verb given in *OED.*

211 *high Behests.* Cf. *PL* XI.251: "Heav'n's high behest."

225 *Tract.* Cf. *Castle of Indolence*, I.lix.9 and note.

228 ff. Cf. the description of the Nile in *Summer*, 803-21, and, for the description of the cataracts in 11.229-32, *Summer*, 819-21:

> "down the *Nubian* Rocks
> From thundering Steep to Steep, he pours his Urn,
> And *Egypt* joys beneath the spreading Wave."

For Thomson's use of the Nile as a symbol for the source of national prosperity, cf. the apostrophe to Independence, *Liberty*, V.129-35;

> "Of *publick Freedom*, hail, thou *secret Source!*
> Whose Streams, from every Quarter confluent, form
> My *better Nile*, that nurses human Life.
> By Rills from Thee deduc'd, irriguous, fed,
> The *private Field* looks gay, with *Nature's* Wealth
> Abundant flows, and blooms with each Delight
> That *Nature* craves."

Accounts of the Nile could of course be found in many places, but Thomson's source here is probably John Harris, *A Compleat Collection of Voyages and Travels* (1705). Thomson used Harris for certain passages on Africa in *Summer* (1727) and possibly for additions to the 1730 version of *Winter*. (See *Background of Seasons*, pp. 139-40; Horace E. Hamilton, "James Thomson's *Seasons*: Shifts in the Treatment of Popular Subject Matter," *ELH*, XV[1948], 113-18.) For the turning of the river, ll. 228-29, cf. Harris, I, 391: "Some have thought the Course of the River *Nile* may be diverted another way; but those places where 'twas to be done, are not now subject to *Ethiopia*, and the King has no Inclination to such a Project." For the cataracts, cf. Harris, II, 428: the tributary branches unite at Meroe to form one river, "which after many Turnings and Windings comes to a great Mountain, across which it runs with a violent Torrent, and afterwards falls down with a furious Cascade into *Aegypt*." Later in the same passage it is said that the Nile is not very rapid, "unless it be at its *Cataracts*, where it falls from so great an Height, that the Noise of it is heard at a very great Distance." Line 233 connects of course with the ancient mystery of the sources of the Nile, and is paralleled in *Liberty*, II.48-50 and IV.604-05: "The *whisper'd* Tale, / That, like the fabling *Nile*, no Fountain knows." The exact meaning of Thomson's "trac'd him from the Sky" is not clear, but perhaps it is a fanciful reading or explanation of the name "Mountains of Luna" or "Mountains of the Moon." Cf. Harris, I, 316, of the Nile: "it seems, the Ancients were not well acquainted with its Source; for some pretend that the Lakes from which it springs derive their Original from the snow that falls from the Mountains of the Moon." For the "untill'd Harvests" of 1.235, cf. Harris, I,372: "When the River is retir'd within its bounds, their Sowing follows, which is done without Tilling, only throwing the Grain on the Mud, and Rice on the Water."

248 ff. Cf. Thomson's account of the destruction of Roman virtue by luxury, *Liberty*, III. 372-84.

271-73 For the figure of the sun, cf. *Liberty*, III.113-15.

274 For the theme of Northern liberty in Thomson, see *Background of Liberty*, chap. vi.

291 The convening of Parliament January 21, 1729. See Introduction, p. 157.

RULE, BRITANNIA

1-6   For the allegorical tableau here briefly indicated, see examples in Hans Marcus, "Die Entstehung von 'Rule Britannia,' " *Beiblatt zur Anglia*, XXXVI (1925), 30 ff., 78 ff. Cf. especially Jove's survey of the future course of empire in Congreve, "The Birth of the Muse":

> "Proceeding thus, he many Empires pass'd;
> When fair *Britannia* fix'd his Sight at last.
> Above the Waves she lifts her Silver Head,
> And looks a *Venus* born from Ocean's Bed.
> For rolling Years, her happy Fortunes smile,
> And Fates propitious bless the bounteous Isle;
> To Worlds remote, she wide extends her Reign,
> And wields the Trident of the stormy Main.
> Thus on the Base of Empire firm she stands,
> While bright *Eliza* rules the willing Lands."

A. H. Krappe ("The Origin of 'Rule Britannia' Once More," *Beiblatt zur Anglia*, XLIII[1932], 256-60) argues that the parallel with the sea-born goddess is not so relevant to the imagery of Thomson's opening stanza as Pindar's lines on the emergence of the island of Rhodes from the sea, Seventh Olympian Ode, 53 ff. Helios, the sun-god, chose the island for his own and "wedded the nymph of the isle." The parallel is interesting, and, while it is not clearly a source, serves to bring out the point that Thomson's ode presents simultaneously the goddess Britannia and the island Britain, and blends the two without fully developed allegory. We may compare and contrast the elaborate pageant in *Liberty*, IV.393 ff. The goddess Liberty approaches the "happy Isle" with her train, and is addressed by "the Genius of the Deep" (Neptune) in a long speech which opens with these lines:

> "By Fate commission'd, go,
> My Sister-Goddess now, to yon *blest Isle,*
> Henceforth the Partner of my rough Domain.
> All my dread Walks to Britons open lie."

3   *the charter of the land.* Cf. the Hermit's soliloquy, Act II, Scene 1, in the manuscript version (Huntington Library, Larpent MS 27):

> "Fair Freedom! sovereign boon of heaven,
> Great Charter, with our being given."

Britannia's Charter is the title of a small collection of songs published by S. Gamidge, Worcester, with "Rule, Britannia" standing first.

12-15   J. Churton Collins (*Ephemera Critica* [1902], pp. 324-25) points out a parallel with the figure of the oak in Horace, *Odes*, IV. iv, imitated by Thomson in *Liberty*, III.361-66. The tree, shorn of boughs and leaves by the axe, puts forth fresh shoots with renewed vigor. A closer parallel appears in *Aeneid* IV.441-46, thus translated by Dryden:

> "As, when the winds their airy quarrel try,
> Justling from every quarter of the sky;
> This way and that the mountain oak they bend;
> His boughs they shatter, and his branches rend;
> With leaves and falling mast they spread the ground;
> The hollow valleys echo to the sound;
> Unmoved the royal plant their fury mocks,
> Or, shaken, clings more closely to the rocks:
> Far as he shoots his towering head on high,
> So deep in earth his fixed foundations lie."

216

Cf. *Britannia*, 200-01; John Hughes, "Essay on Allegorical Poetry," in Spenser, *Works* (1715), I, xxvi: "[Chaucer and Spenser] seem to have taken deep Root, like old *British* Oaks, and to flourish in defiance of all the Injuries of Time and Weather."

This stanza is imitated in the speech of Liberty in Richard Rolt's *Eliza* (Haymarket, 1754):

"Swell, ye huge Billows; blow, ye furious Blasts,
Of *Spanish* Tyranny, and *Romish* Pride:
Ye shall not move me! Like these mountain Oaks,
I'll rear my Front sublime, and bear the Storm,
Which, by its Rage, shall stronger fix my Root."
(p. 5)

17-20   Omitted in Larpent MS 27, submitted for licensing by Charles Fleetwood, February 9, 1740[-41]. This copy contains three acts, the first and third corresponding to Acts I and II of the published version. Act I of the manuscript corresponds exactly, line by line and page by page, to Act I as printed. Evidently the licensing copy was made after the publication of August 19, 1740; it is an extended version planned for the public stage. In this version the stanza directed against "haughty tyrants" may have been omitted out of deference to the censorship.

24-25   Cf. *Liberty*, V.64-65: "All Ocean is her own, and every Land / To whom her ruling Thunder Ocean bears."

27-28   The traditional connection between freedom and literary genius. See *Background of Liberty*, p. 13.

29   *Blest isle!* Cf. *Liberty*, IV.408: *"yon blest Isle"*; V.633.: "Their own blest Isle." Cf. also *Britannia*, 85: "the glad Isle"; *Liberty*, IV.394: "the *happy Isle*"; IV.461: "this favour'd Isle"; *Summer*, 1595: "Island of Bliss!"

29-30   *Liberty*, IV.473-74, refers to Britannia as "the fair *Guardian* of an Isle that boasts, / Profuse as Vernal Blooms, the fairest Dames."

Index

References to Spenser, Milton, Pope, and Thomson in the Explanatory Notes are not indexed.

INDEX